State Lines

A · WARDLAW · BOOK

# State Lines

COMPILED AND EDITED BY

## Ken Hammond

FOREWORD BY LEON HALE

ILLUSTRATIONS BY ROLF LAUB

Texas A&M University Press
College Station

The paper used in this book meets the minimum requirements
of the American National Standard for Permanence
of Paper for Printed Library Materials, Z39.48-1984.
Binding materials have been chosen for durability.

LIBRARY OF CONGRESS CATALOGING-IN-PUBLICATION DATA

State lines / compiled and edited by Ken Hammond ; foreword by Leon Hale ; illustrations by Rolf Laub. – 1st ed.
    p.   cm.
    Selection of nonfiction columns from State lines, a
weekly feature of Texas magazine, the Sunday supple-
ment to the Houston chronicle.
    ISBN 0-89096-557-9 (alk. paper). – ISBN 0-89096-562-5
(pbk. : alk. paper)
    1. Texas–Social life and customs.   I. Hammond,
Ken, 1943–  .
F391.2.S7   1993
976.4–dc20                 93-3512
                                    CIP

# Contents

# CONTENTS

# In Defense of the Essay—A Foreword

The pieces collected in State Lines—all of them, including this one —qualify as personal or familiar or informal essays. There. I've used the term right here in the first paragraph to show that we don't need to be afraid of it.

Some of the best and certainly the most entertaining prose in American letters has come to us in personal essays. Yet a great many readers are put off by that word, *essay*. Mention it in a social gathering and watch for the small frowns from those who associate the essay with the dreary hours they spent grinding out school assignments.

I know people who will say they've had nothing whatever to do with essays since they were required to write their last one, to get a grade. And these are pretty good readers. They may even have on their shelves the books of E. B. White, who for almost half a century was probably the foremost essayist in America. And they'll be worshipers of Mark Twain, but you won't catch them calling him an essayist.

Even the new *Encyclopedia Britannica* doesn't call Twain an essayist. Calls him a humorist, writer, newspaperman, and lecturer. My guess is, if Mark Twain had never written one novel he'd still have risen to literary eminence due to his essays, in which his sense of humor soared the highest.

I don't mind speculating that the apparent widespread discomfort with the term *essay* has something to do with reports I keep hearing that the form is dead. The essay dead? Not to me it isn't. The essay is everywhere.

Which brings us to the questions of what makes a piece of prose an essay, and why is it so called?

Back to my *Brittanica:* "ESSAY: a literary composition of moderate length, dealing in an easy, cursory way with a single subject, usually representing the writer's personal experience and outlook."

Coming from an encyclopedia, that sounds fairly harmless. And my personal definition of the essay is even simpler. I see it as nothing more than good conversational prose. Talking well in print, about a particular subject. Perhaps telling a story, as if you might be trying to entertain friends sitting around a fire. Recalling an incident of your youth that helped shape what you have become. Defending your position on a matter of current public interest.

Or writing a letter. My guess is that those who say they don't want anything to do again with essays may have written some fairly good ones in personal correspondence. The best essay I've read in recent times was in the form of a six-page letter from a woman explaining why she hadn't been able to repay the money I lent her a few years ago to get her husband out of jail. That letter would fit nicely into the compilation of essays in this book. I would include a part of it here if it weren't a personal letter.

To assign the credit (or the blame) for the term *essay*, we must go back to the sixteenth century and a Frenchman by the name of Michel de Montaigne. Montaigne is often called the originator of the essay. He did name it, all right, but I have trouble accepting that one person sat down and invented the form. No style of writing is more natural, and I think people were scribbling essays centuries before Montaigne, without calling them anything special.

Montaigne was plagued most of his life by poor health, but he was lucky that his family was rich. He received a fine private education and spent half his life sitting in a chateau near Bordeaux, France, one of the finest parts of this world, thinking and studying and writing his essays. The summer of '89 I spent a while near there and didn't want to leave. I wanted to buy a house in the middle of all those vineyards and stay and write the story of my life. I couldn't afford to do that, but Montaigne could and did.

There's a French verb, *essayer*, which means "to try." Montaigne labeled his compositions *essais* because he saw them as attempts to express satisfactorily his thoughts and to relate accurately his experiences. And often discovering, in the process, what his thoughts actually were and what his experiences really meant. He didn't mind wandering away from the subject, and was willing to confess toward the end of an essay that he may have changed his mind about the matter since he began. But literary critics seem to agree that Montaigne wrote in a vivid, delightful style.

He died in 1592, and along behind him came Francis Bacon, who wrote in a more formal fashion and about heavier subjects but became England's first great essayist. Bacon led a parade of English writers who took the essay to its highest level of popularity: Abraham Cowley, Oliver Goldsmith, Samuel Johnson, Joseph Addison, Richard Steele, Charles Lamb, and Robert Louis Stevenson. In the United States we found the spirit of Montaigne in Ralph Waldo Emerson, Henry Thoreau, Twain, White, and a host of others still writing.

I have saved the *New York Times Book Review* of November 18, 1984, because it contains an essay on the essay by Phillip Lopate, himself an eminent contemporary essayist. One of his points in that piece is that newspaper columnists (or at least the best of them, as he says) are now carrying on the essay-writing tradition of Addison and Steele.

To that I would add that newspapers across the country are devoting enormous amounts of space on their opinion pages to citizens, professional writers or not, who may submit their pieces with a reasonable hope of being published. Magazines, as well (as this book demonstrates), are giving writers an opportunity to take one of old Montaigne's attempts, to record personal thoughts that may be of high interest to perfect strangers.

If you now ask, "Who are the contemporary essayists?" my answer is, "Turn the page. You'll meet quite a few of them in this book."

—Leon Hale

# Preface

As the "State" in this book's title implies, the essays in this collection have to do with both the state of Texas and the state of mind, but not in any stereotypical sense. They are not about the Texas of oil and cattle empires or bigger-than-life characters. Nor are they about Texans as a colorful breed apart. Indeed, some of the essays, such as Martha Howard's recollections of a homeless brother on the streets of Houston, or Marion Winik's sweet-and-sad piece on absent pets, could have come from anywhere.

And yet, in most of these writings, Texas is an underlying element—not flashy and intrusive, but there. In Evan Moore's essay about a chuck-wagon cook on the 6666 Ranch, or in Ben Ezzell's piece about picking cotton in the Panhandle, Texas is the natural arena. And even when setting is not a strong factor, as in Jennifer King Moody's essay on cemeteries, there is a certain flavor, whether traceable to geography, history, culture, or all three, that somehow seems to spring from Texas.

All of the essays in this collection are from State Lines, a weekly feature of *Texas Magazine,* the Sunday magazine of the *Houston Chronicle.* State Lines began in July, 1989, as part of a format change for *Texas Magazine.* It was a collaborative effort. Jane P. Marshall, the *Chronicle*'s features editor, suggested the idea for a weekly essay page. George Rosenblatt, travel writer at the time, coined the title, and then–fine arts editor Michael Berryhill lined up the early contributors, among them Michael Weir, Naomi Shihab Nye, Will Cobb, Charles Clawson, and Marion Winik. A handful of *Chronicle* writers also contributed, and within a few weeks, readers had begun mailing in essays.

In the beginning, we had no firm guidelines for what State Lines should be. The best writing possible—that was our only goal, and it was unwritten. But as State Lines became more popular and the number of unsolicited manuscripts mounted, we decided to draw up some written guidelines, most of which we still use today.

We asked for nonfiction writing, generally no less than a thousand words and no more than twenty-five hundred. We looked for essays based on personal experiences, as opposed to pure introspection or observations on current events.

Childhood memories make up the core of many good personal essays, but we warned writers against trying to share nostalgia without meaning. We routinely rejected (and still do) pieces about wonderful summers spent with grandparents on the farm in the good old days. We want pieces with depth, that make a point.

Also rejected were: newspaper column–type humor about Texas weather, cockroaches, and Houston traffic; inspirational writing; tributes to friends, relatives, and mentors; and editorial comment or opinion on social issues.

More than anything else, "essays should give readers the sense or feeling of sharing something personally held," we told writers in our guidelines. "That doesn't mean opinions or principles; it means feelings and experiences and what those mean to the writer. Just recounting the factual chronology of an experience usually is not enough. There should be some sort of point to it, some reason for sharing it with readers. The writer has to give up something in the essay—a bit of himself or herself through feelings or understanding."

We attracted a wide array of writers, from grandmothers who had never been published to poets and authors. One of the most satisfying parts of my job has been finding good essays by unpublished writers. When I call them to say I want to use their work, the reaction is never predictable. The last one I recall contacting, a woman in East Texas, didn't answer right away, then asked me, "Shall I fall through the floor right now?"

The worst part of the job is rejecting twenty or thirty essays for every one that I use.

Our guidelines don't cover everything. They can't. "We sometimes publish essays that might not measure up to the guidelines in all respects," the guidelines state, "but have other strong points, such as being written with such style and feeling that we overlook weak points in other areas."

When I was selecting the essays for this book, I'm not sure how carefully I followed my own guidelines. In most cases I think I did, but it wasn't like going down a checklist. I think what I did was to pick the ones I like the most, the ones I can read more than once and still come away feeling as if I've read something that, if not altogether new, somehow still "seems" new and fresh. That may not be the best definition of good writing, but it's one of the best I know.

−Ken Hammond, editor
*Texas Magazine*

# Publisher's Acknowledgment

The Texas A&M University Press is privileged to add its imprint to this Wardlaw Book. The designation claims a special place in the list of Texas A&M publications.

Supported with funds inspired by the initiative of Chester Kerr, former head of Yale University Press, this book, along with its companion volumes, perpetuates the association of Frank H. Wardlaw's name with a select group of titles appropriate to his reputation as man of letters, distinguished publisher, and founder of three university presses.

Donors of these funds represent a wide cross-section of Frank Wardlaw's admirers, including colleagues from scholarly presses throughout the country as well as those from other callings who recognize and applaud the many contributions that he made to scholarship, literature, and publishing in his four decades of active service.

The Texas A&M University Press acknowledges with profound appreciation these donors.

Mr. Herbert S. Bailey, Jr.
Mr. Robert Barnes
Mr. W. Walker Cowen
Mr. Robert S. Davis
Mr. John Ervin, Jr.
Mr. William D. Fitch
Mr. August Frugé
Mr. David H. Gilbert
Mr. Kenneth Johnson
Mr. Chester Kerr
Mr. Robert T. King
Mr. Carl C. Krueger, Jr.

Mr. John H. Kyle
John and Sara Lindsey
Mrs. S. M. McAshan, Jr.
Mr. Kenneth E. Montague
Mr. Edward J. Mosher
Mrs. Florence Rosengren
Mr. Jack Schulman
Mr. C. B. Smith
Mr. Richard A. Smith
Mr. Stanley Sommers
Dr. Frank E. Vandiver
Ms. Maud E. Wilcox

Mr. John Williams

Their bounty has assured that Wardlaw Books will be a special source of instruction and entertainment to the reading public for many years to come.

State Lines

# He Always Comes Home, in Memory

ALLEN WIER

One of my favorite photographs of my daddy is the same sepia, olive-drab tint as the Army Air Corps uniform he wears in the picture. On cardboard-brown boxes stacked high as his waist, a woman's disembodied hand holds an opener over a can of Falstaff beer. OPENS LIKE A BOTTLE, the boxes declare. Looking like the inverted funnel that caps the Tin Man in *The Wizard of Oz,* one of these cans of Falstaff, opened, sits on the boxes. Barely visible at the top of the photograph, my daddy wears, at a jaunty angle, a "garrison" or "overseas" cap like a manila legal envelope split open lengthwise and put on his head. Below the cap, his ears stick out, pushed sideways by a wide grin for me, beside him in the picture.

Like some short star (Alan Ladd held by a leading lady or in the grasp of a desperado), I stand on a table with the beer boxes to get almost eye to eye with him and match his grin. Light glints off the beer can, off a ring on Daddy's hand, and in our dark eyes. After he died, I retrieved the photograph from deep in a drawer.

"May I take this one of Daddy and me?"

Mother said, sure. "But, that's not you. You weren't born when that was taken."

My mother doesn't know who the photogenic toddler is, grinning with my grinning daddy. Things are not always as we imagine or remember or want them to be. I kept the photo anyway. It's still one of my favorite pictures of Daddy and me.

Like Wiers before and after him, my daddy was born and raised in the Hill Country town of Blanco. Daddy hung out at the general store his daddy ran, swam and fished in the Blanco River, and made out with girls in the cemetery. Repeatedly hitting the moving target of (he claimed) young Lyndon Johnson's buggy after Sunday services at the Methodist church, my daddy wielded a wicked

3

slingshot. He graduated from Blanco High School and hitchhiked over the Devil's Backbone to college in San Marcos, until 1938, when he joined the Army Air Corps and left Texas.

When Daddy got out of that Air Corps uniform, he rode a Mexican train from Tierra Blanca to Veracruz and roamed the jungles looking for flowers and ferns for the wholesale flower business in Texas. My mother and I divided our lives between Texas and Mexico. Each time our tourist visas expired, we had to leave Daddy and our rented rooms in an old colonial mansion in Mexico City for the house we owned in San Antonio. Alone in Mexico, my daddy always found adventure.

Near Tampico one night, bandits rode out of a cloud of mosquitoes and crowded their horses around his jeep on a tiny ferryboat. After the crossing, the bandit leader paid the toll for his men and for Daddy's jeep. One morning, Daddy opened his eyes to a swaying overhead light. Then the bed bucked him out of it. The earthquake jammed his door shut, and he was about to jump from a window when a tremor opened the door. Another time, on a train to Mexico City, my daddy sat up all night arguing politics with an enormous Mexican who turned out to be the painter Diego Rivera.

These stories were added to Texas stories. A man named Lackey, who lived between the Pedernales River and Hickory Creek, shot his niece, his brother, and four others one morning in 1885, then cut his own throat but lived to be lynched from a live-oak limb. One afternoon, Bonnie and Clyde roared through Blanco, a storm of bullets shattering the drugstore window where Daddy stood reading a magazine. A September night, Daddy and Tom Kidder hit a big buck on the way home from San Antonio and used oatmeal to plug the holes the antlers punched in the radiator. I never asked how he happened to have a box of oatmeal along, but every time we drove to Blanco to visit Grandmama, I tried to guess which tree was the Lackey tree, and I listened for the faint echo of Tommy guns and watched for deer suddenly in our headlights.

Years later, I learned the Lackey tree was north of Blanco, above Paradise Hollow, but the facts of my daddy's stories were less important than their drama, their fictional truth. Those tales and the cadences of his talk were part of my Texas history.

My life has taken me to live in different places, but I always come back to Texas, in memory, in dreams, and in storytelling.

Possessed by the voices and the textures of the Hill Country, I do not possess a ranch to return to, but I do possess the place in my imagination. The rock buildings – cafes, bars, filling stations – the gnarled live oaks, thorny mesquite, and persistent cedars; rough hills and limestone ledges; dry creek beds and flood-swollen rivers; the twangy poetry of Texas talk – especially story-telling talk – all this moves me, has for me a special sense of its own, what Henry James calls "a mystic meaning to give out."

My first novel, *Blanco,* renders a mythologized Blanco, a blending of fact and fancy, the result of experience filtered through years and miles. In the card catalog in the Blanco library, after the entry for *Blanco,* someone has typed: "A novel of the Wier family of Blanco." That sounds almost Faulknerian, makes the family sound more prominent than it was. I am bemused, pleased even, by the library's audacity, by the assumption that my novel is about "the Wier family" – factually inaccurate but mythically true.

For several years now all the Wiers in Blanco have resided in the cemetery, where many stones bear the family name. On one of those stones is my daddy's name: Ralph A. Wier. Daddy, like his daddy, Herb Wier, came there before his grandson was born. Until a couple of years ago, when I passed the responsibility on to a son, I was (so far as I know) the last living progeny. The Wier name, in our immediate family, stopped with me. While my wife, Donnie, was pregnant I teased her with talk of heading for Texas once her labor began, so our child would be native-born. As things turned out, he'll have to become a naturalized citizen. I'll pass along all the stories, make sure he learns our Texas history. Bring him back enough, I figure, he'll pick up the twang.

Most of my friends think Texas, all of Texas, is flat and brown, windswept and barren, a scene from the movie *Giant.* That vision of Texas looms large in the national mythology. I remind them that things are not always as we imagine. I tell them to picture those color prints in the backs of old Bibles: pools of clear water surrounded by sun-bleached white rocks, goaty hillsides, oaks twisted by wind and dwarfed by drouth (Texas' natural bonsai – one reason Texans look so tall in the saddle), dusty oak leaves the color of olive trees and dark cedars giving off their biblical aroma.

That cedar smell puts me in Grandmama Wier's cedar closet in the frame house on Highway 281. Sold, pried up and hauled to a lot across from the funeral home, remodeled and painted the pale brown of old photographs, it is no longer Grandmama's house. Where it once stood, there's a car wash. But as soon as I leave town, limbs from the hackberry tree they cut down clatter against the front windows in the howling memory of a blue norther. Out of sight, I see it clearly.

A sepia birthmark, my personal country goes with me. No matter where I live, I watch for bluebonnets every April. I cross all rivers on low water bridges or on crowded Mexican ferryboats. After dusk on any highway, I'm wary of leaping deer. All my camp fires smell of burning cedar, a scent of Holy Land.

# A Child's Growth Rings

BOBBYE S. WICKE

Hurricane season returns to southern coasts like the family's black sheep, bringing memories and adventure, gifts and trouble – some years only a tease, other years a milestone. My first hurricane is a tangled memory of cats and a baby and wind and water, a memory to be unraveled years later and fall into place like a darker growth ring in a tree.

All that was left of the cats after the hurricane ended and my mother's allergy to cats began was a snapshot of a girl about three or four years old wearing a sunbonnet and a smile, with three cats spilling over her arms. The snapshot has turned dirty brown, but you can see that the sleepy tangle of dangling legs and tails and heads is a black-and-white spotted cat, a pale cat that could be yellow, and a mottled cat that might be a calico. The baby came a few months later, but he is part of the hurricane memory, too, because I thought that he would be like the cats, cuddly and purring, and that I could dress him in doll clothes like the cats. He was none of those things. Instead of purring, he burped and cried, smelled bad sometimes, and I wasn't allowed to touch him.

The hurricane ended a lot of nice things on our bayou, where the water was shallow and warm, and so clear that you could see oysters, crabs, and tiny worms on the soft, silty bottom. Most of the homes on our street had long, narrow docks like railroad tracks running far out into the water, with little shelters at the end for boats and for sitting with cool drinks on hot afternoons. We didn't have a dock, but there were plenty to choose from, and I played on the docks and paddled around in the bayou whenever I could slip away from the maid.

Sometimes an old lady whose home commanded a view of most of the waterfront phoned my house to complain that my discarded clothes were trespassing on somebody's dock, and I was in the water again. More often than not, the maid didn't answer or the party line was busy, and then the old lady called the sheriff, who always called my mother at the school where she taught before he went to see if I had drowned. That sequence of events caused bad feelings between my mother and the old lady and the sheriff and the maid, and especially my father when he came home. The domino effect of those feelings ended with me, as the only socially acceptable outlet for everyone's anger and frustration, shut in the closet until bedtime. The tiny, dark hall closet was the stuff of which lifelong nightmares are made, but the lure of the bayou was stronger than my fear of the dark.

Our bayou was twenty miles from open waters, so no one paid much attention to news of a hurricane dithering around in the Gulf on its way to Mississippi, several hours away. One morning there was no maid and no breakfast waiting in the kitchen, although I had overslept. My mother and father were still home, frowning at the radio over their coffee cups. The radio played long enough to warn that the storm had gathered speed during the night and had taken an unexpected turn toward us. Then my parents worked in silence fastening things down and shuttering windows. Shingles flew off the roof as fast as my father could nail them back on; water trickled through the ceiling into pots and pans and blew in under the door and around the windows, soaking the towels and newspapers my mother wedged in the cracks. The day turned cold, dark, and as wet as the bayou.

Grown-ups came with armfuls of food and drink, laughing at the great blast of wind and water when the door was opened and at the battle to close it again. When darkness fell, the women played bridge and the men played poker by the light of kerosene lamps, while the hurricane made landfall on our part of the coast. There were no other children for company; and eventually I grew used to the rattling of the house and the howling of the wind, and slept.

When I awoke the sun was shining, the electricity was back on, and sleeping grown-ups lay everywhere. I went outside in my pajamas to find my cats. The black-and-white cat and the yellow cat were huddled damply together in the garage, and I brought them into the kitchen and poured a bowl of milk for them. I found my favorite, the calico cat, lying cold, wet, and unmoving under a bush, and I brought her into the kitchen, too, to warm her up.

I went back out to see what everyone was walking around looking at. Bits and pieces that had been docks and parts of houses were scattered up and down the street and floating in the bayou. Although the docks and boats were gone and the bayou had turned ugly, all the people on the street were smiling and talking to each other. The people who usually were the meanest were laughing and hugging each other; one of them even hugged the old lady, who had come down off her porch for the first time ever. Up close, the old lady was small and round, and not at all cross.

Then screams stopped the laughter and talk, and sent people running toward my house. The old lady ran, too, jiggling up and down like a puppet. I ran after them, but they were much faster and some of them were coming back down the sidewalk before I got there, laughing again, although the screams continued. I wriggled through legs and around skirts into the kitchen, where the warm smell of something roasting in the oven reminded me that I hadn't had any breakfast. My mother was leaning against the refrigerator with her eyes tightly closed and her mouth wide open, screaming. I could see way down her throat.

My father's face was dark and red; he was holding my mother's shoulders and shaking her.

"Shut up!" he kept saying. "Go to your room. I'll take care of it." She didn't stop for a long time, not until he shook her so hard that her head bounced off the refrigerator. She opened her eyes then and saw the people, some of whom turned away, embarrassed, but still laughing. When she saw me, she began to scream again.

"I'll take care of her, too," my father shouted, and he pushed my mother out of the kitchen toward their bedroom.

One of the neighbors stepped forward then and opened the oven door. I could see that I had made a dumb mistake, like the maid did sometimes when she warmed up cold things. I had put the dead calico cat in there.

# When King Kong Was Young

BOB LEE

*All heroes don't have to be people—for instance, there are Winnie the Pooh, Lassie, Mickey Mouse, Bugs Bunny and King Kong. But all people are possible heroes.*

—DA MAYOR OF FIFTH WARD

It was one of those beautiful summer evenings, a night you wished would never end. I sat out in the backyard, watering the lawn in the twilight, glancing up to see the setting sun glinting off the skyscrapers downtown. That night, I was baby-sitting with my nephew Little Thurman. As I watched the sun set, all he could talk about was world wrestling and, in particular, Hulk Hogan coming up on TV.

"Maybe the kid will get tired and fall asleep," I thought as I started making the popcorn. Little Thurman was still talking about wrestling. He asked me, did I know someone named Andre the Giant? I turned to him and said, "Have you ever heard of the greatest of all giants, King Kong?" Thurman looked puzzled.

I went on to say that when I was Little Thurman's age, the heroes of the day were Mickey Mouse and Bugs Bunny. My mom used to tell us, "You boys eat your spinach so you can grow up to be like Popeye." I sure didn't want to be like Popeye, so I hated spinach. I remember my dad reading about Bagheera, the sophisticated panther, who was Mowgli's friend and tutor in *The Jungle Book* by Kipling. But King Kong was the ultimate. King Kong was stronger than Hulk Hogan, Batman, Superman, Spider-Man, Mr. T, Godzilla, and RoboCop put together.

"Do they sell him at Toys R Us?" Little Thurman wanted to know.

I said, not to my knowledge.

"Then why haven't I ever heard of him, Uncle Bob?" he asked.

"It's because for the last five years (Little Thurman turned six in August), your mom has made you go to bed before nine o'clock," I said. "But when you are with me, there is no such thing as lights out and go to bed. *King Kong* is coming up at 12:30 tonight."

"Can I stay up?" he begged.

I said, "Sure," and he jumped into my arms and gave me a hug. I continued to sell King Kong. "My boy," I said, "it took the entire U.S. Army and Air Force to bring King Kong down. Hulk Hogan may be a hero here, but Kong is known all over the world, and he was a god in Africa."

When I was Little Thurman's age, I can clearly remember my first time watching that tragic movie with my dad. The ending still brings up a tear. I was sitting on Dad's lap, and we were cheering King Kong on as if he were Joe Louis fighting Max Schmeling. When Kong fought the dinosaur to protect the nice lady given to him as a bride, I felt a double sense of pride that Kong was both strong and willing to die to protect the woman.

The movie, made in 1933, is finally being recognized as a classic. Channel 20 in Houston once devoted a beautifully produced tribute to it. Not only was the movie a modern twist to the "Beauty and the Beast" story, but it was the first film to use special effects in creating the monster dinosaurs, leading to all the great horror films of today—all of which I try to catch.

My buddies and I would always talk sitting in the ditch, and not one looked upon King Kong as a villain. We thought of Kong as children today look at the late Jim Henson's wonderful Muppet characters. Henson created the Cookie Monster, Big Bird, Kermit, and Miss Piggy. To us, King Kong was an overgrown Winnie the Pooh with muscles. In May of 1990, not only did we lose Jim Henson, but we also lost the ex–Yankee outfielder—the greatest ever to play for the Yankees—Charlie "King Kong" Keller, who played for the team from 1938 to 1948.

Admiration for King Kong cut across all race lines. Keller was a white man, but blacks looked on Kong as a strong hero from Africa. In some places in America, the opening of the movie in the 1930s caused race riots, as certain whites looked on Kong as a symbolic "black power" threat to white supremacy.

King Kong was what we boys in those days called a freestyle climber. His climbing skills were envied by every boy and tomboy.

After seeing the Kong movie for the first time, I went outside my house early the next morning to climb the sturdy old oak tree in front. I soon got so I could climb up in about five or ten minutes, even though the first six feet of the tree were limbless.

When I reached the top, I felt like the Prince of Fifth Ward. I was ruler of all I surveyed. I pretended that the old oak could understand my chatter. Even my dog, Red, was constantly barking up at me and trying to climb or jump up the tree.

My mom knew I loved that old tree and thought it was my second home. What she didn't know was that I was practicing to climb the Esperson Building.

I can remember taking my friend Wilbur to my favorite spot in the old oak.

"Look there," I said, pointing toward the Esperson Building. "That's the Empire State Building where Kong fought the bad guys."

Wilbur would sadly say, "Yeah."

Somehow we thought if we could climb it, we would save Kong, or make the movie have a different ending.

No one could tell us the Esperson Building wasn't the Empire State Building. It was the tallest and most beautiful building in Houston at the time, with its little domed temple on top.

In the evenings, when the great Texas sun was setting over the Esperson Building, the view from my tree was breathtaking. That building was made for dreams of climbing, of adventure, and freedom.

Years later, I took my first business trip to New York, and as the plane flew into the city, my eyes were glued to the monument as I got my first glimpse. After I finished my business, I took a ride in the elevator up to the top of the Empire State Building.

Quietly, I stepped back from the crowd of other tourists and checked out the places where my hero had stepped. There was where Kong had climbed; here was where he tenderly put Fay Wray back on the ledge before he met his end.

Other buildings in Houston today are taller and bigger than the Esperson Building. It's hard to see the Esperson on the skyline now. Transco Tower, with its big searchlight beam at night, would be a perfect setting for Kong.

In New York City, the Empire State Building has been dwarfed by soaring skyscrapers. Those newcomers, though, look too smooth and glassy to climb. A giant like Kong somehow deserves the stylish art deco office palaces of the past.

As I was bathing Little Thurman, I said out loud, "He was a great ape."

"What's a great ape, Uncle Bob?" asked Thurman.

I looked at him, for that indeed was a serious question. I said, "The great ape is, first of all, one of the original inhabitants of Africa. The ape closely resembles human beings. He has a brain, a large brain, and is the most intelligent animal next to humans."

And, I added, "It is believed by many that apes and human beings developed from a common ancestor."

I started to tell Little Thurman about the scientists Louis and Mary Leakey and their anthropologist son, Richard Leakey. In East Africa, the Leakeys found bones of the first creatures who walked standing up, who lived millions of years ago. It is from those bones that the apes and humans are descended.

Other scientists think our most ancient ancestor is a female they call "Lucy." Her bones were also found in Africa. The theory is that all human beings alive today have a little bit of Lucy in them.

Africa is often called the "Mother Continent." When Richard Leakey meets visitors at the airport in Kenya, he always tells them, "Welcome home."

It was fast approaching ten o'clock as I put Little Thurman into his jammies. I knew as soon as I fixed him his peanut butter and jelly sandwich and gave him his milk, he would fall asleep faster than I could say O. B. Williams.

I have never climbed the Esperson Building, and I have never been to Africa. But I have seen and loved King Kong.

Once again, I settled to watch my hero alone – for the sixty-first time.

# Ringing of the Bell Never Ends

### LIONEL G. GARCIA

I was born and raised in San Diego, Texas. San Diego is the county seat of Duval County, whose long history of political turmoil has covered the little town like a black cloud. The publicity of a gang-rape trial a few years ago has further agonized the little community.

But I always say that my parents live there, my in-laws live there, my younger brother and his family live there, have lived there most of their lives, and they are not bad people. My wife and I visit two or three times a year to be with family and friends, to reminisce.

I walked the dusty streets as a child, barefooted, my pockets full of marbles and a spinning top, looking for a game to play. We were carefree then, getting up in the morning, leaving home after breakfast and not returning until dark, all dirty and sweaty, hoping that some supper had been left for us. As we crossed the yard between my grandmother's house and ours, we could hear the voices of our elders as they sat on the porch, my grandmother fanning herself, shedding the intense heat that had consumed her in the kitchen the whole day. Under the stars and amid the sounds of the locusts, they would make beautiful talk, about people alive or long dead, and when there was disagreement about a date, we would run to get Merce, my insane uncle, who knew the exact date of birth of all the family present and gone.

In his youth Merce had been sent to the insane asylum in San Antonio, and, in a short time, according to my grandmother, he had memorized all the streets in the city. If he had a fit during the conversation, we would just let him go running through the

streets as though nothing had happened. Be careful, my grandmother would say. Don't run into anything.

It was easy to laugh and to cry in the dark with the stories.

We were raised with certain traditions that become very mean-
ingful as we grow older. In San Diego, the Spanish priests had
brought over the European tradition of communicating with the
townspeople through the church bell. The good news and the bad
were passed on to us by the ringing of the bell, as the great poet,
John Donne, had so eloquently written about in 1624 in his "Devo-
tions upon Emergent Occasions."

I remember that on Sunday mornings Father Zavala would have
us ring the large sonorous bell an hour before the mass—repeated
metallic peals that penetrated throughout the sleeping town. Every
fifteen minutes he would give the nod, and my brother Dickie and
I, dressed in our starched red cassocks, wearing shoes for the first
time that week, would both hold on to the large rope and tug at
it with all our might, the weight of the swinging bell picking us
up from the floor on the upswing.

Father Zavala himself would ring the large bell to announce
death in the little town, going on and on—a woeful sound of death
that bound the town together. More tragically, the small bell would
ring for the death of a child, a lighter, sadder tone announcing
the unfairness of life. We would stop to hear the sound, taken
from the game of *canicas,* or *trompos,* or *la chusa,* to be reminded
of our own mortality. My mother, Marillita, and my grandmother,
Maria, would stop the old wringer washing machine. The soulful
peals would continue their cry. No words needed to be spoken.
We would run barefooted to the church to find Father Zavala resting against the wall, the old man exhausted from ringing the bell.
He would straighten up, clear his throat, and announce the dead
person's name.

Off we'd run back home, our feet burning on the asphalt under
the scorching sun, reciting the name over and over to be sure that
we would not forget, would not announce the wrong name. One
time we did get it wrong, and my grandmother cried all afternoon
for her favorite cousin until her cousin showed up on foot, asking
for a cup of flour. We had to run away from home for a while after
that one.

Regardless of who died, to my grandmother it would always be a relative. It could be a cousin ten times removed on my grand-father's aunt's side, but it was always someone she knew. And she would cry, not the wails that she made when my grandfather died, but still she cried. And she would get my mother to start crying, both of them trying to clear the tears from their eyes with their soapy hands, feeding the wash into the rollers. Years before, my grandfather had said that my grandmother Maria should hire out for wakes and funerals to prime the mourners, to keep the wails going.

We'd leave our marbles on the ground and run to the printer, who was by now busy laying type for the *esquelas,* the official an-nouncement of death: the person's name, date of birth and death, family, dates and times for the rosary, funeral. He would soak the printer in the blackest ink that he had, trying to contrast the let-ters with the gray background, the letters rolling out as black as death.

It was our job to distribute the *esquelas,* holding on to the car door, standing on the running board, jumping off the car and run-ning to every screen door in town, and slipping the notice on the door handle. We got paid ten cents, fifty if the person was important.

That night Dr. Dunlap would go through town in his car, with his nurse, Clementina, showing him where everyone lived that had called to complain of shortness of breath. Sometimes he had so many people to see he wouldn't arrive until well after our bed-time and he'd catch us asleep. But we would wake up just to see him. To us it was all a game. To Dr. Dunlap it was work, and we killed him with work.

When he took out his magical stethoscope we would all be awed. He didn't have to ask for quiet. You could almost hear my grand-mother's heart beat as she sat straight on her large chair like a queen. He would gently place the instrument on my grandmother's chest and move it around once in a while, asking questions of Clemen-tina. Clementina translated them into Spanish. Had she eaten a lot of fried foods? No, sir. Never. We would laugh. Everything my grandmother ate had lard in it. How long had she felt bad? Since in the morning when she was kneading the dough for tortillas and she had heard the tolling of the bell. Finally, Dr. Dunlap would roll up the stethoscope around his hand and look my grandmother in the eye and tell her that she had the heart of a young woman. What a joy that was. We could go out and play knowing that our grandmother would live to knead more dough.

I visit the cemetery in San Diego every time I go. My father and mother usually go with me to bring me up to date. It seems the proper thing to do, to go to pay my respects to the people there that I love so much: My grandmother, Maria. My grandfather, Gonzalo, who died suddenly coming out of the meat market, clutching his package of meat to his chest. They said he was dead before he hit the ground. My uncle Juan, the musician, next to them, dead at thirty-three. My little sister, Belinda, who died needlessly of dysentery, whom we baptized with tap water because the priest could not come to the house to give her last rites. My uncle Merce, insane, but generous and kind, who used to curse everyone in town and knew everyone's birthday. Next to him Adolfo, his brother—buried in name only, since shortly after buying his tombstone, he was kidnapped from San Diego as a mindless old man by someone who claimed to be his illegitimate son—buried in San Antonio. My great-grandfather, who lived to be almost one hundred years old, who spent a week in agony before he died, while we played marbles outside his window. My aunt Pepa, the crazy one, who lost all her children in one year. The list goes on. Garcia, Saenz. Gonzalez. Garza. Arguijo. Flores. Everett.

The ringing of the bell never ends.

There is a universality of humankind. There are no bad towns. A little town in South Texas is the same as a little town in John Donne's England, where someone also runs to the church to ask for whom the bell tolls.

Some day the bell in San Diego will toll for me. Let the good priest ring it loud and clear. Let the children run to learn my name from the good priest. Let them scatter from the church like summer butterflies, my name on their lips as they run home to pass the word.

As for me, in the end, one realizes that life is made up of priorities. Therefore, I know that I will go in peace. What is important is what I have written that will survive me. What will fulfill the writer's childhood dream of being eternal?

I have found that as great a poet as John Donne was, he was not entirely right. Surely the bell tolls for everyone, but your death does not diminish me. On the contrary, each one of us, in having lived, adds to the soul of everyone else.

# Snakes, Snobs, and Sanctuary

### STEVEN BARTHELME

Now those other classes—the upper class, lower class, and writer class—make me uncomfortable. Once, when I was actually loose inside the River Oaks Country Club—for a friend's wedding—every time I looked up, cops were watching. Or so it seemed. On the other hand, my time in lowlife circles, where casual acquaintances tend to get killed or carted off to Leavenworth, I happily kept to the minimum. Such silliness, part of the male writer's job description, makes the company of writers unspeakably dreary. Blah blah 9mm automatic blah 115 mph blah blah single malt whiskey. I prefer the middle class.

The problem is that the middle class has always made me uncomfortable, too, even when I was ten. All those folks, edgy, trying to find things other people didn't like, so as to have "taste." All those folks, fretful, trying to talk hip, think quick, dress right. Worrying about each other's shoes. All those folks watching all those folks. It was hard to breathe. So, at ten, we hunted snakes.

This doesn't mean we stumbled onto the odd snake now and again. This means we chased those slinky devils all over Harris County, as well as Brazoria, Burleson, Waller, and other counties whose names I have forgotten.

I say "we" because snake collecting was a joint venture with the kid from across the street, a tall boy called J. E. B. Stuart (not his real name). Jeb was Episcopalian and I was Catholic. He was a fan of Robert E. Lee and that fluffy horse, and I defended Grant (my mother was from Philadelphia) and booze. He went to public schools and I went to parochial, and as we were middle class, we were fast friends.

Where Jeb and I couldn't get on foot or bicycle, we had to be driven, by a handy parent or sometimes by an adult snake person.

I remember standing out in Addicks beside a dry creek bed, sun streaming through the leaves of the trees, with some other kids and the khaki man who had brought them, looking at rusted soft drink cans, beer bottles, and scraps of paper. The man was saying, in a voice rich with disgust, but also horribly dispirited, as if the vulgarity he witnessed had been targeted at him personally: "Civilization. Civilization." In feeling morally superior to litterers, he was, of course, far ahead of his time. We, backward, laughed at him behind his back.

We didn't catch anything that day, but on other days we did. Once, near a small farm that Jeb's people owned near Caldwell, we found two beautiful six-foot Texas rat snakes, or chicken snakes, as the locals called them, or *Elaphe obsoleta lindheimeri,* as Linnaeus would say.

That I can remember their Latin name thirty years later illustrates how seriously we took our herpetology. A Texas rat snake is a big, thick-bodied, tan-to-gray individual marked with large brown blotches. We caught these, a yellowish one and a very dark dude, in an old feed shed—one under a hay bale, the other in some burlap sacks. Jeb and I were ecstatic. I felt better that day than on the day years later that I sold my first book.

Another day we caught three speckled king snakes (*Lampropeltis qetulus holbrooki*) in a field where Rogers Junior High School now stands. On many more days the catch was slim or none, and on others the work of snake ownership—feeding, cleaning out cages, manufacturing cages, keeping records, corresponding with other collectors in other states—kept us off the trail.

Most of the time we didn't wander so far afield. We were lucky to live off South Post Oak Road near a part of Buffalo Bayou that by now, I'm sure, is under several trillion tons of concrete and smoked glass. Caught in a gentle arc of the bayou was a large area of sand and willow trees and what, I guess, was limestone, and in among all of these were a half-dozen shallow rain ponds the size of cattle tanks. There were even a couple of tiny, spring-fed streams. To us this steamy, muddy, mosquito-filled swamp was the clear manifestation of God's bounty. The place was the Amazon of ribbon and garter snakes, world headquarters for blanchards and yellow-bellied and diamondback water snakes, and it was ours.

Some of those summers we went to the ponds practically every day. The next street over from ours was one block, recently paved, but unused. At the end of that, you ducked under a barbed wire fence and followed a thin path through tall yellow weeds under a few pine trees, the path running diagonally across the field to another string of barbed wire. Past that there was a steeply declining red clay road, or at least a place where a bulldozer had once been. A thousand yards down this road were the ponds.

So every day, our sticks and old pillowcases in hand, we would head under the wire across the field, under the wire and down the clay road. When we got there, it was hours of painstaking study of each inch of the margin of a pond, or the shallow depths of a stream, slogging foot by foot along the banks, often stopping and staring, although staring doesn't really get it done. Stare, and you miss things—a certain curve, a bullet-shaped head looking out from weeds, something red and yellow and brown hiding motionless in plain sight under the rippling water.

It stays with you. Twenty years later I got a teaching job at a rotgut university in Louisiana. At a party, my host, one of my new colleagues, took me out back to show me his prize tomato vines. I reached out to the nearest bush, grabbed a green snake, and held it up. My new friend jumped. "How did you see that?" he asked, backpedaling. He never stopped talking about it. When I left Louisiana for a better job, a tiny professorship, my girlfriend and I had to return a beloved pet, a Graham's water snake, back to slithering grounds where we had found him.

Last I heard, Jeb had made good in the meteorology business, securely in the middle class to this day. My professorship has made a great many people, notably my family, happy, by making me middle class again—after fifteen years of life without insurance. Middle-class adulthood is easy compared with middle-class childhood, which, I now realize, reptiles were a major factor in getting me through.

Snakes were outcasts, underdogs, losers. No one liked them, and while that didn't give us taste, it did give us an area of expertise all our own. And we found snakes out in the fields and barns and bayous. In so doing, we escaped not only the scrutiny of our parents but also the suffocating middle-class self-consciousness. There was no one among our acquaintances likely to come along and know better. And there was no one to judge our clothes or our slouches or our slang as we dug around under rotting logs or tramped through blond fields or stood silently on either side of a shallow, cluttered, clear stream, looking into the water, hoping.

# When Junior Grew Up

ADELAIDE FERGUSON

I can still feel the sting of the switching I got the time I cut holes in my sneakers so I could put newspaper over the holes like Junior did.

Junior "belonged" to Lois. She worked down the street for the Alexanders and lived in their servants' quarters. Junior's sister, Neecy, worked for us. Junior just bounced back and forth from the Alexanders' backyard to ours. Junior and I were best friends.

Junior was always there at the corner of the alley when I walked home from school. He'd meet me with a cold yam and a square of corn bread to share until the two of us could get to Grandma's "nourishin'" after-school snack. Grandma would sit me down at the kitchen table, but Junior had to eat his out on the back step. I begged to eat mine out on the step with Junior, but I never got to.

Soon as we could get through with being "nourished," Junior and I would streak out behind the garage to see if our tadpoles had grown yet.

Junior's mama told him that if we soaked the hair from a horse's tail in a bucket of water for a week, the hair would turn itself into a tadpole. We'd been waitin' more than a week, but nothin' ever happened. Time didn't cost nothin'; we just left it there to soak a while longer.

Charlie Rand used to come on Thursdays to mow the lawn. Coley Bay was his swaybacked old horse. That's how Junior and I got the horsehair for the tadpoles to begin with.

Charlie didn't have a lot of faith in us kids. He stood watchin' when we inched up on Coley's tail with a pair of scissors. He saw plain as day when we cut the piece of hair off Coley's tail, but he went on about his business too soon to see us lift the flat iron holdin' Coley to his place and toss it in the wagon. If Coley wandered off at all, it wouldn't be more than a block or so. Charlie always caught him anyhow.

Whenever the iceman drove along in his wagon, we'd hang on the tailgate, beggin' for a chunk of ice to suck on. Most times Mr. Radley threw some off. When it fell in the gutter where Coley left his leavin's, we washed it off with the hose and ate it anyway. Mr. Radley was pretty good-natured, 'cept when we hung on the back of his wagon to get pulled along on our skates. He wouldn't move a stitch until we turned loose.

On Saturday, I got to go to the picture show, but Junior couldn't come. He'd wait at the corner of the alley, like always, and I'd come back and act out the show for him. His favorite was Tarzan. That was how I got the big idea that was to cause more trouble than I figured.

We had a big cottonwood tree down at the end of the alley. If you climbed up in that tree, you could see miles around. It seemed like a good idea to me to climb up there with Junior so I could demonstrate the latest Tarzan movie.

We didn't have a rope, but some of the whippier branches of the tree looked like we could just grab hold way out on the end and jump off, and they would carry us down to the ground.

It took Junior six weeks to get over his broken arm. Even though I didn't break anything, I wished I had. The guilt hurt me lots worse than the whippin' I got. Mama said I shouldn't have talked Junior into trying that jump in the first place. There's some things you just can't explain to grown-ups.

There's one thing grown-ups are good at, though. Finding stuff to tell kids to do that keeps them busy forever. Like when Mama told us to take the saltshaker and go sit under the peach tree 'til we saw a sparrow. If we could put salt on the sparrow's tail, we could catch it and make a pet of it.

We kept that saltshaker handy all summer, just waiting for a chance to salt a bird. Sometimes while we waited, we'd pretend to be big fish lying on the bottom of the ocean. The sky was the top of the ocean way up there, and we were way down below on the bottom. The clouds were the waves. It was easy to believe we were drifting along there on the bottom. Easy, that is, until Junior would start gasping for breath and pretend to be drowning. I couldn't stay still after that. He always convinced me that I couldn't breathe under water anymore, either.

On Sunday, Junior's mama, Lois, went to her secret JuJu meetin'. We kids weren't supposed to say anything about it, and we never did. She'd powder her face all white and put on a white dress and take off down the alley for wherever it was the meetin' was held.

Lois would tell us stories about Billy Boy and Half-leg Man and Mr. Clutch, who lived in the attic and waited 'til we did somethin' we shouldn't, so he could drag us up to the attic and eat us. Whenever she left for her meeting, she lit a black candle and set it just inside the door to her quarters. She said the candle kept the bad spirits away while she was gone.

One time, Lois cast the bones for us to tell us how we'd grow up. She took these little white sticks out of a leather pouch she kept in her dresser drawer and rolled 'em out on the bed. I don't know what she saw when she stirred 'em around, but she said for us not to worry, that everything was gonna be jus' fine. Then she'd tell us things to watch out for, like cross-eyed men with red hair. She said they carried the evil eye. Junior and I weren't worried anyhow. We never worried.

Charlie Rand didn't just cut the lawn. Whenever Mama needed a chicken killed, Charlie did the killin'. Junior and I tried to be around whenever chickens got killed. The squawkin' and floppin' was somethin' to see. Mama said Charlie was the only man she knew who could pop a chicken's head off in one twist. Then, he'd hang the chicken up on the clothesline for a while.

It was the pluckin' I hated. When Charlie put the chicken in boiling water to make the feathers turn loose, the smell was somethin' awful. Junior and I would stand there holdin' our noses waitin' for the part where Charlie cut the gizzard out. Grandma said sometimes you found valuables in a chicken's gizzard. We kept waitin' to find a diamond ring. We never did.

On wash day, Neecy would haul out the big boiler and set it on the two gas rings in the garage. Dad liked his shirts boiled stiff as a poker. Junior and I got to punch the shirts down with a cut-off broom handle. Somehow, we never could make all the air go out. The shirts kept blowin' up on one side when we pushed on the other. It got hot doin' that in summer, but Neecy always kept fruit jars of ice water for us, "to keep the engine runnin'" she said.

It was the first day of the new semester at school. It was also the first day Junior wasn't waitin' at the corner of the alley. I started runnin' for home, my heart poundin'. What if somethin' had happened to Junior? But before I reached the yard, Junior stepped out into the alley to meet me. Somethin' was different about him now. I noticed he was holdin' a bundle in one hand. There were tears on his cheeks.

I'd been hurryin' to get home to show him my new Girl Scout uniform. It seemed like I'd waited so long to get to be twelve so I could join. It didn't even seem important now with Junior so sad and all.

He told me he was goin' to have to go live with his grandma now that he was gettin' older. She'd need him to help her, and he couldn't stay around the servants' quarters anymore. When he called me Miss Adelaide, I laughed out loud. I never heard anything so silly in my life. I asked him if I was supposed to call him Mr. Junior now. He laughed out loud. We just stood there laughin' out loud.

It wasn't a bit funny. We knew we weren't goin' to see each other again. I never quit missin' Junior.

# Ritual of the Reading

## RACHEL HERRERA REED

The routine never changed. Each evening I sat on the hot concrete porch steps of our white-framed house. The huge pecan tree shading the front yard brought no relief from the intense heat.

Impatiently, I clutched the round scooped neckline of my sleeveless cotton dress.

"It's so hot! I wish I could wear shorts like my friends," were my unspoken thoughts.

But I knew better than to ask my father for permission to change my hated summer dresses for shorts like those worn by my first-grade friends. His answer would be a quiet, soft-spoken "No." Father never raised his voice to us; but all nine of us, including Mother, knew that his authority was final and absolute. Defying Father was unthinkable.

"Is he here yet?" Mother asked as she swung open the black screen door.

"His iced tea is ready." Her tired voice reflected years of hard work. His iced tea along with a dinner of refried beans and stacks of freshly cooked hot tortillas awaited my father.

Waiting to catch the first glimpse of our father, my family slowly gathered under the massive pecan tree. His appearance never changed. He wore faded brown khaki pants and, in spite of the heat, a long-sleeved cotton shirt. Perched firmly on his head in a no-nonsense manner was his white-and-black pin-striped railroad cap. In one hand he carried his round, black metal lunch pail. In the other hand he had a folded newspaper.

I was always the first to spot him. Happily, I jumped up and ran down the semipaved street. The hot tar mixed with small rocks stung my bare feet. When I reached Father, he solemnly handed me his lunch pail. We never exchanged a word.

Together we walked that last block to our house. His heavy, black boots quickly covered the last block home. I walked rapidly to keep up with him.

His chair and his iced tea awaited him on the front porch. Not speaking a word, he quietly sat down, accepted the glass of iced tea offered by my mother and drank a few sips. A release of tension and heat flowed slowly from him. Taking off his railroad cap, he smoothed the iron-black hair with one hand cooled from holding the glass of iced tea.

His next step was to untie his shoelaces and slowly release his feet from the oppressive boots. My mother quickly picked up his boots and handed them to me. I knew to place them on the linoleum floor by my parents' bed.

Mother returned to her gleaming white kitchen stove and turned up the gas flame under the black cast-iron skillets containing the fideo and the beans.

Dinner was solemn, serious, and quick. Father sat at the head of the square wooden table and was served by Mother. My sisters, brothers, and I joined my father while Mother and my eldest sister rolled out the white round domes of masa. Deftly, Mother cooked the tortillas on the thick, hot comal. The tortillas were hot, crisp, and delicious. Years later, I would learn to add butter to them; but for now I used them to scoop up the beans from my plate.

Mother ate last. My sisters and brothers left the oppressive heat of the house and returned to the shade of the pecan tree.

My father remained at the table finishing another glass of iced tea. The table was cleared. My sister handed Father the newspaper.

He would spread out the pages and, moving his lips, try to teach himself to read. His callused hands tightly clutched the newspaper and, occasionally, he touched a word on the newsprint as if by touching it the word would speak to him.

His lips moved nervously as he stumbled over unfamiliar words. He came to the end of a paragraph and still did not comprehend. With a deep sigh he stopped, clenched his jaw, and with stoic determination reread the article.

Standing quietly in the corner of our tiny, hot kitchen, I finished washing the dishes and drying the large skillets. My father's concentration penetrated the kitchen, and I tried to finish my duties quietly without disturbing him.

Finally, he motioned me to join him at the kitchen table. Together we tried to read and understand the newspaper. Sometimes, my meager first-grade knowledge was sufficient and I sensed his eager, happy excitement when we did comprehend. With deep satisfaction he folded the newspaper as if to say, "I can read."

Then, he turned to me and always asked the same question, night after night.

"Ya has aprendido a leer en la escuela?" "Have you learned to read yet in school?"

I always had to answer "No."

Years later, while a senior at the University of Texas in Austin, I returned one hot summer evening to that concrete porch shaded by the same massive pecan tree. Once again, my father sat on the front porch. But now the iron-black hair had become somewhat pin-striped black and white, almost like his railroad cap.

This time the glass of iced tea was offered to me.

"Como está Don Pedro?" We chatted about relatives, neighbors.

Then, without a word, my father handed me the newspaper.

I had forgotten about those summer evenings and the daily reading lessons. I had forgotten the sting of hot tar on bare feet and the heavy black cast-iron skillets filled with beans.

Glancing at my father, I began to read aloud swiftly and mechanically.

He listened attentively, his head slightly bowed, his eyes downcast. After a few minutes, in a soft, unfulfilled voice, he interrupted me.

"I never learned to read."

Silently, I folded the newspaper and handed it back to my father. Contradicting Father was still unthinkable; but, on this hot summer evening, I dared the unthinkable.

"Padre, you did learn to read—through me."

Choking back the tears—for I knew that he would be irritated at any show of emotion—I awkwardly embraced him.

On that hot summer evening my goodbye to my father was, Gracias.

# Mornings of Tears, Blue Jays

THOM MARSHALL

The woman in the corner house near the end of Conlen Avenue liked her news delivered to the back door. I was glad to do it because she tipped at collection time and she smiled and treated me like a person with a job rather than like a kid with a paper route.

The guy who worked nights in the filling station on 7th Street hated me because of the times I caught him sleeping on the job, lounging back in a chair with his feet on the desk.

One time on Olive Street, the morning after a big thunderstorm, I found a blue jay dozing on a wire fence, not more than three feet above the sidewalk.

Funny, the long-ago scenes and incidents that remain evergreen in the mind. It's been thirty-four years since that first newspaper job. I was thirteen. At the time, I was throwing a route solely for the six dollars and change I made every week. Now I see a number of benefits that had nothing to do with money. The morning bike ride was a healthful exercise routine for a runty, asthmatic kid. The monthly collection chore taught money-handling responsibilities. Keeping customers happy, finding new ones, reading the product, all contributed to the learning and growing process.

But there were these other things that happened – unexpected experiences that must have been important, judging from their indelibility as memories. Perhaps they are tiny pieces of some vast jigsaw puzzle that is yet to be put together.

I can't recall the woman's name, but I remember that beautiful spring morning she was sitting on her back step crying when I brought the paper. I had seen the wreath of flowers on the front door. I had no idea what to say, but it seemed inappropriate to just hand her the paper and pedal away. So I got off my bike and sat down on the step beside her. We just sat there, she crying, me looking up into the new leaves of the big oak tree that dominated the backyard. I listened to her soft sobbing and to the vocal experiments of a mockingbird in the top branches. It was five minutes, maybe; no more.

"Thank you," she said.

And it was OK to leave.

First time I caught the gas station guy asleep was on a similar morning. Again, it seemed inappropriate to just leave the paper and pedal on. So I threw the tightly rolled daily hard against the station's metal door. It was even louder than I expected. The guy jerked as though he'd been jabbed with an electric cattle prod. He jumped to his feet, fear and anger distorting his face. His expression was almost one of pain, and I decided later he must have had a hangover.

As I pedaled away, trying to look nonchalant, he ran to the door and jerked it open. But he didn't yell after me or anything. And I knew he wouldn't complain to the distributor I worked for or try to get the station owner to cancel. If he did either, he would have had to admit to sleeping on the job.

A couple of other mornings I caught him aslumber and repeated the door-banging scenario. I had to. I can't explain the compulsion, but it wasn't just orneriness that made me do it. It was bigger than that. It was my paper route. It was my time of morning. Sometimes I'd spend the entire hour throwing papers and never see another person. A certain feeling of power came from that. Banging that guy awake was a way to flex it.

I never saw him again after the last morning I did it. They started closing the station at night. But probably the door-banging didn't have anything to do with it. Probably it was lack of business.

When I happened upon that bird sleeping on the wire fence, I stopped my bicycle maybe a foot from it and just stared. Its feathers were all ruffled up from the hard storm not long past, giving it an unpreened, disheveled appearance. Branches and leaves had been knocked from the elm trees and were strewn over the street and sidewalk. Wind, rain, thunder, and lightning had made it a rough night on nests.

Perhaps, had its long tail been on the other side of the fence, I could have pedaled on and left the bird undisturbed. But the tail was pointing in my direction. I had to reach out with my right hand and see if I could grip it between my thumb and forefinger and do it before the bird woke up. I did. And then the bird awoke with a peep of surprise and immediately started trying to fly away. I held fast to the tail. I hadn't thought ahead to what I should do if this happened. A heartbeat or two and the bird was gone. I was holding a feather.

I hadn't meant to be cruel. I supposed the bird was all right and would grow a replacement, but I hated what I'd done and would have given the feather back if there had been any way. A sadness about it rode with me for the rest of the route.

Another stupid thing I did was fill my bicycle tires too full. The harder they were, the easier it was to pedal. So I would stop at a gas station and shoot in compressed air until the tires felt solid. No air gauge—I went solely by feel.

And then one early summer day after the route was thrown, while I was taking a late morning nap, I heard a loud pop outside. Like a firecracker or gun in the front yard. I went to the door and looked out. Nobody. Nothing. Just my bike parked in front of the porch. I returned to my nap, but a few minutes later there was a second loud pop, followed by a crashing noise, which I recognized as the sound a falling bicycle might make.

It had been early morning's cold air that I had shot so freely into the tires. And after finishing the route, I'd parked my bike in the sun, which heated the black tires, made that cold air expand, and blew out the tubes and tires. It cost about three weeks' pay.

I can't remember exactly why I quit throwing papers. Perhaps it was having to get up so early every single morning. Collecting the money every month was a real hassle, too. And when it snowed it could be hell if it was the wet and sticky kind because it would pack under the fenders and bind the tires and I'd have to wake mom up to drive me in the car. Maybe I just thought I'd outgrown it.

Other jobs followed—a grocery store bag boy, a butcher's helper, a tractor driver, a body shop flunky, a painter's helper, a flag holder for a crop-dusting pilot. They paid better. But they all lacked the freedom and sense of control. And I never had another chance to grab a sleeping blue jay by the tail.

# For Mr. Turtle, and Others

## MARION WINIK

Flat goldfish floating at the top of the bowl. Stiff cat hanging from the chain-link fence. Weary dog driven, hot-nosed and trustful, to the vet for the last time. The Easter bunny that drew blood from a childish thumb and disappeared, cage and all, the next day.

The crazy fox terrier who did not want to be dressed up as King Henry the Eighth, who divebombed the sprinkler, who terrorized the slumber party, who went after Scott Sugarman bare-toothed and growling and was sucked by Mr. Sugarman's righteous wrath into the back of a pet control truck.

The gerbil Rock, mate of Roll, chased under the living room couch by the cat, where, safe at last, he keeled over from a heart attack. That same tabby, emaciated after three months in the woods, suddenly mewing at the door just as we were leaving for Disney World; entrusted to a neighbor, she had to be buried in the garden while we were gone.

Tangled, decrepit, barely mobile Scotch and Soda, dead within days of each other in the Dallas backyard where they lived together seventeen schnauzer years.

If childhood pets teach responsibility, they also teach the limits of love. To feed and to walk and to brush and to sift through the litter box, not just when you feel like it but every day, every day, every day because THIS IS YOUR PET YOU TAKE CARE OF HIM DON'T YOU THINK I HAVE ENOUGH TO DO AROUND HERE?

Go on the paper, Buddy. On the paper, do you hear? No, don't eat those shoes. Don't chew on the electrical wire. GET OUT OF THE STREET, BUDDY! HURRY! HOW MANY TIMES DO WE HAVE TO TELL YOU?

But ultimately all our affection and careful custodianship cannot keep Buddy alive, and only the meanest person would use the words "road kill" to describe an animal killed in the road.

Dustin, Tiger, Missy, Brandy, Pumpkin, Buzz, Noodles! Shep, Schnapps, Zeke, River, Conga, Rufus, Ali Baba, Fluffy the Whore. The names echo through the neighborhood, the plaintive whistles from yard to yard, the simple signs stuck hopefully on phone poles. VERY FRIENDLY. WHITE WITH BLACK SPOTS. GENEROUS REWARD.

Every day at dinnertime she runs the electric can opener by the open window, hoping the lost kitty will dream of a blue dish of moist tuna and come limping home. She would like to wear a silver bracelet like the one she had for a soldier missing in Vietnam – BUTTERBALL, and the date he disappeared, stamped in capital letters in the metal. He might turn up even now, she thinks. And can't help slowing down to look when she sees a white cat in someone else's yard.

It is less complicated to love a pet than a person, but it takes more imagination to mourn one. How can a grown woman properly express her grief over the death of a cockatiel?

I think back to Mr. Turtle, his head tucked in once and for all, laid to rest in a small box by child mourners in black witch gowns from last Halloween. The Irish wake for the Irish wolfhound. The Jewish social worker who sat shiva for a faithful Dane. Jeff, who buried Lucia in the piney woods near a stream, a Doberman outfitted like Cleopatra with studded collar and fresh-picked flowers, favorite possessions and snacks for her journey to the afterlife, poems by Wallace Stevens and Dylan Thomas copied out on slips of paper, read by Jeff and his girlfriend over the grave.

My friend Paul Basil lost his dog Lilly five years ago. Paul drew lines with people but never drew a line for that dog, a sleepy black Lab with a white star on her chest. She suffered his human sweethearts with patience, knowing their tenure in her water bed was only temporary. Sure enough, each girl eventually left in despair. God, Paul, I only wish I was that dog.

At the end, he nursed her and cleaned up after her without minding and never wanted another dog again. For months he was awkward with the sorrow of it, the back of his truck as empty as his heart.

One Saturday night Paul was driving home from New Mexico, and a drunk heading the other way crossed over into his lane and hit Paul's car at a hundred miles per hour. I see the accident over and over in my mind, and sometimes I see it like this: Just as the headlights blinded him, as the terrible noise began, that tunnel of golden light you hear so much about opened up in the roof of the car.

Floating out of the contracting front seat, the sudden shards of glass and metal, he soared straight up above the highway into the West Texas sky. And as he moved out of the tunnel through the luminous gateway, Lilly stood there waiting, her brown eyes wet, her nose lifted high, her whole stumpy body wagging with anticipation.

# The Widow Who  Lived on the Hill

EDWARD SWIFT

My mother and father met quite by accident, or so everyone in the family has said. Mother was never convinced of it. She always said that some things were meant to be. My father, from Pennsylvania, was stationed in Bastrop, Texas, during World War II, and my mother, who was born in a sawmill community in East Texas, was introduced to him by a first cousin. My father's name was Edward Franklin Swift; my mother's, Pearl Elizabeth Brown.

When they met, Mother was a telephone operator in Livingston. That was her first job, and for the rest of her life she talked about the thrill of placing long-distance calls. "Hooking people up across the country was like traveling," she would say. "In those days, talking long-distance was like going somewhere you've never been before."

Because telephone operators make very little money, Mother, living in a rooming house, decided to cut her expenses even further by occasionally sharing her landlady's bed in order to make room for unexpected travelers. Mother often told me that her landlady was very fat and ignorant of personal hygiene. Throughout her life she would suddenly remember the woman.

"Honey," she would say, puffing on a Lucky Strike, "it makes my skin crawl to think about sleeping with that sorry old thing. Your father came along just in time."

Many years later, after my father was killed in combat, Mother and I were driving through Cleveland when she suddenly stopped the car in front of a hotel. "I've got to show you something," she said. We got out of the car and stood on the sidewalk.

It was a summer afternoon in the early fifties, and Mother still had that war-bride look about her. She was dressed in a suit from the forties. Her hair was held back by tortoise-shell combs. Her seams were perfectly straight and her lips and cheeks discreetly rouged. For a while she studied the front of the hotel, and then she pointed to a window on the third floor.

"That's it," she said. "That's where your father and I spent our first night together; we were madly in love."

That day I heard, for the first time, an almost tangible sadness in her voice, and for the rest of her life I continued to hear it. Even when she was happy and making jokes, which was often. Even when she was dancing the Charleston, which she loved passionately, she was surrounded by sorrow, which she tried, sometimes successfully, to conceal. The truth is, she never fully recovered from my father's death.

"You don't recover from something like that," she would say. "You just go on the best you can."

Her darkest periods of mourning, although severe, were never debilitating. Never did she take to her bed and weep. Never did she sit down in despair. She kept moving. She kept busy. She would get all dressed up just to go to the grocery store, and although her mood might seem lighthearted, the darker drama going on inside would gradually escape almost unnoticed.

Everyone encouraged her to remarry, everyone except my grandmother. We lived with my grandparents. Grandfather, who was often lost in reverie, died in 1952, and my grandmother lived another twenty years. She was diabetic, terrified of being alone, and was never as sick as she pretended or as well as she might have wished. She lived under the fear that my mother would recover from my father's death, remarry, and abandon her.

"Your place is with me," Grandmother would say. "I'm the one who really needs you."

Even without my grandmother's pressure, I don't think Mother would have remarried. Contrary to what Grandmother believed, I don't think Mother had much interest in men or physical love, even though she had many handsome suitors. My paternal grandmother in Pennsylvania begged Mother to marry one of the eligible bachelors.

"Pearl," she said, "you will always be my daughter, even if you marry someone I don't like."

But Mother said she had never met anyone quite like my father, and for that reason she chose to remain single. She called herself "the old widow on the hill." We did not live on a hill, but that made very little difference to Mother. She liked the phrase. It rolled off her tongue, and she enjoyed saying it.

At the age of thirty she would amuse herself by saying, "Get out of my way, Mr. So-'n'-so. I have things to do today and cannot be bothered with you, for I am nothing but an old widow who lives on a hill, and I deserve some respect."

While chain-smoking her Luckies—a habit she picked up from my father and never dropped—she would make good use of her eternal widowhood. "Don't you even so much as think of taking advantage of an old widow who lives on a hill four miles outside the Woodville city limits," she would say to anyone she thought might cheat her. There she would stand, in the face of God if she had to, and in a melodious voice, demand her rights.

Although her heart was often aching, she would flash her bright smile, her opal rings, and her scarlet nails, which she said were "long but not vulgar." She would lift her lightly painted face in order to catch the best light, and, blowing smoke through her nose like a dragon, she would tell the banker exactly why he should give "the old widow who lived on the hill" a loan.

To my knowledge, no one ever refused her. The men in Woodville called her Miss Pearl, and although she sometimes lost her nerve, she had them believing that she was, underneath it all, a tiger ready to claw her way out of any cage.

I believe she was willing to claw her way out of any cage except the one she lived in, created in part by my grandmother's often feigned dependence upon a caretaker, and my mother's need to have something, or preferably someone, to occupy every minute of her time, particularly during those first few years after my father's death. Grandmother wanted constant attention, and she said that Mother was the only daughter out of three who knew how to give it. Her security was severely threatened by Mother's astounding beauty, which drew a number of eligible bachelors to our door.

One by one they would come calling, and Mother would turn them away while Grandmother watched with her small stinging eyes. Often, with Grandmother looking on from another room or listening from the porch, Mother would charm her suitors with her limited but fashionable wardrobe, her opals, her pearls, her intoxicating smile, and by what appeared to be self-assurance but was often merely a charade.

She also charmed the men by the way she smoked cigarettes.

Careful to display her varnished nails, she would hold a Lucky Strike between her thumb and index finger and slowly bring the cigarette to the center of her painted lips. I don't think she thought of smoking as unhealthy in those days. I don't think she thought of it as sexy or glamorous either, but when Mother lit up, men turned to stare.

She could blow the tiniest smoke rings and enjoyed demonstrating this practiced skill in public. Surrounded by dozens of little rings of smoke, she would suddenly look around and say: "Why on earth is everyone staring at me with intentions? All people want to do is stare at a widow, and the only way they know how to stare is with intentions; what is the world coming to? All people want to do is stare and stare, especially at widows; what is so interesting about a widow anyway?"

As children, my cousins and I were mesmerized by Mother's long, cadenced sentences with endless repetitions and questions inserted into the middle of statements. We were amused, too, by the sight of her tall, thin body moving at top speed through the house or across the yard.

"I'm all akimbo today," she would say, her threadlike arms going off in every direction imaginable. "Just look at me, I'm akimbo."

We loved the word akimbo almost as much, if not more, than she. For a brief time, it was her word. Using it made her laugh, made us laugh, and it was our laughter that provoked her to escape into even greater animation. While watering the yard she might suddenly break into a spastic Charleston, drenching us with jets of water and sending Grandmother scurrying from the front porch where she often sat engrossed in a romance magazine.

"Look at Mama run," Mother would say, pointing with the garden hose.

Mother had a stock of words that she always mispronounced, but there were three words she would mispronounce with a vengeance. She always said "mysteeris" instead of mysterious, "ba'zeer" instead of brassiere, and "Ba'zil" instead of Brazil. We children would often engage her in conversations requiring her to use one of these words. It wasn't difficult because Mother was always willing to follow our lead.

"All I want is to be a mysteeris person," she would say, knowing it would please us. "And if my eyes were as pink as an albino's I would be mysteeris."

My mother and father only lived together a few months. When he was killed in the war, their honeymoon was still going strong, and for the rest of her life she carried only the finest memories of him.

One day when she was painting her nails, I said to her, "No one could be quite that wonderful. Had you lived together a little longer you would have seen another side of him."

"No," she said, carefully picking up a cigarette while her nail polish was drying. "That's not it. There's much more to it than that, so much more until I can't explain it right now, so I won't even try to."

In her heart she was convinced that my father and she had been made for each other, that their marriage had been fixed in the stars, and she continued believing this the rest of her life.

Because my father had predicted his death, Mother believed that he had had the gift and curse of prophecy. He was a master sergeant. I was eighteen months old when he was killed in action in Burma. When he said goodbye to my mother for the last time, he told her that he would not return.

He had a premonition of his death. He just knew. "Some people know these things in advance," Mother always said. His last words to her were, "Take care of my boy."

At the time of my father's death, we had not yet moved to Woodville. We were living in Camp Ruby, a sawmill community of itinerant log cutters who were supervised by my grandfather, Isaac Elton Brown. A camp is exactly what it was: a cluster of thrown-together houses, all unpainted, with tin roofs, all resting a foot or more off the ground on hickory blocks.

We were there for only a few years, only until a small number of trees in that part of the Thicket were cut and hauled by rail to Camden, where a team of albino Negroes worked at the sawmill.

Mother was born in Camden in the year 1919. The albino Negroes were engraved in her memory, and she talked about them all her life. She said that many of them had come from Ba'zil. She said that their eyes were pink and mysteeris, and that you could not tell if they were looking at you or not. She said that white people had severely mistreated them, and therefore, they had quick tempers and were prone to carrying knives and clubs.

She also said that they sunburned easily, and that they seemed to know things ordinary people did not know. She said that my father had the same power.

# A Mission Completed for Doll

SUNNY NASH

In the 1950s and 1960s Iola, Texas, had a one-pump filling station and a general store that sold cloth by the bolt, nails by the pound, flour and meal by the sacks, eggs by the crate, potatoes by the bushel, beef and pork by the sides, and beans, beans, beans, and more beans by the scoop.

There were no fast foods, no slow foods, no foods to go, no foods to stay, no exotic foods. The nearest hamburger was thirty miles away at the Bryan Dairy Queen, and I once had greasy fries at a Houston drive-in restaurant. To some older Iola folks, those fried potatoes may as well have been in France. They didn't eat their potatoes cooked that way. And they'd never been to a big city, and many had no plans of ever going. They spent an occasional out-of-town Saturday night slow-dragging to scratched juke-box records in a Railroad Street beer joint on the lower end of downtown Navasota.

Livestock had dirty watering holes with green slime. Bees buzzed about their private hives on Mr. Hopkins's farm. But Iola had no swimming holes or swimming pools, no amusement parks or regular parks, no minigolf or maxigolf, no Little League or big league, and no camp, summer or otherwise.

Because no one I knew in Iola had air conditioning, summer heat forced us and everyone else out of the house to catch a breeze and entertain on Saturday nights. Odorless smoke from a barrel of burning cow chips chased mosquitoes and spiraled into a starry sky. Watching smoke disappear above, I saw more stars from Aunt Celia and Uncle Finner Mitchell's aging front porch than I had ever seen anywhere. Sitting for hours gazing upward, I hardly noticed weakened boards moving under my bottom when somebody bounced across the floor.

Some evenings we kids caught fireflies and stashed them in a mason jar. Pairs of curious eyes circled the glass, watching mysterious glows until taillights dimmed. Then we lost interest and bet on which mossy old man playing checkers could spit tobacco farthest from the porch. By sunset, neighbors wandered over carrying cold drinks and old quilts.

Show time! Here comes Cousin Roy, everybody howled, getting up from their reclines and pointing down the dusty road at a tiny silhouette struggling to keep his guitar out of the dirt. Rhythmic feet disturbed loose dirt on the grassless lawn, sweaty bodies swayed, and sticky palms clapped when closed-eyed Cousin Roy sang low-down blues after low-down blues to his out-of-tune picking.

Iola was a good summertime place for me, my grandmother said. There were normal children there. I lived in Bryan with my grandmother, my mother, and my brother, two years younger than I. Mostly, it was my grandmother and I, though. My mother traveled much of the time, carrying my brother to doctors in Houston and Galveston.

To get to Iola, we took Highway 21 east toward Madisonville as far as the tiny settlement of North Zulch, where we took Farm Road 39 about ten miles south to Iola. Dotted with farms and fields of cotton and corn, areas around Iola were home to many of our relatives, making it easy for us to catch rides going one way one day and the other way another day.

If a family lived in or near Iola, the family either owned a farm, worked on a farm, or left town. Some families who were not landowners hired themselves out as field hands to plant, chop, pull, and pick cotton. I remember hearing about women field hands in the old days using water breaks to nurse their babies and others becoming mothers between the rows. Uncle Finner harvested peanuts on the few acres he owned.

On Saturday mornings, Aunt Celia packed lunch meat and bread in a cardboard box. The family piled into an old car, little ones sitting on the big ones' laps. Uncle Finner drove them into Bryan to shop. Aunt Celia had to estimate her children's clothes sizes. They couldn't try clothes on for fit, touch any merchandise, return items for exchange or refund, use public restrooms, or eat in cafes. After the family had shopped, they stopped at our three-room house to visit, eat their sandwiches, and use our two-hole facility in the backyard before returning to Iola in the early afternoon.

On Sunday mornings, the Mitchells and their neighbors went to Saint Louis Baptist Church, located on the property with Iola's two-room school for colored. Sunday school, singing, preaching, shouting, and tossing coveted coins into the collection were followed by box lunches under churchyard shade trees. Children played while men carried boxes to makeshift tables. Women arranged food and fanned flies from the fried chicken. We kids were worn out and fell into silent slumber on rear pews long before the pastor preached his evening sermon from the pulpit.

By 1953, the only black children in Iola were my cousins, the Mitchells—Earlene, Charles, Berta Marie, Freddie Mae, Otis Leon, Brenda Kaye, Finner, Jr., and J. W.—and two other cousins, Woodrow and Clifton. Only Earlene, Charles, Berta Marie, Freddie Mae, and Woodrow were school age. The loss of one student would close Iola's colored school.

One Saturday in June, 1954, before my fifth birthday, Aunt Celia left thirteen-year-old Berta Marie at our house. She didn't feel like shopping. When Berta Marie lay across our grandmother's bed in the living room, it was clear why everyone called her Doll. Hardly blinking her long black lashes, Doll's huge eyes stared at the wilted flowers on the cracked wallpaper beside the bed until her family returned.

By Monday, Doll was ill. The closest doctor who would treat her was in Navasota. Uncle Finner begged a day off from his job at the filling station. The doctor said he found nothing. Back home, Doll worsened. Over a two-week period, Aunt Celia and Uncle Finner took her back several times. Finally, the doctor admitted Doll into the hospital. Before her examination, Doll asked her father to take her home. She said her bellyache had gone away.

After the doctor examined Doll, he told Aunt Celia and Uncle Finner that Doll's problem was her appendix. Uncle Finner held Aunt Celia off the doctor, who confessed that although he believed it was too late to save Doll's life, he would perform surgery, anyway. Hoping for a miracle, the weary couple agreed. To everyone's astonishment, Doll came out of surgery alive. In her room, she whispered to her mother that all she wanted was sleep. Aunt Celia watched Doll fall asleep for the last time. For weeks, Aunt Celia wept, moaning sometimes in her sleep. Her intense pain was caused by more than grief. Believing the doctor had neglected Doll, the whole family was bitter.

By the middle of August, however, the Mitchell children had to face their new plight. Doll's death released Iola from obligation to educate its black community. Officials advised the teacher to find a new position, and they closed the school forever. Aunt Celia and Uncle Finner visited nearby towns. The poorly financed Richards School for colored accepted the children. Roof and walls leaked. Light and ventilation were inadequate. Teacher quality was questionable. Out-of-date textbooks were discarded property of other schools. And there was no public transportation.

Uncle Finner bought an old car hull, rebuilt an engine, and taught Charles and Earlene to drive. Always uneasy about her children's safety since she lost Doll, Aunt Celia worried. Wringing her hands, she peeked through the porch screen periodically and watched Uncle Finner work on the car until the children's dreaded first day of school in Richards. Accepting her children's new routine with great apprehension, Aunt Celia cried after they left and fretted until they returned.

On chilly school mornings, Earlene helped Aunt Celia make oatmeal and biscuits. Freddie Mae helped pack sack lunches. Charles was by his father's side checking tires and oil. Woodrow met them out front and they were on the highway before first light. They traveled sixty miles a day round-trip in rain, fog, or ice and almost always in darkness. For most of the school year, night still rested on the Iola school when the Mitchell children passed on their way to the Richards school for colored. Night already rested on the Iola school when my cousins passed on their way home from Richards. With their right to an education threatened by their sister's death, my cousins made going to school a mission for Doll.

Earlene graduated in 1957, Charles in 1958. Woodrow took over driving. By then, the rest of the Mitchell children and Clifton were in school. When I had vacation days, I went to school with them. My school was the lowest quality Bryan offered, but it was better than the school my cousins attended in Richards. Because of something to do with taxes in 1961, they changed from Richards to Normangee, which did not provide an improvement in schools. When Woodrow moved away in 1962, Freddie Mae became driver until she graduated in May, 1964.

In June, 1964, Iola officials visited Aunt Celia and Uncle Finner.

In light of civil rights developments, they invited Otis Leon, Brenda Kaye, Finner, Jr., and J. W. to attend school in Iola. After ten years of out-of-town schools, Uncle Finner and Aunt Celia accepted, but not without reservation. Aunt Celia's fears that her children would be mistreated were somewhat arrested when Iola teachers and students seemed to be making a sincere effort to welcome the children. Brenda Kaye, Finner, Jr., and J. W. graduated from Iola High School. Otis Leon attended, but died in 1965 from an injury he suffered while playing football at the school.

Like Doll, Otis Leon and many others had been eulogized at Saint Louis Baptist Church next to the closed colored school. Earlene's wedding in 1959 and many others had been held there. Family reunions had enlivened the property annually until 1976. Friends and relatives said so long to Uncle Finner there in 1982. By the time Aunt Celia died in 1987, however, government had assumed management of the school and church grounds, where the history of Iola's black community lay. Today the property has been established as the city's garbage dump.

Doll's death compelled her sisters and brothers to finish school. Although the Mitchells boast no war heroes or superstars, diplomats, or millionaires, among them there are no dropouts, an extraordinary achievement in a time when the world did not care.

# Punching the Bag of Happiness

### LIONEL G. GARCIA

We never had a newspaper in San Diego, Texas, the little town where I was born. We didn't have to. All the daily news was passed on by word of mouth.

And, of course, there were several people in the town who were more respected as chroniclers of the news than others. For example, a distant uncle just couldn't help being a liar and he delighted in making up stories—lies about someone dying, someone running off with another woman, someone in jail—passing them on to whoever was around the streets in the early morning and then waiting during the day for the lie to take hold. These rumors, lies, were called *borregos,* or sheep, for reasons known only to the old people of the town. My mother hated him for having that particular flaw in his character. "I can't stand him . . . not even in a photograph," she would say.

Now if you want to talk about reliable, Alfredo Gomez was reliable . . . and good. You could go to the bank with everything he told my father. I never knew Alfredo Gomez to not have the news right, something that we can't even say about our most respected newspapers and television news today. But of all of them, the chroniclers of the town, the most respected and revered was Tio Amando, the butcher. My father would get up very early to go to work in Alice, but before he left, even before breakfast, he would drive to Tio Amando, who with his son Amandito butchered the beef for the day. He knew exactly what had happened during the night while we had been happily asleep. He knew the inside of politics, who was composing lampoons for whom, who was having affairs, who had been in a fight at what beer joint and last, the worst of all, who had gotten killed in a fight. In his own version of a newspaper comic section, he would throw in the latest

45

joke or two. My father would come home from the meat market, sit down and eat breakfast, and tell us all what Tio Amando had reported for the day.

Tio Amando was also a sage in those days, although we did not know it. Once, on a hot August afternoon, as he sat outside the meat market fanning himself with his blood-spattered apron – he had eyed us going by, a group of us, young, healthy, cutting up – he imparted to us one of the wisest bits of advice that we would ever receive. He took a long look at us and shook his weary head, sighed about his lost youth, and said, for all Main Street to hear, "Take advantage of your manhood right now, sons . . . for soon it will be gone." It's not often that a man gets such good advice, and for free.

In those days I had made up my mind that I wanted to be a boxer. Every Friday night, my uncle Maitias and I would sit by the radio, the room darkened for effect, and we would listen to the fights. The names were so good: Joe Louis, Sugar Ray Robinson, Jake LaMotta, Billy Conn. I wanted to be Kid Gavilan. I wanted to be a fighter. There was nothing in the world that I wanted more.

My grandmother thought that I was crazy for going around punching at the air everywhere I went. "The child has gone crazy," she said, shaking her head at me. "But just you hit something in this house and break it and let's see what a fighter you are," she warned me. My mother, hearing the warning, agreed. "That goes for me, too," she said.

That summer I worked the milk-bottle concession stand at the annual Cotton Fiesta, and with the money earned I ordered two pairs of boxing gloves from the back of a Captain Marvel comic book. I waited for months for the gloves, and when they arrived, my mother had a fit. Not only did she not agree with what I had done, she couldn't believe I had bought, with hard-earned money, two pairs of boxing gloves made of cardboard leather. My grandmother was more understanding, and I was allowed to keep the gloves. My brother Dickie and I would box in the backyard, the gloves unraveling as we fought, but since he was left-handed, I could never figure out what he was doing.

That was the least of my problems, though. I had the habit of closing my eyes when I boxed. If that wasn't bad enough, I lowered my head as though I were going to butt my opponent, and in this position, with my eyes closed, flailing away at the air, I was an easy target for anyone.

My life changed one Saturday afternoon at the old movie house. The Pathé Newsreel came on, and there on the screen was Sugar Ray Robinson training. I was mesmerized by the talent of the man. I wanted to be Sugar Ray Robinson. He was hitting a punching bag so rapidly and with so much rhythm that I figured that was my problem. I needed to train on a punching bag. Which is where Tio Amando comes in.

Tio Amando worked his butcher shop on demand. Since his cooler was very small, nothing was killed and butchered unless he was running out. In other words, if he didn't have what you wanted, you bought what he had. Nobody had ever heard of sirloin or rib-eye. I don't know what ever happened to those cuts of meat. They must have been there. Every cow is the same. But we never saw those cuts of meat. They disappeared mysteriously when he butchered. He did delight in selling my father the spleen, an organ so tough and undigestible that it required hours of boiling and a very long time to chew and assimilate. "So that you can make saliva," he would say, slapping the package as he handed it to my father.

When he needed to butcher an animal, he and his son would get up early and drive to his ranch just outside town and they would slaughter what they felt they could sell. They would haul the carcass into town on the back of the pickup truck and cut it right there behind the cooler, Tio Amando all the time gathering his news from the locals who came by, stopping now and then to give a couple of whacks to his knife against the cold steel. By seven in the morning he was so full of news that he could burst.

On Saturday afternoon, my father showed up with a big grin on his face. He had a surprise for me wrapped in butcher paper. He explained to my mother that he had told Tio Amando of my wanting a punching bag, and Tio Amando had thought for a while, had rubbed the stubble on his chin, and had said, "I'll take care of the little scoundrel." He reached into the cooler and grabbed the hind end of the cow, cut into it and wrapped the portion for my father to take home.

Now my father grinned happily as he placed the package on the kitchen table, my brother Dickie and my sister, Sylvia, and I waiting patiently for him to open it up. My heart jumped in the joy of anticipation as he unfolded the paper, unwrapped the contents and before us, on the table, we saw for the first time an undefinable mass of gray fat. My father picked it up and said, "Inside all this fat is the bladder of the cow. All we need to do is take the fat off." My brother and my sister made some excuse and left us to study the problem. My mother had left awhile earlier.

That afternoon we stripped the fat off the bladder, and at least it looked as if it had possibilities. It was round, sturdy, made of leather. When we were through, my father looked at me and then at the mass of tissue before us. I knew what he was thinking. Who was going to inflate it? My father did that, not hesitating, having a few beers in him already. Remember, it was Saturday. He blew it up as fast and as hard as he could so that he would not have to do it again. Immediately the smell of urine took over the whole yard. He took a long piece of string and tied the narrow end shut, and sure enough, I had what looked to me to be the perfect punching bag. We walked over the yard wondering where we could hang it, and eventually we agreed on the clothesline. He tied it there, and we both stepped back and admired the way it looked, almost translucent, like a balloon made of animal parts.

I went over to the bladder, reached back and hit it with all my might, my eyes wide open. The impact of the blow sent the bladder twirling around the clothesline and the old remnants of urine flying in all directions, burning my eyes. I spat, smelled my hand, and made a face. "Don't worry," my father advised me, "that will go away after a while. . . . It has to. Nothing lasts forever."

I stayed there and hit it several more times, now with more of a light tap than the heavy blow I had first given it. I was no fool. The next day I could hit it harder, but the air somehow was escaping, and with my father gone, I was left to inflate it myself. When I did, I tasted the bitterness of urine that had stagnated out in the open, that had impregnated the old bladder since the moment the animal had been slaughtered. I realized then how much my father loved me to have been the first one to blow it up. I knew then that I could never let him down.

From that day on I would dance around the bladder, now light and flapping in the wind, tapping it lightly just like Sugar Ray Robinson, and in time the smell was gone, the smell from my hands was gone, and every time I hit it I rejoiced in the whomping sound that it made. In time it became so dry and translucent that I could see through it and every day that I hit it, it would resound even more, like an aging tympany, filling the neighborhood with a melodic bass well into the night.

I never became a boxer. My nose bled all the time and it scared my mother and she took the tattered gloves away from us.

Tio Amando, every time he saw me, would take up a boxer's stance and jab at me and say, "Come on. Throw your best at the old man. Let's see how well you can do."

I never asked for anything else again in my life.

# The Boy Who Saved Pecan Pie

MICHAEL BERRYHILL

The best pecan pie in the world is made by my Yankee mother using my father's mother's recipe. My grandmother was a country woman from the little North Texas town of Petrolia in Clay County. Some of the cookbooks I have unsystematically searched say that the most frequent problem with pecan pie is making it too sweet. But many other things can go wrong with pecan pie.

Everyone knows that a bad crust kills a pie. Nonetheless, millions of people continue to make and even sell, in restaurants and bakeries, bad crusts.

I am not going to explain crust. That would require research worthy of theologians. The argument would be worse than the one about whether to cut egg noodles when they are wet or when they are dry. If you don't have a good recipe for crust, find one before making this pie. All I have is a recipe for the innards.

Here are some of the wrong things that are put into pecan pies: light syrup, brown sugar, molasses, maple syrup, honey, cream cheese, buttermilk, cornmeal, chocolate, bourbon, rum, kahlua, other kinds of nuts, raisins, and even Pecan Sandies cookies. Until the world—OK, I'll be more modest—until the state learns how to make basic, quintessential, don't-ever-change-this-recipe pecan pie, why should it be messing around with these deviations?

Critics of the news media, make a note in the margin here. I blame us, the mass media, for these deviations. We have lost track of the fundamentals. We have made people bored with their ordinary lives. Because of us, vast numbers of the public are into hang-gliding and cosmetic surgery. Imagine the damage this quest for the new has done for the understanding of pie.

If we acted responsibly, we would quit publishing any other pie recipes until we were sure our readers had this one down.

But before I can give you the recipe, you are going to have to listen to a story about it. I call it, "The Boy Who Saved Pecan Pie."

Back when I thought in images and not in words, my father bought a new blue Studebaker pickup with red wheels. Before it could get very dirty from being on the job, he built a wooden frame on the truck bed, covered it with a dark green tarpaulin, and stretched it tight with ropes threaded through brass grommets. Into the back of the truck he placed a double-bed mattress, several pillows and a thick stack of patchwork quilts.

There were three of us children: I, the oldest, Barbara, and David. We all got in the back of the truck with my mother and cuddled under the heavy warmth of the quilts. It was autumn, a cold front had blown through and we had hours to drive from Houston to see Grandma in Petrolia.

Petrolia. The name evoked the essence of Texas. A name like Coaltown in the mountain states. It was flat and bleak, a wide spot in the road that had sprung up on some long-ago oil strike and was just hanging on. A store or two remained open, but most of the buildings were boarded up.

My grandparents lived in a small white house fronted with wooden pickets whose white paint had been sanded gray by the wind. You passed through a rickety broken gate, its foot planted firmly in the mud, its slanted top worn smooth by hands.

The yard was planted completely with flowers, flowers as tall as I was, which was not very tall, but tall for flowers. They presented a bewildering array, some of them bright red and purple and blue, and worked by bumblebees. Others were withered and stale.

My grandmother was cooking. When I was not looking, one of the men had caught and killed a chicken in the backyard, and she cleaned it. She showed me the egg yolks from inside the body. The hen would have laid them if we had not picked her for dinner.

My grandmother wore rimless glasses and coiled her long, gray braids in compact masses on the side of her head. At night she would sleep out back with Barbara on the sleeping porch. It was insulated merely with a double thickness of fine mesh screen through which the world looked weird and wavy.

Grandma would stand in a white flannel nightgown patterned with small flowers, warming herself before the long fingers of flame that shot up the ceramic face of the gas fire. Slowly she unraveled the gray braids and brushed out her hair. My sister would brush the lower ends, as high as she could reach. Carrying hot water bottles, they would tread carefully out to the cold double bed stacked high with quilts.

I slept where my father had slept when he was a boy, on a cot in the small room just off the kitchen that also serves as a pantry and storage area. The house had no plumbing. A big pot of water rested on the kitchen counter from which we would drink from a communal dipper.

After fried chicken and biscuits and cream gravy with dark flecks of chicken skin and pepper in it, creamed corn, cole slaw, sweet pickles, and sliced tomatoes, we ate pie. I was standing on the kitchen linoleum and could barely see the top of the table, and someone gave me a piece.

Pecan pie was my discovery. The adults were eating it, of course, but they didn't notice it like I did. If I hadn't been so persistent, pecan pie would have been lost with other of my grandma's secrets. But I saved it for the world.

I immediately begged my mother to bake it. We went home and weeks passed and she did nothing about pecan pie. We ate our usual meals, oven-fried chicken, green beans and new potatoes with ham, roast beef with potatoes and carrots. David tried to eat all the carrots, but we stopped him. The day after they were first served, the roast beef and vegetables became stew with biscuits.

No pecan pie. I was not a whiny kind of boy. I had a simple request. I adored grandma's pecan pie. Wouldn't mother make it?

My mother said she would get the recipe. The first time she made it, she was too busy and harassed with raising us. She left out the eggs. The result was gooey and tacky, like stiff candy. We rolled it up into little balls, laughed, and called it pecan taffy.

Finally she made it right, just like it is supposed to be. The pecans were native and fresh and crumbled by hand. No humpbacked, halved pecans sat conspicuously on the top. Its insides were a gelatinous, brown goo of perfect consistency and moisture. Its sweetness mounted straight up to the permissible limit, then backed down a notch. It was best served, I decided, at room temperature.

A longtime friend of the family always asked my mother for two of these pies for Christmas, not gifts that you buy at a store. I couldn't understand why he just didn't ask for the recipe and get his mother to make it.

Here's what goes into it: ½ cup white sugar, 2 tablespoons butter, ¼ teaspoon salt, 2 tablespoons flour, 1 cup dark Karo syrup, 2 beaten eggs, 1 cup broken native pecans, ¼ teaspoon almond extract. (Some people substitute vanilla for the almond extract, but I have already remarked about deviations.)

Cream the butter and sugar. Add the beaten eggs, flour, salt, extract, and syrup. Stir with a spoon until well mixed and add pecans. Pour into an unbaked pie shell and place in an oven that is a little hotter than 350°, but not at 375°. Bake about forty-five minutes. A knife will come cleanly out of the center when it is done.

Sure, this recipe can be messed up, especially if you make a bad crust, or try to bake four at once and haven't compensated by making the oven a little warmer. My nightmare is that I have left something out and will ruin thousands of Christmases. So I am calling my mother one more time to check the ingredients.

Other recipes, I notice, call for entire cups of sugar. Well, no wonder other pies are too sweet. Others call for more eggs and more butter. To paraphrase the modernists, sometimes more is too much. None of the thirty or so recipes I have seen includes the flour or the almond extract. Maybe they are the secret ingredients. By the way, you could easily ruin the pie by adding too much almond extract.

I called my mother again, and the recipe is true. Some of the things in my story "The Boy Who Saved Pecan Pie" are not true, but I'm not going to say which ones.

# A Boy and His Stick Horse

BOB LEE

Recently I made what is now the routine trip to my people's farm in Newton County, deep behind the timber curtain in East Texas. I do the chores for my elderly relatives. I usually cut wood and stack it for my ninety-eight-year-old aunt, who still uses a wood stove. I mend fences, cut grass, and go into Jasper to pay bills and shop.

I learned to love the forest as a child, taught by my uncle, De-Witt Adams, who died this year at age eighty-nine. He was simply one man among many in that part of East Texas who struggled through a life as a logger, hunter, farmer, horseman, and cattle-man – supporting his family in the best way he knew.

To me, Uncle DeWitt was King of the Forest. He taught me the sounds of the Big Thicket: birds, frogs, farm animals, crickets, rushing waters, and my aunts, Shug and Odell, singing. He lived a simple, communal life and was almost totally self-sufficient. The only things he didn't make on the farm were coffee and salt.

Our land has always been a haunting and mysterious place and is to this day. Uncle DeWitt was born there in 1900, and died there, looking out the window of the house he built into the trees. He had a love affair with the forest. It was tough, like any love affair.

He once told me that after slavery many blacks of that county went deep into the forest and formed little settlements. The Thicket offered places to fish, good land to farm, logs to build homes, grass for cattle and horses, wild game to hunt, and springs for water.

Uncle DeWitt thought the forest was God's country. When I was a little boy, even I believed Newton County was the Garden of Eden. It was a paradise, a place where legends and tall tales, dreams and romances existed.

Most of all, Uncle DeWitt taught me the sense of freedom and

self-reliance that comes from living in the woods and doing everything for yourself.

Many times I'd planned to take my nephews and niece to East
Texas with me to get them started into loving the forest. But I'd
say no, I'm going all alone and have this paradise to myself just
one more time.

This weekend, however, I took along my five-year-old, curious,
energetic nephew, Little Thurman. The weather was beautiful this
day, and as I worked, he followed in my footsteps, asking childish
questions. "What's this, Uncle Bob? What's that, Uncle Bob?" He
was in my way, all the way, like a fat little puppy.

"That's an anvil, son; it's been in our family since slavery times,"
I told him.

"What's inside there, Uncle Bob?" he asked.

"That's where we cooked sugar cane and made it into syrup,"
I replied.

Then he asked, "What's that, Uncle Bob?"

"That's where we made our cornmeal. It's called a grist mill. Your Uncle DeWitt was the only man in many counties who made his own cornmeal. The skill goes back to our ancestors."

I walked back into the forest to see how the garden was growing. Little Thurman followed me like Winnie the Pooh follows Christopher Robin. The garden was green with tomato plants, onions, cucumbers, squash, and turnips, and I could see the tracks of the thieves: opossums, raccoon, and deer. I pointed this out to Little Thurman.

As we walked barefooted through the cool soil, I asked him, "What's your favorite toy?"

"Robots, a toy dragon, spaceships, my toy computer, Hulk Hogan, and laser guns," he answered with excitement.

"But where are your stick horse, cowboy hat, and six-shooter?" I asked.

"Stick horse?" he asked, laughing. "What's that?"

That was more than I could let pass. I picked up a broken rake handle, tied my handkerchief around the top end, and mounted my horse. "Whoa, boy," I ordered. Little Thurman looked puzzled, then asked: "What's that, Uncle Bob?" I whinnied, slapped my horse's rear, rose up like the Lone Ranger, and shouted: "This is a stick horse!"

My horse took off like Secretariat at the Kentucky Derby. Dust and Little Thurman trailed behind me, crying, "Let me ride the horsey!" My stick horse made a stop, then began to buck. "Whoopee, whoa boy," I shouted to Little Thurman. "Get back, he's mean. He might kick you."

"Let me ride, Uncle Bob," Little Thurman begged. With one jerk of my bridle, the horse stopped bucking, and we ran toward the house, with Little Thurman close behind. I dismounted and tied my stallion to the front gate. Little Thurman ran up, sweating with excitement.

In the yard I found an old broomstick, then I got one of Uncle DeWitt's ancient, colorful ties to act as a bridle. This new stick horse must have looked like a Shetland pony to Thurman.

I gave full instructions to Thurman before he could mount: number one, don't lay your horse on the ground; number two, tie him to the fence so he won't catch cold; three, don't bring him inside the house because mothers don't like animals in their homes;

four, stay on the trails because horses are afraid of snakes; and five, your horse will ride only you, not two.

"So come on, Uncle Bob," Thurman said.

"Whoa, horsey, what are you going to name him?" I asked. He said "Boy!"

I advised him to ride slow and hold the bridle tight. He mounted Boy, gave his horse a slap on the rear and took off as if he were riding for the pony express.

As Little Thurman rode and played on his stick pony by himself, I recalled my former constant companions on the range. My brother Thurman rode a fine horse he called Fury. Our kid brother, El Franco, was made to be the Indian. It's a known fact that no one who played Cowboys and Indians wanted to be the Indian. But if you wanted to play with the big boys, you had to start out as the Indian. I would tie chicken or turkey feathers to El Franco's stick stallion. I would also paint his face with shoe polish and stick a feather in his hair.

It wasn't long before El Franco loved playing the warrior of East Texas with his broken BB rifle in one hand. Mounted on his beautiful stick horse, Little Ribbon, named after Aunt Odell's real horse, Ribbon, a fine Appaloosa given her by Uncle DeWitt, El Franco was constantly on the warpath. He would ambush us as we brought the settlers through his territory. He never won because we had Roy Rogers six-shooters with endless bullets. And, of course, we had the cavalry.

Riding and fighting Indians and outlaws all day, we got pretty hungry and thirsty. We kept our pockets filled with the tea cakes Aunt Odell lovingly baked, and we drank from the creek that ran through our land.

This particular Saturday as I raised my head to see Little Thurman on his imaginary pony cross the same cattle guard my brothers and I had bridged years before, I thought to myself: Laser guns and spaceships in East Texas? When all these beautiful stick horses are available for riding?

I watched Little Thurman disappear as he dashed down the road into the Big Thicket, and I shouted after him: "And, rule number six, this time around, try *not* to fight with the Indians!"

# The Books of Summer

MARGARET SYMMANK

In the summers I never went much farther than I could walk. I walked to the store for jawbreakers and comic books, to Bible school, where I sang, "Roll away, roll away, roll away – every burden of my heart roll away," and every two weeks, I walked to the bookmobile.

The road that led to the store and Bible school and the bookmobile ran three-quarters of a mile from our house to the post office – a narrow, rock-topped, too-hot-for-bare-feet piece of county right-of-way parallel to the Santa Fe Railway.

From the road, I waved to accommodating engineers who traveled the rails from Galveston to Houston and Lord only knew where beyond that. Very far, I was certain. The boxcars swayed along the tracks – clanking when empty, bumping when full – headed for places distant and dim. Roll away, roll away, roll away.

I'd been to Galveston for Christmas shopping, sampled the wonders of the candy counter in Sears, and roamed the endless, shell-spattered beaches in summer. I'd seen Houston a time or two. It was fast and noisy, and people wore their Sunday clothes no matter what day it was. I knew I wasn't ready for that. Maybe someday – when I knew things. Knowing things came from books, and books came from the bookmobile.

It was an awesome creation. Huge and square and green and tan, it parked itself in the shade by the post office two Saturdays a month. It had wheels and doors that opened like a school bus but bore no other resemblance to that very distant kin. Inside, it was a room. Not a vehicle at all, but a real place with shelves of books all the way to the ceiling, and lights and a tiny oscillating fan that stirred the dim air breathed by all the visitors in all the other places the bookmobile stopped.

At one end of the room was a little set of steps that led up to the driver's seat. There was no rail or chain to keep people from going up the steps and having a look around. Such a trespass was unthinkable. The driver always walked over to the store for a Nu-Grape, then sat leaning against a sycamore trunk smoking Luckies while the line of applicants for library books snaked in one door of the bookmobile and out the other. Ten, maybe fifteen minutes was the limit allowed inside. The ever-present press of those behind, waiting their turn, frustrated the brief quarter-hour in the bookmobile world.

A sustained and reverent hush filled the small cavern, its walls bumpy with book spines. Visitors shuffled the length of the room, transfixed by titles, offering and receiving whispered counsel.

"If you'll check out *Anastasia* for me this time, I'll let you get a book on my card next time. If you get that one, don't read it before you go to sleep, or you won't."

The books were there for the taking, but choosing was agony. Four. Only four at a time to keep for two weeks. One had to choose carefully. Trouble was, once the book had been read enough to know if it was the right one, there was little left to be read at home. Yet it was impossible to put the book back on the shelf half-read. Sometimes, the only thing to do was to act on blind faith, or maybe a word of wisdom from a fifth-grader whose name appeared on the checkout slip in the front pocket.

My selections made, I faced the trial of the checkout desk. The librarian sat behind it. Serious and graying, she embodied all the authority vested in her by the Galveston County Library System. She wore navy or brown, buttoned and cuffed even in August. She would sometimes stop, rubber stamp lifted in midair, and peer deep into my soul to determine if the book I had chosen was on my reading level. A second-grader dared not attempt to pass herself off as going into fourth.

There were two ways to walk home. I could trot along the dusty, narrow shoulder of the road—the quicker to arrive home and be at the tempting stories tucked under my arms. Or, I could start reading as I walked, stepping too high or too low over the uneven ground while the words bounced in and out of focus, stark against the glaring page.

The best stories happened far away, in places real or not so real.

Places past the boundaries of the known world—beyond Houston or Galveston. Places somewhere along the distant reaches of the Santa Fe Railway—across the bumpy brown waters of the Gulf of Mexico. Albuquerque, Shangri-La, the moon. Places where possibilities were wonderfully frightening, where I might someday be plunked down to live out adventures and do great deeds millions of miles from chores or arithmetic or similar pressing problems.

My transport was simple and sure—long afternoons spent stretched on a quilt under the trees, lulled by the sway of leaf-filtered sunshine across the mesmerizing words on the page. Roll away, roll away, roll away. The effect was consistent, the results reliable. Every burden of my eight-year-old heart always rolled away.

By the time I could reach the top shelves without effort, standing head and shoulders above the better part of the bookmobile crowd, the summers had grown shorter. The world was miraculously reduced to a manageable list of continents and oceans suspended in a universe whose orbs I could comfortably name. The conductors on the trains rarely waved from their rocking cars, or at least, not that I noticed.

The books were thicker now. The far-away places named within their pages were unquestionably real and had come frighteningly close. Wounded Knee, Hiroshima, Auschwitz.

More frequently I rode instead of walked. With friends, with boys, or taking the wheel myself. Once, during a summer storm, when I drove past the post office, the somber, dark form of the bookmobile sat beneath the thrashing sycamores. Its doors were sealed against the ran. It glistened and seemed oddly small.

I don't remember when the bookmobile stopped coming. The last summer before I drove away, over the railroad tracks to places very far and very real, I think it may have parked there by the post office once or twice.

Then the reading changed. It was now the means rather than the once-glad end I'd come to know every two weeks. I plowed through volumes etched with eye-squinting print—heavy, weighty, bound as though they meant business. Descartes, Kant, Nietzsche. Sometimes the heavy books would slip onto the floor unseen by eyes closed beneath lids every bit as heavy. In dreams I rode the bookmobile. Seated in the sacred seat, I steered along the railroad tracks, rocking off to some unnamed land, reading books on any level with wild abandon. Roll away, roll away, roll away.

Through the years, I've seen a bookmobile once or twice. Not mine. A sleeker, fuel-efficient model, air-conditioned, tinted windows, slipping through the traffic en route to some nameless little town. There must be children there. Lined up. Waiting. Waiting for the bookmobile to take them far away.

# Traffic Rogues of Richmond

### RICK BASS

We weren't bad kids. Sometimes we'd drink a whole six-pack of
Budweiser among the five of us. Didn't much like the taste. Three
of us were seniors and two were juniors. We car pooled to Robert E. Lee High School from the west side of town.

David (burly and gruff) was the leader. Then there was Mark
(frail and hippie cool, with a glass eye); Stuart (supercool, wore
expensive sunglasses); Steve (the jock); and me (the intellectual).
We would not have associated otherwise – especially not the juniors
and seniors – but the car pool, well, we had to. Economy.

Do people car pool anymore? This was so long ago that we had
eight-track players in our cars. We all drove beat-up cars and lusted
after women – girls – and new cars. You can imagine the conversations. We were driving horrible old cars that did not express our
true wild hearts, not in the least. In fact, we were driving old
ante-cars. And dating old ante-girlfriends. What a barbaric age,
adolescence.

Houston gasoline was cheap in 1973 – thirty-nine cents a gallon,
I think. I know there are people who remember it being a nickel a
gallon, which is like it being free, but thirty-nine cents wasn't bad.

I sound like a grandfather. It was only sixteen, seventeen years
ago.

The cars we ferried each other to school in were horrible: bald
tires, steaming radiators, dragging mufflers – and we weren't doing
it to be cool, or quaint, or rustic, or tough. They were just ancient
cars. One frosty morning my old Ford caught fire, and we had to
lift the hood and put the fire out by throwing shovelfuls of dirt
on the engine while all the other motorists gawked, but wisely
kept going.

The wonderful thing about the car pool was that not one of

us would have had a thing to do with any of the others under more normal conditions. It was daring what we were doing, crossing boundaries. Of course, in the hallways, we'd never acknowledge each other, never even nod or say hi. But before and after school, it was like family—a squabbling family, to be sure—always deviling each other about our eccentricities, knowing exactly what to tease each other about. We'd tease Stuart about his dark glasses, Mark about his sissy puka shells or whatever those things were called, Steve about his weight lifting, and me about my driving. I was the youngest, and clumsiest. I'd bounce the car off curbs in my wide sweeping turns, much to the delight of others. And David? Nobody teased David about anything; he was huge and "adult," deep-voiced and cynical. Weary, already.

Westheimer was three wide lanes then, not four skinny ones, and no one was on the roads at 6:30 or 7:00 in the morning. We'd glide down Westheimer unencumbered, hitting all the green lights, seeing them hanging one beyond the other, all the way down the long runway of Westheimer. In the early morning fog the road was just plain empty, and there were green lights as far as we could see, so it was like fish running to the sea.

There was a field across from the high school. The Field, it was called, and because it was always raining in the winter and spring, The Field (long since developed into a shopping mall with pizza and tropical fish) was always muddy.

On dry, sunny days most of the students parked in The Field because the meager parking lots were full.

We parked there every day, rain or shine. The more mud, the better.

We hated our old cars. We could never injure them enough so that they would stop running.

It became a code of honor to park in The Field—to start at one end and make it all the way to the other end.

Anyone who did not at least try was, clearly, not a man.

The teachers and other students would watch in horror from the windows as great plumes of mud churned into the sky, completely obscuring our presence. Almost always, it was raining, and there would be a sheet of rain between us and the school, so that those in the school could barely see us. With the school looming in front of us, dull and flat-walled, it looked like some kind of penitentiary.

We'd go to class muddy and with our hearts still racing. Never learned a thing, except how to drive in the mud. There was one French teacher—the real thing, with a French name even—who was particularly horrified by our actions. He would hiss "Cad!" whenever he saw one of us in the hall. His second-floor window faced The Field and he took the savagery of it, the mindlessness of it, personally.

Another thing we'd do with our cars—discovering our powers and theirs, the power of a free, open world and cheap gas, simultaneously—was what we called, in reverent and yet ominous tones, The Block.

It was even more barbaric than the mud-rutting.

The trick was to raise tempers, create havoc, and spawn chaos and dissent.

We'd drive as slowly as we could alongside another slow-moving vehicle (the two side-by-side, one-way lanes of Richmond were particularly good for this) and then cackle like mad hyenas, as our bounty, our treasure, collected behind us like shrimp in a net. It was best if we knew someone who was blocked behind our barricade. We kept score: twenty, twenty-five, thirty cars "blocked" were respectable numbers, with us leading the way, creeping, like pied pipers.

Needless to say, I'd be less than amused if someone did this to me today. But back then, the city was not in so much of a hurry. There wasn't, believe it or not, a really serious traffic problem, and it was good, clean, perverse fun. David one time was able to block forty-three cars before losing them as he went through a traffic light.

The most exciting thing we ever did with our cars was a city-wide block, the day of final exams one spring. We were seventeen and eighteen years old. I wince to think that we might have been so immature at such an advanced age, but we were.

We left our neighborhood at the same time, with synchronized watches, as if on a bomber mission, or like a pack of wolves, hunting. Each of us drove his own beat-up car with cardboard taped over the license plates.

David, Stuart, and Mark—the seniors—took the three eastbound city-bound lanes of Westheimer at eight in the morning. Steve and I, peeling off from the pack and scooting down Gessner to pick up the two eastbound lanes of Richmond, did the same.

We crept.

It was biblical. It was as if the Red Sea were behind us, the morning sun glinting off all those trapped cars and all the writhing souls inside them. It was as if we were leading them ever so slowly at four, five miles an hour into the promised land. Steve and I, cotton-mouthed, fear-hearted, but loyal and committed, glanced over at one another at times, grinning nervously. At other times we pretended to be nonchalant, as if not realizing what was going on: just out for a slow drive.

The horns behind us sounded like – an air raid? New York City? Baying hounds? We imagined that, over all the noise, we could even hear the far-off strains of horns, many more horns, over on Westheimer.

It was like being in love – that kind of commitment, that kind of loyalty. Knowing we had to all stand together and keep the seams plugged, or all would be lost, and the city would slip through.

At 8:25 A.M. we made our escape – punched the accelerators and sped away; took back routes to the school and did not park in The Field, but in the secluded anonymity of nearby apartment complexes. We sauntered into school wearing dark sunglasses, whistling, but with hearts still racing, and still able to feel, or imagine that we felt, the trembling, furious buzz of the city's anger, like a hive of bees.

All we wanted to do was see how much traffic could be stacked up on those two roads; all we wanted to see was, just once, wall-to-wall cars, glittering bumper to bumper, in our young city, on those fast, open streets.

Be careful, as Tobias Wolff, and others, say, of what you wish for.

# Arms and the Man

## DAVID THEIS

The first killed deer I distinctly remember seeing was shot by a young friend of my family. He had the nice mythic name Kit, and I remember him – thirteen, crew cut, athletic, red-faced – bursting into the bunkhouse of our parents' shared South Texas deer lease, where I, nine, and habitually dreaming, sat with my father and Kit's father. The two men were about the same age, but my father, with his deep-set, harrowed eyes could've been my friend's parent instead of my own.

Kit shouted several times that he'd hit a buck, and we all ran out of the bunkhouse for my father's light blue pickup. Much later I learned he used to win barroom bets against strangers, for despite his great bulk, he could pull off his boots and outrun them. But now he lumbered just ahead of me. I had to ride in the truck's back and braced myself against the cab as we sped bouncing over hard dirt roads toward the spot where Kit had shot his deer. There they got out to look for some trace of the animal's path. Again I ran behind, and strained to see the blood that the fathers bent over. They followed its trail in the direction Kit pointed, and I could hear them call out when they found another trace.

I lingered and stared down to where the first stain was supposed to be, but couldn't find it. I must have made a ten-foot circle but found not one drop of blood. Kit and the men ran past me back to the pickup. I saw no choice but to operate on the faith that I, too, would one day see.

The adults understood the deer's trail, and my father found his way to a farm-to-market road that led to the other side of the lease. There, just beyond the bare trees, in a drainage ditch beside the road, lay Kit's deer, dead now, with one eye dangling from its socket by a fine pink ribbon of muscle. I wondered if the eye were dead too, or if, freed from the body, it watched as the adults bent over the ruined head and counted the points of its antlers.

The next season my eight-year-old brother came to join us at the lease. I was too old now to evade the hunting itself and wander alone, looking for javelina tracks, imagining I found them or even the fossilized print of a dinosaur. The hunting I had mastered still led me into the preserve of boys and their imaginations, rather than that of men and completed acts.

My brother was ready, though, and late one afternoon he, my father, and I sat hidden behind a large dead bush. My brother had a little .22-caliber rifle, while I carried a .410-gauge shotgun loaded for deer. I had fired at plenty of tin cans in my life, but the gun across my knees still seemed quite apart from me, so that I felt lost, still blind, when my father bent his head and whispered, "Do you see her?" I squinted through the bush but saw nothing.

"There," he said, "at the edge of the trail. She's looking to see if it's clear for her buck to follow."

So now I'd have to shoot, and I squeezed my gun but still saw nothing but the branches in front of my face.

"She's coming across now," my father whispered. "You've got to be awake."

"I can't see anything," I finally whined.

"Get your gun ready," he said, then whipped his own 30.06 carbine up in a quarter-arc from his bent knees to his shoulder. Without taking time to aim, he fired. My gun still rested on my knees and I winced at the report.

My father stood, exultant. He'd hit a buck on the dead run without even properly aiming. My brother shivered in excitement and I, frustrated, stood to follow them toward the deer.

"He's still alive," my father said, and now that I finally saw the animal stretched out on the hard ground, I watched as its legs pedaled in little circles, as if it were trying to dog-paddle out of the already great, dark-red pool.

My father pointed out the bullet hole at the base of the deer's long neck. I nodded and looked, but somehow the animal didn't seem real to me. Maybe it was just my age and discomfort with the world, or my fear of our logical next step, or the odd, dreamy silence, but that buck was the most abstract thing in the world, and no amount of blood pumping from the base of its neck could make him alive.

"And look at this," my father said. "He's a freak."

The deer's antlers, instead of branching apart, had grown and twisted together.

"I've never seen a rack like this," my father said, himself nervous now. "We'll mount him for a trophy."

It made sense that when a deer finally lay dying at my feet it would be a freak, his thoughts turned in on themselves. Maybe he was even a messenger, warning me of the inherent strangeness of the world I was about to enter. The pool of blood extended now toward our tennis shoes and my father's boots, and my brother wanted to finish it off.

"No," my father said, then turned to me. "You're the oldest."

He said this with all possible generosity, even repeated that he'd never seen such horns. He told me to aim just above the shoulder to the heart so that the head would be preserved. I lifted my gun, pointed its barrel down at the still pedaling animal.

At forty-nine, my father had hair as white as the snow that never fell here, and some days he could scarcely move, though I didn't know that then. Maybe he felt something in his bones. Maybe he wanted to hurry me along.

There was no question of not shooting, but I looked away as I fired. My blind shot hit the deer in the back of the head and broke the bone connecting the two antlers. I looked up just in time to see one horn, blown apart from its mate, hurtling end over end into the trees.

"What did you do?" my father said, and his knees buckled. The deer shuddered quietly and died. My brother glared at me.

"Dad should've let me kill it," he said.

Back at camp my father was kind, and announced that I'd shot a buck. At the same time he didn't try to make it more than it was, and I was grateful for that.

A month later his blue truck ran off a bridge. I've never learned exactly why. That midnight, when he hadn't come home, my mother checked first for his deer rifle to see if he'd left on an impetuous hunt, and came back trembling into my bedroom when she found it. I never hunted again, though every now and then my brother and I fired his gun in the open country behind our house.

I got to where I could tolerate its kick, as well as the cleansing point of pain its explosion left in my ears. But I was firing into nothing, not even aiming at trees, and so I told my brother the rifle was his.

# The Almost Unbeatable Long Shots

### C. C. RISENHOOVER

When I was growing up, baseball was the center of my being, the reason, I believed, God had put me on this earth.

The only problem was that when school ended in Jasper in 1954, the year I was seventeen, so did organized baseball. There was no American Legion team that year, no youth baseball of any kind for someone my age. It simply promised to be a long, hot summer of backbreaking work with a logging crew, with no evening or weekend baseball to ease the aches and pains.

There was, however, one hometown team that would be playing that summer – the Jasper Steers.

The Steers were about as good a semipro team as ever took the field. Some said there was nothing "semi" about them, that they were pros through and through. The Steers had it all: good hitting, pitching, and defense. When touring, major-league all-stars played the Steers during the off-season, the Jasper team usually came out on top.

While the Steers carried the name Jasper throughout the country, the team wasn't exactly the chosen ambassador of the city fathers. The reason was obvious.

All the players were black.

The Negro American League was breaking up, and many of its players found their way to teams like the Steers. Some of them were good enough to play in the majors, but there was a quota system then – whether the czars of baseball admit it or not.

All of the guys who played for the Steers shared my dream of playing in the majors. Second baseman Jackie Robinson of the Dodgers was their role model. And though I wanted to play for the Yankees, pitcher Robin Roberts of the Phillies was mine.

I'd had a good season pitching for the Jasper High School Bulldogs, but that all ended in May. Then something happened that changed my prognosis for summer. It did more than that. It changed my life.

Elmer Simmons, a black pulpwood contractor who owned the Jasper Steers, asked me to pitch a game for his team. And he offered to pay me fifty dollars.

Now it might not be a big deal today for a white boy to pitch a game for an all-black team, but this was 1954. It would be another fourteen years before Jasper's schools were integrated.

If I'd lived in one of those white houses in town, Elmer probably wouldn't have asked me. But I lived in a gray Milltown house, separated only by a railroad spur from the red Milltown houses occupied by black workers and their families. I played unorganized baseball, basketball, and football with black kids. I went to their high school games. They went to mine.

We were integrated before integration. We just never gave any thought to going to school together.

Elmer wasn't one of those alleged "agitators," a Yankee who had come South to cause trouble between the races. He was local, a man who had grown up poor, but who had become a success through hard work and perseverance.

A lot of whites resented Elmer because he drove a new Cadillac, had a big house and plenty of money. For the most part, the resenters lived in the white houses in town, and looked down their noses at everyone who lived in Milltown. Most of the Milltowners thought it was cool that the richest white people in town couldn't outdo Elmer.

Elmer loved baseball, had been a pitcher when he was younger, and I don't think he'd ever missed seeing me pitch a high school game in Jasper. (He also owned the baseball stadium where my high school team played.)

Elmer saw something special in me, which made me feel special because the man was known for his baseball knowledge. He thought I was destined for the "Bigs."

There was some hullabaloo about me pitching for a black team, and on a Sunday at that, but it didn't come from my parents. And the fifty dollars was more than I would make for a week of logging or for working at the sawmill. I never gave any thought to how playing for money would affect the remainder of my high school eligibility.

The minor league team we played that Sunday was all white. A lot of local whites showed up. Some were supportive. Some came out of curiosity, and others came to see me pounded.

I woke up that morning with a high fever, but wasn't about to complain. There was no way I was going to be scratched. It was stifling hot and humid, perfect weather for a fever.

I had watched the Steers play before and knew they were good, but you never really know how good your teammates are defensively until you see their work from the mound. In the first inning I was throwing batting practice pitches, and the opposition hit some shots. My outfielders flagged down balls that would have gone for extra bases if I'd been pitching for the high school team.

We won 3-2 in thirteen innings. I pitched the entire game and ended up in the hospital with bronchitis.

When I got out of the hospital a week later, my legs were like rubber. And Elmer Simmons had another proposal for me. The Steers were going on a two-month tour, and he wanted me to go along if I could get permission from my parents.

My folks weren't exactly in love with the idea, but Elmer talked to them and they agreed. I guess they figured I'd spend the summer moping if they didn't.

In that summer of '54 I was, for the first time in my life, color-blind. I think my teammates were, too. The summer wasn't about racism or a white boy playing on an all-black team. It was simply about baseball, unity, pulling together. I was proud to be wearing a Steers uniform, to be part of the package.

There were, of course, incidents—mostly racist remarks by whites and blacks who couldn't comprehend the kind of understanding that baseball can bring to guys who love the game.

In Louisiana and Texas we played against all-black teams. I stayed in black hotels and ate in black restaurants. Some blacks may have resented it, but my teammates were protective.

At one game a black fan became verbally abusive about my color, and I had to keep my teammates from causing him bodily harm.

Because my legs were still weak from the bout with bronchitis, I didn't pitch until we moved into Oklahoma. It was a memorable game for a number of reasons. I gave up the first home run of my career. I'd never allowed one in high school. I also hit a ball off the wall and was thrown out at first because I couldn't run.

When the opposition realized my legs were gone, the bunting began. Fortunately, I'd already pitched six innings, and we were ahead when I was relieved. I got credit for the victory.

I'd like to say I was the best pitcher on the team, but I wasn't. The best was Wacoan Alvin Jackson, a left-hander who went on to pitch for the Pirates and Mets and became pitching coach for the Baltimore Orioles.

Because we played for a percentage of the gate, and often to empty seats, money was tight. Each of us was supposed to get two dollars a day for meal money, but sometimes we didn't get that much. There were times when we didn't get any. First priority for money was gas and repair for the rickety bus that would take us to the next game.

There were days when we didn't eat, sometimes a couple of days in a row. We often slept on the bus. Showers became a luxury.

One of my best friends on the team was the late Vernon Hicks. He was then, and for years afterward, a coach at Moore High School in Waco. He was the most educated among us, knew the odds were against him, yet he pursued the dream with enthusiasm.

I intended to keep in close touch with Vernon, but like a lot of other things, that became secondary. We talked by phone a few times over the years, but I never saw him again after that summer of '54.

My professional summer made me ineligible for my senior year in high school, but I later had tryouts with the Pirates and Athletics. But the pain in my shoulder and elbow could not be hidden.

It's hell to be washed up before you're twenty.

Nothing I've ever done in my professional life has been as satisfying as playing baseball that summer. It was then I learned the lengths to which men will go to reach their dreams.

We were all long shots. But we pulled together and shared what we had. We had a togetherness that better-fed, better-equipped, and better-rested teams couldn't approach. We had, for a summer, something few people ever experience: we were almost unbeatable.

# Leaky Roofs and New Beginnings

WILLIAM COBB

Our family always fantasized about moving. We lived in an old wooden house in San Antonio for many years, a house whose roof leaked during thunderstorms. We would scatter pots and pans around the living room to catch the drips. At the beginning of the storm, when the pots were empty, the many drips and pings sounded like music. My mother said it was a pretty sound, if you ignored the water marks on the ceiling, which looked like coffee stains. It was a large house with wide hallways, a fireplace, and windows in every room. It smelled of cedar paneling and mothballs in the hall closets. But it wasn't good enough.

We used to play a game called "When We Move," in which we would try to outdo each other in our fantasy places to move to. Most of these were either in the mountains or at the sea. "When we move," said my sister Lisa, "we'll be able to go swimming every day and we'll have a sailboat, snorkel and flippers. When we move, I'll have a collection of seashells and go surfing every day and have a tan and ponytail, like Gidget."

"When we move," I said, "we'll have a waterfall at the end of Main Street and in the distance, we'll see snowcapped mountains. We'll only have to go to school two days a week, and then, half the time, we'll have recess, when we move."

We never considered our stepfather being caught up in this dissatisfaction. Glen seemed forever obsessed with a scheme to make money, to make a "killing," but it was always in weird and farfetched ways. He invested in penny stocks. He collected rare coins. He was an amateur archaeologist and had the notion to breed Rottweilers. But none of the schemes ever panned out.

Until one day, when he was picking us up at a public swimming pool, he said, "You know, when we move, you'll probably be able to swim every day." We asked if he was joking or what. We're not really moving, are we? When?

Glen reached out and rubbed the windshield with the back of his hand, because it was fogging up in the rain. "You'll find out soon enough." We found out later he had a new obsession. He had gotten into an argument with his boss at the Pearl Brewery where he worked. So he decided to quit his job, move to the Gulf Coast, and open a restaurant in a small fishing town called Fulton, right next to the slightly bigger town of Rockport.

At first we lived in an old motel, the kind that sprang up during the Great Depression; they were called motor courts. It looked like the Bates Motel in *Psycho,* only it didn't have a scary mansion behind it, and in front was Aransas Bay, with short, gentle waves, row after row of faded fishing piers, their posts covered with barnacles and oyster shells. We lived so close to the bay that we heard the constant sound of slow waves slapping at the shore through our open windows.

Fulton seemed not so much to have been built as to have been washed up by the sea. All the buildings were weather-beaten, warped, and gray. The streets and parking lots were filled with seashells and fish skeletons; sea gulls swooped in the sky above. In the convenience stores, the clerks sold live bait.

Glen quickly began work on the restaurant. He had bought a hamburger hut for next to nothing and decided that he would build out from there, using that as the kitchen area. But when we got there it was just a crummy, tiny little hamburger hut, built for selling tourists fast food in the days before everything was a Wendy's or a Burger King. It looked like a concession stand at a football stadium.

"Someday this is going to be a first-class restaurant," he said, standing in the oyster-shell parking lot, gazing at the cinder-block hut, which had the prices of french fries, malts, lemonade, and cheeseburgers painted on the walls.

"Sure, Glen," we said, sipping our chocolate shakes. But secretly it worried us that the man who owned it before had died.

But there was no stopping Glen. Around the hamburger hut, he poured a concrete slab, a foundation for the other dining room of the restaurant. The air above the wet foundation filled with a wet mud smell, the smell of something taking shape. Before it dried, we scratched our initials and the date in it.

The sea was brown that summer, the surf choppy—waves that didn't move forward but just stirred up the sand. The air had the sharp tang of the ocean smell in it, a fishy smell. One day a tide brought in millions of jellyfish—pulpy white alien-looking creatures, trailing wedding veils of stinging, threadlike tentacles, pulsing slow and graceful and sinister. For a time, the gulf seemed malignant, filled with poison and danger: stingrays whose barbs broke off in your foot, crabs that pinched, currents that sucked you under. A woman's arm was bitten off by a hammerhead shark, and we watched her husband crying by the police car on the five o'clock news, a surfer in the background, pointing out to sea. Portuguese men-of-war washed up on the beaches so that you had to watch where you stepped to avoid the purple and blue air bladders, the powerful venom in their tentacles.

In the fall Lisa and I started school in Rockport-Fulton High, and in all of our dreams and all of the times we were playing our "When We Move" game, we had never anticipated such a change. The new school shook my view of the world. I had always assumed that I would get good grades, go to college later, and assumed that everyone else wanted these things too. That's what it had seemed like at my school in San Antonio.

All of these seemed like false assumptions in Rockport. Many of the students had failed several grades and hated to read. Some of them were seventeen years old in the ninth grade and bigger and meaner than me. They sat in the back row of my math class, chewing gum and whipping their forearms with leather thongs. This was a sign of toughness. They raised huge welts on their arms and showed them off. They wore dark sunglasses and slept through history. They spat on each other in physical science.

The high school looked like any other, except that it was near a swamp. Mosquitoes thrived in the stagnant water of the many puddles and swamp grass. After lunch it was hard to pay attention as everyone scratched mosquito bites and stared at the algebraic equation written on the board and hoped they wouldn't be called on.

And there were alligators. Once, during P.E., John Watson hit a pop fly, and Richard Chernovski, in left field, was running to catch it, then stopped and just watched the white ball bounce into the green field of grass. We all watched as John loped around the bases easily, everyone yelling at Richard to get the ball and throw, but he shook his head. As John whooped and hollered running into home, Richard jogged up to second base, where the coach was standing, playing ump.

"Coach," he said, and paused. He was out of wind, and taking deep breaths between his words. "There's a gator out there, right next to the ball."

We walked out to look. "Nobody get too close," said the coach. But the warning was unnecessary. We were all about fifteen yards away, and from that distance, the alligator looked like a big black lizard, only it wasn't moving. The softball had rolled to a stop about three feet from it. We stood in an exaggerated circle around the alligator and the softball.

"Maybe it's dead," said someone. "It's not moving."

"I was right up on it before I saw it," said Richard. "I swear to God it opened its mouth and like to have bit me, if I'd gone any closer."

The coach slapped a mosquito on his neck. "Let's come back for the ball later. He'll probably be gone in a while."

After that, the outfielders were always a little jumpy.

During the fall semester, the restaurant was finished to the point that people could sit at tables, although in the back of the dining room you could still see sawhorses, and in the daytime, hear the whine of the power saw. We nailed black felt tar paper on the roof. Inside, we put rolls of fiberglass insulation between the studs, then covered it all with paneling. We bought tables and chairs on credit. We had menus printed, and matches. But still we had no business. The front wall of the restaurant was filled with windows, and at night we watched the few cars on Fulton Beach Road drive by, hoping one of them would turn in.

On evening late in November a storm came in, and it rained with the force of a hurricane. There was only one pair of snow-birds (winter Texans) having dinner, and Lisa and I and my mother and stepfather stood by the windows and watched the storm. "Isn't it pretty?" said my mother.

As we stood there, watching the slanting rain in the white head-lights of the cars, the streaking red of the taillights following them, and stretching out on the wet black asphalt behind them, we relaxed for a moment in the first big rain since the dryness of summer.

Then the roof began to leak.

First we heard the drips and noticed drops spotting the stainless steel tops of the saltshakers, then all around us vertical rivulets and streams began to appear, until soon we had to place pots and pans throughout the dining room and kitchen to catch all the rain.

Glen was defeated. "Maybe this wasn't such a great idea after all," he said. His shoulders slumped as he mopped the front dining room. With a crash of lightning, the power went out. After we helped the elderly couple out to their car with flashlights, we sat in the darkened dining room, listening to drips and pings all around us.

"I bet the power is never coming back on," said Lisa.

"I guess I didn't do such a good job on the roof," said Glen.

But mother broke out the candles, and soon the dining room was filled with light, and the drips from the ceiling flashed through the light all around us, and she hugged Glen and told us not to worry; things would be OK.

"I don't like living here, Mama," said Lisa suddenly, almost in tears. "It's so weird and creepy. There are snakes everywhere."

"It's just so different, honey. You'll learn it has its good side."

"But no one believes in anything here," I said. But my mother shook her head. In the candlelight, her green eyes were clear and steady.

"Yes they do," she said. "You just don't know them well enough yet."

I'm still not sure whether she was right or not; but we didn't move away after that, and before too long our restaurant began to make a little money, although never a "killing." We never really liked working there, my sister and I, but we developed a crowd of goofy regulars, and sometimes had fun with them. And I remember that night, while the lights were off, my mother held me so tightly that my face was smashed against her neck. I felt her ribs, and as I did, was filled with a definition of faith in the cradle of her bones.

# A Father's Legacy of Land

TERESA KYLE CAGE

All his life, until he died at eighty-five, my daddy liked to brag that he still slept in the same room he was born in. That room is in an old house on a farm in East Texas that was settled by my great-grandfather in 1839.

While I was growing up, I could not understand the pride my daddy felt about the place. The house was a simple dogtrot design, a rectangle building with an open-air hallway cut through its middle. The hallway and the high ceilings in the large rooms kept the house cool in summer, but it faced directly north, and in the winter, cold wind whipped down the hall and whistled through the cracks in the walls.

My daddy inherited the house and surrounding acres when his father died. When he was thirty-nine he met and married my mother, the sixteen-year-old daughter of a family from Louisiana who had come to work on the farm. That was in 1929, just days before the stock market crash. The Great Depression came and went, causing little change on the farm. My folks were used to hard times. In 1932 their first child was born, and then four more over the next ten years. It would be twelve more years before I came along.

While my sisters and brothers were growing up, the family raised cotton and tomatoes for market, but supporting a large family by farming was harder for my dad than it had been for his father. Daddy hired himself out to others when work was available, which was seldom, and when money was short, which was often. During World War II, he went to Houston to work in the shipyards. My mother stayed home and kept the family and farm together. When it finally became too much and she wrote my father that she and the kids were moving to Houston, he gave up his job and came home. Somebody had to be there to watch the place.

In 1952, their oldest son was killed in a hit-and-run accident. My mother was still grieving two years later when she realized that no, she wasn't experiencing menopause at forty-one. She was pregnant with me. My dad was sixty-four and proud as punch. My nearest sibling was twelve years old and reluctant to relinquish the title of baby of the family. She graduated from high school and moved away the same year I started first grade.

Growing up together on the farm, my sisters and brothers had roved the land like a tribe, working in the fields, swimming and fishing in the creek, picking wild plums and berries, and teaming up with cousins for picnics and parties. They carved their initials in the name tree–an ancient beech on the bank of the creek.

I roamed the farm with my imaginary friend Carmen. (I was never hungry for a cookie but always eager to take one to Carmen.) With just one child at home, my parents had more time to spend with me. At the first sign of spring, my mom and I would head for the woods to search out the tiny wild violets and to enjoy the heady fragrance of yellow jasmine and honeysuckle climbing and winding through the tall pines.

Spending time with Daddy usually meant a fishing trip to the creek. We'd find an empty tin can and dig up earthworms from the yard, then he'd shoulder our switch cane poles and we'd walk the trail to the creek.

My parents had given up raising crops for market by then, but we still grew nearly all our own food. My dad would hitch up our mule, Old Kate, to the plow and turn the sandy soil. I liked the feel of the fresh plowed earth—hot and dusty on top, cool and moist where the plow cut its path. In the same fields where my brothers and sisters had worked hard chopping cotton, I built frog houses by sticking my bare foot into the furrow, covering it with dirt, then slowly removing it to form a little cave.

Weeks before the garden vegetables were ready to pick, the wild dewberries ripened. We picked our way through the sunny briar patches until our Mrs. Tucker's lard buckets were full. Bigger and sweeter than the wild dewberries were the tame blackberries that my mother had planted in a row by the garden. After they were baked into a berry cobbler, you couldn't tell which was which.

When the corn stalks grew tall and green, I enjoyed walking through the shady rows picking ears with the longest, prettiest silks. I pretended I was an Indian maiden as I wove the sticky red-gold silks into braids on my corn shuck dolls.

Early mornings in the summer we would go to the field to pick the ripened produce before the heat of the day. Heavy dew covered the plants and soaked our shoes as we gathered cream peas, black-eyed peas, purple-hull peas, pinto beans, lima beans, okra, tomatoes, squash, onions, potatoes, corn, cantaloupes, and watermelons. In the afternoon, the front porch was the gathering place for shelling peas or shucking corn. Then there would be hot times in the kitchen while my mom blanched the vegetables before canning or freezing them. At the end of summer we always had a full freezer and a stock of vegetables and jellies put up in jars.

But there were some things we couldn't grow—flour, sugar, cheese, and Prince Albert tobacco, to name a few—so sometimes on Saturdays we went to town. Daddy would saunter over to sit on the whittlers' bench by Wall's Drug Store and talk with the other old men while Mama and I did the grocery shopping. Sometimes she and I went to the drugstore for a strawberry ice-cream cone.

Our livestock consisted of Old Kate, a small herd of Hereford cows, some colorful chickens that ran free over the yard, and an occasional hog. One autumn, I watched in horror through the kitchen window as my father shot and slaughtered a hog.

When we wanted chicken, the job fell to my mother. She used to corner the unfortunate chicken, then catch it by the neck and swing it around and around until it was dead. I watched only once, because the memory of it lent an off-taste to the chicken and dumplings on the Sunday dinner table.

Nature always controls a farm's fate. A late freeze, too much or too little rain, and a garden can be wiped out. Daddy might get cussing mad over a freeze or a drought, but he harbored a real fear of storms. As soon as he saw a dark cloud and heard rain hit the roof, he'd go through the house closing the windows and latching the doors. Add a little hail or a stout wind and he was ready for us to go to the storm cellar, a hole in the ground about six feet square. Mama wouldn't go; she said it was damp and snaky and she would rather take her chances in the house, but I thought it was an adventure. Daddy would squat down with the rope on the door wound tightly around his hand and the door pulled almost shut. I stood behind him peeking out the crack watching the storm.

The world seemed a magic place in the late afternoon after a spring storm. The sun setting below the storm clouds shot bright light through the heavy, freshened air and reflected off the brilliant new green of the grass and trees. The whole world basked in a vivid green glow. A rainbow sometimes arched across the sky, and later, as the sun dropped below the horizon, the clouds grew pink, then red, then blue and purple as darkness fell. At night, we often heard a pack of wolves yipping in the distance. On clear nights, the sky was full of stars and I would twirl around and around with my head back and my arms spread out until I was so dizzy I would fall down.

But as I grew into adolescence, I lost some of the magic. By then Daddy was in his seventies, and all the farm activity was slowing down. I realized that my home life was different from that of most of my friends, and I did not want to be different. I wanted my parents to sell the farm and move to town. My daddy had always been a colorful character, and he became even more of one as he grew older. I was mortified when he would be standing on the porch dancing a little two-step when the school bus drove me home in the afternoons. (Probably my sister had been just as embarrassed as a teenager to find me standing in the yard showing off my latest Hula-Hoop trick when the bus brought her home.) Somehow the three of us survived those years.

Like my sisters and brothers before me, I moved away from the farm when I finished high school. My daddy died three months after I graduated from college. When I was born, he didn't believe he would ever see me grow up, and he didn't. Growing up is a relative term. My daddy saw me grow older, but he missed seeing me grow up. That happened when I realized the sacrifice he had made by hanging on to his farm—our family legacy—so that he could pass it down to his own children, as his father and his father before him had done. Daddy was not a gambler. He held onto that land, his only valuable possession, never risking it for anything. He knew if he held on, he'd have something important to leave to his kids. But my great-grandfather and my grandfather left not just land, but a way of life. In the old days a man could survive and raise a family off the land—growing their own food and selling timber and cotton for spending money to buy clothes and shoes.

People leave the farms now for jobs in town, at the lignite plant, or out on oil rigs in the Gulf. Nobody grows cotton in East Texas anymore, and the tomatoes in the grocery stores are shipped in from California.

The farm and the house are still there. The name tree is still thriving on the banks of the creek. My name, and the names of my sisters and brothers, and now, our children, are carved into that tree. Someday, we will inherit our ever-dwindling share of our great-grandfather's farm. Like my daddy, we will probably hang onto it, through thick and thin, because it's a family legacy. And we will leave it to our children. But if that's where the legacy ends, so be it. A family heritage has more to do with people and memories than with places and a little piece of land. Still, I hope no one ever cuts down the name tree. Let it die a natural death, just like the old way of life on the small family farms of East Texas.

# Trees Rooted in Time

## MICHAEL HARGRAVES

The trees, like so many things that make up our childhood, were killed by progress. Their deaths were planned twelve miles away in the county seat by people who had never seen them; condemned by those who had never stood in their comforting shade or listened to them whisper to the wind in their lisping, leafy voices. They didn't die because of passion or anger or prolonged age or for any reason that would have been understandable. They died because they were in the way.

During my childhood in the plains country of the Panhandle everything had seemed large, but the trees were the largest of all. And when I returned and saw that the house we had lived in was actually small, and the barn and the silo made monstrous by youth had shrunk while I had sprouted, the trees still loomed at the end of the field as large as I remembered them. By their very continuity, they had the power to reassure that things, after all, hadn't changed that much. They were a link with a past where everything seemed simple and sure, and were undiminished by time or memory.

The trees were sixteen cottonwoods that had been planted in a straight row at the end of the field to serve as a windbreak by some unknown settler. They were bordered on one side by a wide, shallow irrigation ditch and on the other by the country road that was to be widened in the name of progress. By the time I became acquainted with them as a child, they were almost one hundred feet tall and six feet thick, and had long ago overreached their original purpose. But because of their existence, other life flourished in myriad ways, and they provided an oasis for nature in a landscape otherwise dominated by the agricultural hand of man.

Protected from the burning prairie sun and drying winds of summer, willows, hackberries, and viburnums grew in random profusion under the dappled canopy of the big cottonwoods. In the rank shade of these bushes grew even lesser plants. Ferns, wild strawberries, and foxtail grass rooted in lush abundance. Mushrooms and toadstools sprouted in the damper spots and competed with the Indian pipestem for the deepest shade. Where the willows huddled too closely to the ditch and made the water shallow with their roots, cattails waded out and defined where the deeper water began by their abrupt absence. There were piles of rocks that had been removed from the fields and scattered about, and in summer these were covered by thick tangles of wild morning glories. Humped among the trees, they formed verdant mounds liberally sprinkled with fragrant, trumpet-shaped flowers.

There was life of a quicker sort that made a home in this green retreat also. Under the rich, moist soil, earthworms were always abundant, and on the carpet of leaves above, mice and shrews rustled about on private errands. The rock piles were jointly shared by snakes, ants, and chipmunks, while an occasional prairie dog made his burrow-home beneath them. Wrens and song sparrows occupied the wild berry bushes and competed melodiously with each other against the humming chorus of the bees. In the top of the highest cottonwood a pair of red-tailed hawks raised their yearly brood in a pile of sticks. During the day, they slid high above the surrounding fields, shrieking to one another in their high-pitched voices, while at night, the frogs called throatily to their mates as they squatted among the cattails. Rather than a barren line of trees at the end of a dusty field, this was a green clump, a veritable riot of vegetation, a miniature forest filled to bursting with life, and all of it suckled by the sixteen cottonwoods.

As children, my chums and I played among the trees. We caught frogs to take to school there, and it was there that we had our first rueful encounter with a skunk. During the winter the trees were magically transformed into the Yukon Territory and, huddled around a willow twig fire, we held off wolves and bears with our cap guns. One summer the trees were the Sherwood Forest. With our home-made hackberry bows, we lurked among the foliage and killed the king's deer at our leisure. The sheriff of Nottingham and his men—disguised as schoolgirls carrying dolls—were pelted from the safety of the trees with blunted, willow arrows as they skipped down the dusty county road. Only a few years later—and yet all of us suddenly much older—these same girls would join us among the trees in the warm summer evenings. As we lay in the grass and giggled, the arrows we had shot at them were returned to us from another bow and, transfixed, we succumbed to the sweet pull of spring, while the whippoorwills thrummed the dark prairie sky above us.

The day the county road crew picked to remove the trees was one I had also chosen to visit the old homestead and see friends I'd lost contact with over the years. A childhood companion and I were driving down the dusty road and, seeing the men and collection of yellow heavy equipment gathered in the shade of the cottonwoods, we decided to stop and see what they were about. They were, they told us, preparing to remove the old cottonwoods so the road could be widened and paved. Stunned, we decided to sit in the shade of the truck, out of the way, and watch the demise of our old friends.

With a loop of steel cable about his waist, one of the workmen scaled the first tree. When he had climbed as high as he could with safety, he tied the cable securely around the trunk and scrambled down, his climbing spikes dislodging chunks of deeply grained bark as he descended. The other end of the cable was then trotted across the road and into the adjoining field and fastened to the rear of a road grader. On a signal, the grader began inching forward, gradually taking the slack out of the cable and applying tension to the crown of the tree where it was secured. When the proper amount of tension had been attained, several of the other crewmen attacked the opposite side of the tree with large chain saws. As the saws bit deep, more tension was applied by the grader until, with an ominous cracking, the giant toppled over and slammed onto the road with a whooshing roar and a cloud of gravel and dust. The crewmen with the saws then methodically dismembered the tree, and a front-end loader picked up the large sections and dumped them into a truck to be trundled away.

One by one the trees fell, but not without a fight. Once, a large hornet's nest was dislodged from the branches, and all work stopped as the men ran whooping among the equipment, cursing and flailing their arms, as one of the smallest residents of this tiny Eden made a last-ditch defense of one of the largest. On another occasion, work stopped when a chain saw, biting its way toward the heartwood, found one of the large nails we'd used as children to make a ladder to our treehouse. But the chain was hastily replaced and the trees continued to fall.

When the last giant had fallen, bulldozers removed what other growth would interfere with construction, and dynamite was used to blast up the large, spreading stumps. The little vegetation that was spared eventually succumbed to the freezing wind of the harsh prairie winters and the direct glare of the summer sun. Later, a passing motorist would flip a cigarette out of his moving car, and the last evidence of this lush haven would disappear in a roaring funeral pyre—a delayed, fiery requiem for the trees.

The trees aren't gone, though. They still rise beside the dusty road in my mind as majestic as ever. Safe from government officials and lightning, they stand reaching their feather tips upward in my past and, through the magic transcendence of memory, loom across the years casting a cool, dappled shade on my present. Somehow, they had taken root in the small boy who played beneath them, and there they still grow: tall, stately, and alive.

# Beaches: A Door into Childhood

BARBARA KARKABI

For years I have hated Texas beaches, comparing them to the pristine, dune-covered beaches of my Cape Cod childhood.

Every year, as soon as school was out, my family made its annual trek to the Cape. We left the hot, noisy, dangerous streets of Manhattan's Upper West Side, not to return until the day before school opened in September. The Cape and its beaches were our refuge, the yard we didn't have for nine months of the year, the place my mother considered home.

We went to the beach every day that it wasn't raining. Sand piled up in the car and stayed there until a frantic clean-up before my father arrived for weekend visits. Although we were "summering on the Cape," it wasn't a luxurious life. We lived in the part of my grandparents' ramshackle, two-hundred-year-old farm house that had not fallen down.

We pumped our own water from a well. We strolled down a path to an outhouse. We had no television or telephone—partly calculated, I now realize, to keep away New York City visitors.

So it wasn't luxurious. It was old-time Cape Cod, a real world of working people—plumbers, electricians, fishermen, small farmers, the backbone of the Cape—a dying breed there now.

Until recently it was a scene that looked the same for as long as I can remember, an anchor of stability in a changing world: winding country roads and an old farmhouse overlooking a cranberry bog. The nearby beach where Indians once camped was a wild and solitary piece of land known as Sandy Neck. Sand dunes the size of houses stretched for miles, covered with stubby crab grass and wild beach plums.

To me it's never been just a pretty sight, but a door into my childhood.

That's probably why my first sight of Galveston left me disappointed. There are many things I have grown fond of in this state that I moved to almost twelve years ago, even some that I will miss if I leave – but its beaches are not one of them.

I had rushed to the beach, eagerly anticipating my first visit to the exotic-sounding Gulf of Mexico. The wild surf lived up to my expectations, but that was about it. The water was muddy, the beach was flat, the sand was packed and dark – covered with flattened splotches of tar that got all over my feet, remnants of a late seventies oil spill in the Gulf.

I sat on the sand; it felt like concrete. I decided to try the water, but for someone used to the more frigid waters of Cape Cod Bay, the Gulf was as warm as bath water. Then I saw a round, bloblike creature floating next to me.

"What's that?" I screamed.

"It's a jellyfish," a friend informed me.

I'd heard about them but never seen one, as jellyfish rarely visit the cold waters off the Cape. I ran out of the water with a speed I never knew I had. I sat down on the sand and tried to relax. The sounds of an engine made me look up to see a car heading straight toward me. What, I thought, was a car doing on the beach? I frantically scooped up my towels and left. It was several years before I returned.

Beaches have always been important to my family. They're not just places to go where you get a tan – that's just a small part of the whole experience.

My Victorian grandmother's favorite beach outfit was designed to avoid the sun and to embarrass her grandchildren, or so we thought. She was born in England in 1884 and to protect her peaches-and-cream complexion, she sat under a large beach umbrella, holding a smaller umbrella over a head that was already protected by a hat. Instead of a swimsuit, she wore a blouse covered by a sweater, an ankle-length skirt, thick stockings, and black-laced shoes.

Like us, she loved the beach. But when she went, she spent much of her time making dire predictions about the consequences of sunburn. She blissfully ignored the fact that her three grandchildren had inherited the olive complexion of my mother's Portuguese whaling ancestors from the Azores. Unlike my grandmother's, our skin was made for the outdoors and rarely burned.

Probably her warnings were just jabs at my mother's "scandalous" Mediterranean connection.

As I get older, I have come to realize that the beach was a symbol of escape and freedom. For my mother, who grew up in a Cape Cod world that looked down on her half-Portuguese background, it was a place she could escape the racism and connect with her seagoing blood. She went to the beach in good weather and bad, and especially loved the ocean on its wildest days. It was a memory passed down from one generation to another—a gift that linked us all.

When my mother was sick with the cancer that finally took her, she longed for one more visit to her favorite beach. Instead, confined to her bed, she had to be content with the memories she dictated for me to enter in a book called *Grandmother Remembers:*

"One day my father came to me and said he was going to show me a sight I would never forget. We drove for a few miles and then we had to walk because there was no road to Sandy Neck then. I was in junior high school and it was a misty fall day. I'll never forget topping that hill and seeing the sand dunes stretching for miles. What a sight, it was wild and beautiful. But things don't stay the same, they change."

Well, sometimes they do and sometimes they don't. Certainly, the Cape has changed, a victim of the overdevelopment that plagues so many tourist meccas. The beaches are more crowded, but thanks to strict state and federal laws they have remained close to the beaches of my childhood memories.

In part, it's those memories that keep a running debate about beaches going between me and my husband, a native Texan.

While he appreciates the beauty of the Cape's beaches, he longs for the warm Gulf waters. To me, the Cape water is cool and refreshing; to him it's like being doused in ice water. He views swimming on the Cape as an ordeal that can be done only in the high summer—which lasts for about two weeks in August—after a great deal of shrieking, arm-waving, and teeth chattering. People nod sympathetically when I tell them he's from Texas.

When our daughter was born, I worried that I wouldn't be able to get her up to the Cape often enough to share my childhood experiences. As a working mother, there would be no way I could ever give her three months of solid beach time. So I dutifully made the Galveston trek, watching as she tottered around the beach with a shovel. I worried that she might be run over by a car (an ordinance passed some years ago restricted the use of cars on certain beaches), stung by a jellyfish, or cut by a stray piece of glass. But she has learned to watch where she walks.

Recently she has become old enough to enter the family beach debate. During the drive to Galveston, I talked longingly of Cape Cod beaches and she nodded patiently. But when we got to West Beach, collected sand toys and inner tubes, and began to walk, she looked up at me and said: "Mommy, isn't the beach beautiful?"

Puzzled, I looked at the flat stretch of beach that I have complained about for so long. There were no huge sand dunes you could roll down till you got dizzy from laughter, no sense of the Atlantic stretching forever till it meets Europe and the past. It was no different than it's ever been.

Then I caught a glimpse of her eager face as she raced toward the sand. Whether I liked it or not, this was her beach, her childhood experience, a little simpler and less complicated than mine, perhaps, but that's OK. I could share it with her or be left out.

In the eyes of a child, all beaches are beautiful. I've even begun to think that maybe the Cape waters *are* a bit chilly. And the last time I was there, I saw a restrictive sign prohibiting practically everything on the beach except sitting and swimming. So I am learning to look at Texas beaches all over again. How nice if it turns out to be a new door into my childhood, right in my own backyard.

# Field Trip

NAOMI SHIHAB NYE

Only once did I ever take a large group of children on a field trip. I took a creative writing workshop to a printing office to see how pages were bound together to make books, and our cheerfully patient guide chopped her finger off with a giant paper cutter.

I had not prepared the children for experiences beyond typeface, camera-ready copy, collation. Standing toward the back like a shepherd, I felt their happy little backs stiffen at the moment of severance. A collective gasp rose from their throats as a blot of blood grew outward in a rapid pool, staining all the pages. Cupping her wounded hand against her chest, the woman pressed through the crowd, not screaming, but mouthing silently, "Hospital. Now. Let's go."

The children stood motionless, suspended. The motion of the workers was like the flurry of feathers and wings when anyone steps too quickly into a chicken coop. People dialed, then asked one another why they were dialing. Couldn't they drive her to the hospital themselves? Someone at the emergency room said to place the severed finger on ice, and a man who, moments before, had been tediously pasting up layouts ran for ice.

One boy tugged my shirt and croaked, "The last thing she said was—you have to be very careful with this machine."

Someone dropped a ring of keys, and I immediately crawled around on the floor, reaching under a desk for them. It felt good to fall to my knees. For a second the stricken woman loomed above me, and I stuttered, apologizing for having distracted her from business, but she was distracted by something else.

"Honey, look at that thing!" she said, staring into the cup of ice where the index finger now rested like a rare archival specimen.

91

"It's turning white! If that finger stays white, I don't want it on my body!"

We laughed long and hard and straight, and the children stared, amazed. Had we lost our senses? That she could joke at such a moment, as the big fans whirred and the collating machines paused over vast mountains of stacked paper . . . I wanted to sing her blackness, the sweet twist of her joy, to call out to those boys and girls, "This, my friends, is what words can do for you—make you laugh when your finger rests in a plastic cup!"

But she went quickly off into the day, and I shuffled an extremely silent group of budding writers back onto our bus. I wanted to say something promising recovery, or praising our guide's remarkable presence of mind, but my voice seemed lost among the seats. No one would look at me.

Later I heard how they went home and went straight to their rooms. Some had nightmares. A mother called my assistant to say, "What in the world happened on that field trip? Sarah came over today, and she and Molly climbed up on the bed and just sobbed."

At our next meeting we forgot poetry and made get-well cards. Or come-together-again cards. May the seam hold. May the two become one. They thought up all kinds of things. I had been calling the printing office to monitor her progress, and the reports sounded good. The students had been gathering stories: someone's farmer-uncle whose leg was severed in a cornfield but who lived to see it joined; someone's brother's toe.

I went to her home with a bundle of hopeful wishes tied in loops of pink ribbon. She was wearing a terry-cloth bathrobe and sitting in a comfortable chair, her hand hugely bandaged.

She shook her head. "I guess none of those cute kids will ever become printers now, will they? Gee, I hope they don't stop reading and writing! And to think of it happening in front of such an interested audience! Oh, I feel just terrible about it."

Reading their messages made her chuckle. I asked what the doctors had said about the finger turning black again. She said they thought it would, but it might be slightly paler than the rest of her hand. And it would be stiff, for a long time, maybe forever.

She missed being at work; vacations weren't much fun when they came this unexpectedly. The pain had been excruciating at first but was easing now, and wasn't modern medicine incredible, and would I please thank those kids for their flowers and hearts!

Once I'd dreamed of visiting every factory in town, the mattress factory, the hot sauce factory, the assembly line for cowboy boots, but I changed my mind. Now I took my workshops out onto the schoolyard, but no farther. I made them look for buttons and feathers, I made them describe the ways men and women stood as they waited for a bus.

By the time our workshops ended that summer, we felt more deeply bonded than other groups I'd known. Maybe our sense of mortality linked us, our shared vision of the fragility of body parts. One girl went on to become one of the best young writers in the city. I'd like to think her hands were blessed by our unexpected obsession with hands.

I continued to think about field trips in general. In San Antonio, school children are taken to the Hall of Horns, where legions of exotic stuffed birds and beasts and fish stare back at them from glass habitats; to the missions, where the Indians' mounded bread ovens still rise from parched grass; and to the Alamo, where David Crockett's fork and fringed vest continue to reside. Here, we say, for your information, soak it up. See what you can learn.

It was not always predictable. At the state mental hospital, my high school health teacher unwittingly herded us into a room of elderly women who'd recently had lobotomies, just after telling us doctors didn't do that to people anymore.

On the day Robert Kennedy was shot we found ourselves, numbed, staring at vats of creamy chocolate brew at the Judson Candy Factory. The air hung thickly around us. It didn't make much sense to consider all that work for something that wasn't even good for you. A worker joked that a few of his friends had ended up in those vats, and no one smiled.

As a child I finally grew brave enough to plot a camping trip years after my friends had first done it—to Camp Fiddlecreek for Girl Scouts. I'd postponed such an adventure because of a profound and unreasonable fear of spiders. I felt certain a giant spider would crawl into my bedroll and entangle itself in my hair the moment I got there. The zipper on the sleeping bag would stick, and I would die, die, die. Luckily I finally decided a life without courage might be worse than death, so I packed my greenest duds and headed to the hills.

The first night I confided my secret fear to the girl who slept next to me. She said she'd always been more scared of snakes than spiders. I said, "Snakes, phooey!"

The next day while we were hiking, a group of donkeys broke out of a nearby field, ran at us, knocked me down, and trampled me. My leg swelled with three large, hard lumps. I could not walk. I would have to be driven back to the city for X-rays. My friend leaned over my bruised face, smoothing back my bangs and consoling me. "Donkeys! Can you believe it? Who could ever dream a donkey would be so mean?"

So began a lifetime of small discoveries linked by a common theme: the things we worry about are never the things that happen. And the things that happen are the things we never could have dreamed.

# A View from a Catwalk

BARBARA WILSON SHALLUE

Leaning on the metal railing of a platform high above the ground, I lift my hard hat to slick my sweat-soaked hair off my forehead. I yearn for a breeze. The summer sun is pounding me into the grating. In the distance, construction workers scramble around an ethylene unit being built next to our syngas plant. Dust clouds swirl behind bulldozers. The huge furnace structure looks like a medieval castle among the tall columns and round, spiked tanks surrounding it.

"You gonna transfer over there?" asks a voice. It's an instrument technician squatting on the grating, putting a flow transmitter back in place.

"No. Not if I can help it," I answer. "I helped start up this place, and that's enough for me. Climbing columns checking for leaks doesn't sound like fun anymore."

"How long you been here?" he asks.

"Twelve years."

"How old are you? You must've been just a baby when you started."

"I'm thirty-one now—nineteen when I hired on."

He tucks his wrench into his tool pouch. Using the pipe, he pushes himself into a standing position. "Right outa high school, huh?"

"Just about."

We take our locks and the chain off the valves protecting the transmitter from the methanol in the piping. I slowly open them, checking for leaks, then call the control room by radio to make sure the transmitter is working. I sign off the work order and watch the contractor's yellow hard hat bob as he skips down the six flights of steps.

I move up to another level, the highest in my area. A whiff of rotten eggs hits my nose then disappears—hydrogen sulfide. I've been looking for that leak for weeks with no luck.

Taking in the view, I see chemical plants stretching to the horizon in all directions. Down on the Ship Channel, a tugboat is pushing a barge to our dock.

Where have the past twelve years gone? After high school I spent three unhappy semesters at the University of Houston on a scholarship for chemical engineering. I didn't like the control the department had over me and my studies.

I gained twenty pounds during a summer semester of calculus II and physics before I finally decided to quit and get a job at a chemical plant. I could earn enough to support myself and go back to college on my own terms. After two months as a welder's helper at a muddy, mosquito-infested construction site, I was hired to help start up a new methanol plant. The company had the time to train an inexperienced nineteen-year-old female, as well as a sociologist, nurse, ex-Marine, grocery store manager, and other greenhorns of all races, ages, and nationalities.

I supported myself quite well, thanks to the long hours we worked. But I had no time to go back to school. When the pace slowed, I married and helped send my husband to college. Twelve years and two babies later, I am staring over the same old railing.

It's hard work, physically and mentally. I swelter in long-sleeve coveralls in the summer. Sweat blurs my vision through my safety glasses, which constantly slide down my nose.

I dream of the days north winds blow across the water and turn the gray steel structures into winter wonderlands. Gigantic icicles decorate each landing, turning deadly as the temperature rises and they crash to the ground. Ice coats the metal grating of the stairs and catwalks. Shivering under layers of long johns and sweat suits, we slip and slide, trying to keep the pipes thawed and the plant running.

A movement on the rocks far below catches my eye. An old friend is waving. I wave back, thinking about the people I've worked with. You can learn a lot about someone during long talks on top of the cooling tower at 3:00 A.M.

Sharing and conquering fear also pulls people together. Five years ago, my friend on the ground was knocked off his bicycle by a hydrogen explosion. Two nights later, I explored what was left of the burned area. The stench of charred wires and insulation hung in the air. I felt nauseated climbing a dark twisted stairway, finding my way by flashlight.

It was a miracle no one was killed. A valve we had to turn several times each shift was found fifty feet away. The heavy steel doors leading into the boiler lab were embedded in the counter where a technician would stand to run samples. Part of the top catwalk where I often stood on nights thinking and staring at the full moon was missing.

A year later a tower of fire surged skyward following an explosion in the carbon recovery area. It's too big for us, I thought, as

I ran toward it in my heavy steel-toed boots, my tool pouch banging against my leg.

But fire school every year trained us too well. I donned my bunker gear and followed my friends into the labyrinth of pipes and supports. Shadows danced around us where the light of the fire couldn't reach. My muscles cramped straining to hold the hose. The flames gorged on the tarlike residual oil, which oozed nonstop from the blown pump seal. Every so often a loud wail would rise above the roar of the fire like an Irish banshee, then fade away.

This is it; I'm going to die, I'd think, expecting a new explosion. I thought of my husband and my baby son, my friends and family. My eyes stung and my head ached from the fumes, but there were no more explosions. The fire finally died, the metal cooled, and we laid down our hoses.

Thinking of the explosions, I remember not to linger in one spot too long. I head to the cold box area. I hear a buzz and see a red light blinking on the carbon monoxide monitor in my chest pocket. I readjust the yellow barricade tape to warn people away from the leaking valve. It's supposed to be fixed during the next shutdown, when we clear the equipment for maintenance and repairs. No telling when that will be. We're making too much money right now to shut down.

Under the grating near the leaking valve is a small vessel where two welders died several years ago, overcome by nitrogen during a shutdown. By the time I reported for the night shift, the Life Flight helicopter had come and gone. I can't pass the spot without thinking of the two men, and picturing the area as I found it; discarded needles and bandages littered the grating and the rocks below. My first job that night was to clean up the mess.

Trotting down the last flight of stairs, I adjust my earplugs against the assault of noise and merge into the shadows of the pipe alley. I whisper a prayer, the most important part of my routine round: "Thanks for keeping us safe one more day, Lord."

# Stooping to Earn a Dollar

BEN EZZELL

Working in the cotton patch in the early 1930s, the years of the Great Depression, was a powerful aid to ambition. Mine was to get out of there as quickly as possible, and to get as far away as possible from wherever cotton was grown.

Picking cotton (or more accurately, pulling bolls, because not much cotton was being "picked" in the Panhandle of Texas in those years when the price hovered around four cents a pound) was not an elevating job. Growing up in a small town in the Texas Panhandle, not on the farm but close enough to it to find employment there, I learned about cotton economy the hard way – in the cotton patch, where I spent the fall years of my high school career.

Our school geography books used to picture cotton picking as it may have been in the Deep South, with cotton pickers (generally blacks) working between rows of luxuriant cotton plants waist-to-shoulder high, standing erect and stuffing the fluffy fibers into baskets they carried nonchalantly on one hip.

It wasn't that way in dry-land West Texas. Our cotton grew in rows all right, endlessly long rows, but it grew close to the land, standing eighteen inches or less above the hard ground. To harvest its bounty, we cotton pickers spent the long days on our knees, literally, pulling ten- to twelve-foot sacks and standing erect only when the sack was full, and then only long enough to tote it to the wagon, weigh it, and empty the contents. We worked steadily, head down, crawling between the rows and dragging that sack, snapping off the cotton bolls which, after frost, were sharp as knives, and stuffing them into that long sack.

We worked from sunup to sundown – steadily, monotonously, miserably – to earn perhaps a dollar a day, five and a half days a week. Saturday was payday. Nobody worked on Saturday afternoon; then we went into town and spent our hard-earned money. Sundays were days of blessed rest.

Pulling bolls was miserable work, and we were poorly paid, but so were the cotton farmers who hired us. Cotton was a stingy crop, always at the mercy of the elements on the one hand and the boll worms and weevils on the other, and in those years of drought and dust even a rare "bumper" crop brought the farmer little cash.

The going rate during my own hard-scrabble years as a cotton puller ranged from 15 cents per hundred pounds to 35 cents. A grown man who was a hard worker and adept might gather a thousand pounds or more in a long day's work. At 35 cents, that fellow might take home $3.50 a day. Farm kids who were adept and hard-working might pull six hundred or seven hundred pounds. Being a skinny kid who was neither farm-bred nor very adept, my maximum was five hundred pounds or less, and that maximum depended on a law of economics I learned in the cotton patch: it was a disgrace to work for less than a dollar a day.

So when the going price dropped to 20 cents per hundred, I'd go to the field before dawn and work until after dark to get five hundred pounds and earn that dollar. But when the price was 35 cents I could (and would) take it a little easier and earn that bottom dollar with only three hundred pounds of cotton on the wagon. Obviously, I was not a farmer at heart.

But I was fired with ambition, an ambition to get out of that cotton patch and find an easier way of making a living.

In those depression years, however, most of the kids in a rural community worked in the cotton patch in the fall. Prices were too low, and wages too small, to import harvest labor, so the custom was to start school classes in August and dismiss school for six weeks or so when the cotton harvest started so that everybody who was big enough could go to the fields.

This was a basic democracy, and the cotton patch was a great leveler.

It was also "stoop labor" at its meanest, in West Texas anyway. We bought our own cotton sacks at the beginning of harvest—heavy white duck sacks that would hold up to one hundred pounds of cotton bolls at a filling—and the first two days of work were usually devoted to paying for the sacks and the cotton gloves, which we wore out quickly. Kneepads were fashioned usually from scraps of old patchwork quilts, fabricated at home to protect the knees on which we crawled.

Lunches were packed in brown bags and eaten in the field. Not much time could be lost for lunch breaks if that dollar was to be earned at the prevailing wage.

And there were no such niceties as the field toilets government regulations now demand for farm laborers. Privacy was a pile of tumbleweeds at the nearest fence row. And the code words for the person leaving the cotton sack to head to the fence were "going to catch a rabbit." There was no peeking; cotton pullers had to keep their heads down anyway.

We weighed and dumped our own sacks into the mule-drawn wagon, which was parked in the field, and recorded the weights on the Big Chief tablet nailed to the side of the wagon. It was all handled on the honor system, but the farmer checked the total when each load was hauled to the gin, and woe be to the harvesters whose totals checked out short when the load was weighed on the gin scales. We kept each other honest in order to keep our jobs.

At noon on Saturdays, each hand turned in his weights, and these were checked against the weights recorded at the wagon. If all was in balance, it was payday on the spot, and we headed for town with the $5.50 in our jeans. We learned in those days what "minimum wage" really meant.

The money may have been meager, but it was mighty in that depression economy. Not much of it ever went into bank accounts – banks were not especially friendly to teenage customers in those days, and not overly trusted, for that matter. But we learned a lot about managing our own economy, and managing it carefully. When you've put in a fourteen-hour day in the cotton patch earning a dollar, you tend to be pretty selective about how you spend it.

Most of the money went for necessities: clothing for school, maybe a new pair of shoes for Sunday, possibly a new set of tires for the bicycle or a can of Neverleak to repair the old ones, or a warmer jacket for November mornings. Some of it was tucked away for Christmas gifts. And a little of it was spent on the spot for entertainment, not much because the Saturday movies cost only a dime, and a date with the girlfriend could be managed with nickels for Cokes or ice cream cones.

With those depression dollars everything was relative. A little could go a long way, and a little was what we had most of.

The cotton patch was a stern taskmaster. After a long day in the field even the youngest at heart had little energy for anything else come nightfall. The routine was to get home at dusk for supper, listen to the radio for an hour or so (we'd never heard of television in those days, but we could listen to "Amos 'n Andy" or "Jack Benny" or "One Man's Family" or other family-style entertainment) before hitting the hay. Morning came early in the cotton patch. And on Saturday night, knowing we could sleep a little late on Sunday, we might stay up to listen to "The Shadow," a thrilling mystery show on radio.

A lot of graduates from those cotton fields were fired with enough ambition to send them off to colleges and careers far away from the cotton patch. And now, after more than half a century, I still keep my distance from anyplace where cotton is king; and when I drive through cotton country during harvest season, even now when cotton picking by hand is a thing of the past and harvesting is done with mechanical monsters, the sight of those long rows of cotton makes my back ache and my knees sore.

# The Last Time I Saw *Elissa*

GUNNAR HANSEN

Call me Gunnar. Like many sailors, I have wondered what going to sea on a square-rigger would be like. I've sailed a number of different boats, from sailing dinghies to fifty-foot ketches with two masts and lots of speed; but I've never sailed anything as large as a square-rigger. These are the ships that excite sailors. These ships are what real sailing is all about.

There are not many true square-riggers left. One of them, the restored 113-year-old *Elissa*, is based in Galveston. So when the chance came to join her crew, I did not hesitate.

I knew sailing *Elissa* would be different from sailing a modern sloop. She was big–202 feet long, with her mainmast 102 feet from the deck. Even the jib boom, which extends out from the bow, reached 30 feet above the water. With all nineteen sails set, she would fly 12,000 square feet of sail. I usually dealt with about 1,000 feet. *Elissa* was going to need all of that sail, too. A million-pound ship doesn't accelerate in a breeze like a small boat weighing one-fiftieth of that and sporting five times the sail area in relation to weight.

On Friday the thirteenth I got my first look at her, docked at Pier 21. She was beautiful in an old-fashioned way: gray, with a graceful curve of deck line, her jib boom projecting steeply from the bowsprit. Except for the deckhouse, she was all deck from bow to stern.

I went below. A carpenter worked alone in the officers' quarters, restoring the teak-and-maple paneling, sawing carefully with a fine-toothed Japanese saw. He appreciated the chance to do a proper job, he said, to work slowly and focus on what he needed to do. These quarters were three times those shared by eight sailors in the fo'c'sle, a confined space where the ship's motion would be uncomfortable under normal conditions and almost unbearable in a sea. I had a berth here until we sailed.

That evening, I joined four others at the mainmast. We passed around some tequila the carpenter had brought. He didn't drink anymore, he said, but this had seemed a special occasion. The taste was sweet and peppery. A light rain began to fall. We jumped to—the hemp lines had to be thrown off the belaying pins. Though most of the lines were synthetic, some were real rope and would shrink when wet. Left tight, they might part or break a fitting or a spar.

The next morning crew training commenced. With *Elissa* tied to the dock, we hauled lines and moved sails. I was lost in the confusion of lines at first. But eventually I found a fine rhythm in hauling on a line, hand over hand. I liked the exertion, the sweat, the tightness of my arms and shoulders. After a while, my hands became stiff and would not close into a fist. My palms were sore from a kind of slow rope burn.

One night after sail training, ten of us went to the Crazy Cajun for dinner. The crew was well known there, and the whole dirty lot of us was made welcome. We talked about *Elissa*. When I asked how they had become involved with *Elissa,* the answers were oddly similar: They had found the ship by accident. And they had become fascinated by something they had not known still existed. They had done whatever they could, shoveling sand out of the old hulk or carrying deck planks. They had not done it so they could go sailing; they had done it for the ship.

Later that night three of us sat on the dock, staring at *Elissa* silhouetted in front of us. "What amazes me is the complexity," one of the others said. "It's quite complex as a whole, but quite simple taken piece by piece."

"Have you seen it silhouetted at sunset?" the third sailor asked. "The rigging is like a cobweb. I always consider myself a spider spinning its web when I'm up there. At night the blocks shine like stars. Sometimes when I'm up in the rigging and swing down and land on the deck, I think to myself, 'Errol Flynn, eat your heart out!' He never had anything like this."

During the training the carpenter had been working quietly below, separate from the rest of the group. The next morning I asked him why he thought she appealed so to the crew.

More than just the ship drew them, he said. It was the water.

"The ocean doesn't have a human scale," he said. "It's still beyond comprehension and always will be. That's why we'll always be drawn to it. I mean, why do you think these people are here? Everybody has a fistful of degrees, but they still want to come down here and work on *Elissa* and sail. Read the first paragraph of *Moby Dick*. That's what he's talking about. That says it."

The last night in port I sat in my cabin, reading. It was small, with one porthole, and in the sticky, still air I felt I was in a Joseph Conrad novel in another part of the world. I pulled myself onto the mattress and listened to the rain sizzle onto the water. The wind picked up and the ship began to move. I went out on deck. *Elissa* was coming to life. I could imagine her surging forward heeled over slightly. The hemp lines had been slacked for the rain, and all above me they danced in the wind.

Finally, the day came. *Elissa* would be towed to her anchorage to prepare for the next day's sail. We cast off the dock lines. As we cleared the dock and began to move, I felt a thrill of excitement. "A true kick in the ass," the carpenter said, standing next to me.

At anchor that night I could not sleep. I lay there sweating, feeling the motion of the ship under me. It was a pleasant feeling, but not enough to overcome my excitement and discomfort. I moved on deck, threw my bag on the main hatch, and stretched out on my back, a life jacket for a pillow. Under the full moon, the shadows of the swaying rigging danced across the hatch cover. In the dim light the masts and yards seemed to reach up forever.

The ship was silent except for the tread of a passing crewman on anchor watch and a sigh from someone sleeping nearby. There were distant sounds, the deep rumble of a marine diesel, the whine of a generator ashore, but *Elissa* herself remained silent. This was like the sailing I knew. This peace, this sense of being within a moment without distraction, was essential to sailing. The wind picked up slightly. It whistled through the rigging, a faint, eerie keening.

The next morning a tug towed us to sea. *Elissa* pitched with a long, slow motion. She raised her bow high as she climbed a swell, then dived, sending waves off from either side. Passengers staggered on deck, trying to keep their feet. This was why sailors walked with an odd, rolling gait, their feet apart. They had learned to navigate a pitching deck without falling.

"Set the main topmast stays'l on the starboard tack!" The sail had begun.

"Fore topmast stays'l halyard!"

"Manned and ready!"

"Haul!"

"Set main t'gallant stays'l!"

Out on the bowsprit I sat astride the base of the jib boom and looked back at *Elissa*. We moved at about eight knots, about what a fifty-footer might be doing under the same conditions. I wanted to feel more of the motion, to get way out on the end. Cresting a wave, *Elissa* dived. My feet rose out of the foot ropes. This was why the jib boom had been called the widow maker, the most dangerous spot aboard ship, reserved for the unmarried crewmen. I went back to the deck.

I stared down at the water, at the bow wave hissing below me. It was so easy to become lost in looking at the water. I did it for hours on small boats. Those had been the finest moments—ghosting down the Chesapeake at three in the morning, or surfing off the top of a wave in a storm at twelve knots, or just alone in the cockpit in the middle of the day, looking out at the empty sea, doing nothing.

I looked up at the sails above me. In this wind they bellied out—pregnant, swollen shapes. This was the part so hard to describe, the mysterious, inexpressible—the swell of the sail, the powerful surge of the ship, the light, the wind, the sound. And out there the sea, gray-green, wave after wave never ending.

I stayed there until called in to tend lines as we sailed to our anchorage.

"Have you learned the mantra of sailing yet?" the carpenter asked when we dropped anchor.

"Yes," I said.

We climbed into the lifeboat for the row ashore. That was the last time I saw *Elissa*. The sky was beginning to clear, a streaking dense blue behind the ship. The sun was on her, and *Elissa's* hull and spars shone. She was alive and still, between storms, balanced, glowing in the light.

# And a Side Order of Courage

## WILLIAM COBB

During the late 1970s, I worked my way through college at a variety of restaurants, from the Hill Country to the Gulf Coast, where fried foods were the catch of the day: fried shrimp, fried chicken, chicken-fried steak, and fried frogs' legs. Usually all of these were fried in the same vat of oil, so perhaps it shouldn't be surprising that people often said the frogs' legs tasted like chicken. But I never agreed with this, unless you're imagining a slimy featherless toad of a chicken that lives in a swamp, and you hunt with a gig. No, I always thought that frogs tasted like exactly what they were—amphibians. Kind of a cross between a duck and an oyster. Now and then someone complained the french fries also tasted like frogs' legs, but what can you do?

The kitchens I slaved in ranged from maybe-sometimes-clean to one of the lower circles of hell, where rogue rats snapped at the Achilles tendons of village-idiot dishwashers, and there were certain pots on the back of the stove you didn't lift the lid on, because you feared the soup. In summer the kitchens were invariably hot, hot, hot, to quote Buster Poindexter, and this heat did nothing to improve the mood of the ex-convicts, drifters, and college bums who comprised the kitchen staff.

We were a surly and taciturn bunch and took a Nero-to-Rome view of food preparation: "Let It Burn." Someone always brought a boombox to work, which we put on the stainless steel counter. We turned up the volume so loud that when the waitresses tried to ask us something, we could only see their lips moving, but since it would probably be some kind of special order—and we never, ever did special orders—what did it matter?

"You want a substitution?" someone would guess, and the others would roar with laughter, slapping each other's tatooed backs. Oh, that was a good one; stop, you're killing me.

In musical tastes we favored the Sex Pistols, Black Flag, Joy Division, and the Dead Kennedys. It was so hot in the kitchen that we wore only shorts and grimy aprons, and to the waitresses, who could barely see our sweaty, half-shaven faces through the steam and smoke of burning things on the stove, the scene was reminiscent of a medieval blacksmith's shop, where Quasimodo, the envious hunchback, toils over his master's armor.

Of course, the fried food—"It says right here on the menu," the customer gesturing angrily—was always "golden brown." Except maybe when we got a little busy or were arguing the nihilism and angst of David Lynch's "Eraserhead" and forgot to check the deep fryer. Then, the food—whatever it was, frogs, chickens, some unidentified fish euphemistically known as "trout"—might be a little darker than, say, the color of my Volkswagen's engine.

And the steaks were always "grilled to perfection." Except maybe that one night at a resort restaurant I had best not identify on the Gulf Coast when I got a little too busy. I was supposed to be training my best friend—who had gotten the job as "assistant chef" through nepotism—how to grill sirloins and T-bones. But we got a little too busy—you might say, in a little over our heads—and before we knew it, there was a row of tickets on the wire above our stainless steel counter, all clipped with clothespins and containing more dinners than we could handle.

So in between chopping tomatoes, tossing fries in the basket and putting the basket into the deep fryer, arranging parsley on the plates, defrosting some hopelessly frozen crustacean in the microwave, and flipping hamburger patties on the grill (this restaurant had a menu approximately the length of *Lonesome Dove*), I grabbed a spatula and went to flip the steaks on the grill, except I pushed at one a little too hard; it stuck, then, boing! popped into the air and sailed behind the stove.

To put another steak on would have slowed everything down by fifteen minutes, and since the major principle of restaurant cooking is, THE FOOD MUST BE SERVED PROMPTLY AND ALL DINNERS TOGETHER, I fished a weak flashlight out of the storeroom and crawled back there. This is where the narrator says: "Sometimes, at night, I wake up screaming."

In between the cobwebs, the lost guest checks (Were the customers ever served? Did they go hungry?), the caps of Bic pens, the stalagmites of stove grease and Jimmy Hoffa's shoes, I spied the steak, not all that dirty, really. I can still remember the look of horror on my friend's face as I rinsed the sirloin and slapped it back on the grill for a little further taste of "perfection."

Accidents were always happening in these assorted dark and murky kitchens full of sharp objects, and we were never prepared for them. Once a coworker sliced his thumb while hacking heads of lettuce for the wagon-wheel salad bar. As he held his bloody hand drip-dripping into the sink, we stood around like contestants on "Jeopardy" and guessed what he should do.

Suggestions included: "Apply a tourniquet!" "Find his pressure points!" "Elevate his feet!" We settled on immersing the bleeding hand in ice and watched as this mixture quickly changed from the clear, crisp vision of a mountain stream to a two-quart saucepan full of Bloody Mary mix.

As the salad man began to grow weak from loss of blood, some bright soul correctly remembered that immersion in ice water was for a burn, not a cut, and gosh, Brad sure is looking pale, isn't he? On another busy night I nearly severed my index finger while chopping an onion, and as it dangled from one tenacious tendon, I opened the first-aid kit only to find the torn wrappers of several Band-Aids and an empty box of throat lozenges.

Fires were even more fun. When the grill at one restaurant caught fire, we all vaguely knew you were supposed to smother it with something, except when we tried to smother it with our aprons the aprons burned, and when we tried to smother it with flour, the flour burned, and when we'd finally figured out the fire extinguisher ("Insert the blue pin into the red slot and pull down on the red lever. . . ."), the overhead sprinkler system kicked in.

It was great experience, as they say, and I'm sure it made a valuable contribution to my character. It provided me with a firsthand view of the capitalist, free-market system, and I'm glad I worked my way through college at these establishments of fine dining. I acquired many ennobling tennets of the Puritan work ethic, although I never felt so much industrious as greedy, since I already had money for school, and this was extra pocket money to afford *Rolling Stone* magazine, cable TV, late-night pizza, and to hone my skills at pocket billiards and Foosball.

Still, I learned many things. I learned "you are what you eat" means absolutely nothing, unless you're a cannibal. I learned that you can't be sure about what genus-species you're consuming, but if you're lucky, you should be able to tell the difference between Mammalia and Amphibia. I learned that in a restaurant that supposedly served "fresh fish," the frogs' legs come from India or Japan, the catfish came from Iceland, and the shrimp from Ecuador. But the mice mated locally.

# A Call and Then, a Duel

CHARLES CLAWSON

Long ago, before traffic, a friend of mine named Cooper would call, day or night, and whisper into the phone something like, "Your biscuit is about to get buttered." This meant that he was going to drive over in his '64 Plymouth Valiant with the plastic-bag windshield and cream my '63 AMC Rambler, which had no back seat, as it sat parked beside the curb. Before hanging up he'd stay on the line just long enough to hear if I'd exclaim, "No, Coop, I've got company," or, "Dinner is on the stove," neither of which mattered, but would add to his enjoyment. Cooper would give me the call three or four times a month. I'd press his button a little less.

It started after I'd been lying in his driveway all day, as we tinkered with the beaters. Cooper had been married almost two years, and I was still making innocuous marriage jokes: "All you need now is a good dog," or, "That yard is crying out for a little white fence." Cooper got real quiet. That evening, in his own particular way of patching things between us, he phoned and said that he was going to drive his Plymouth over the top of my Rambler.

"Not if I catch you first," I said. In truth I always felt on the defensive during the raids, as if I had more at stake.

To accelerate an old and beloved automobile to respectable ramming speed, timing the approach on streets that had stop signs, lights, corners—other cars, too—and to actually barrel headlong into another car, this was not an easy thing. It went against all of one's better instincts. One would find the need to holler and pound the dashboard some.

The crash suit helped. With the thick padding of gloves between my hands and the steering wheel, the cut of the seat belt cushioned to snug restraint, and my head roomed off in the protective helmet, I felt as if nothing could touch me, as if I could bounce from point to point and not feel a thing.

Cooper lived about five miles north of me, on the other side of the Heights, meaning that when one of us got the word, we had roughly seven, eight minutes to get the car started and far enough out of the neighborhood to avoid easy ambush. Imagine sitting down to an intimate dinner when your host gets a phone call that causes him to stand up and mutter into the phone, "You bum," then spring for the hall closet where he pulls on a thickly padded motorcycle jumpsuit, helmet, and gloves, all the while explaining that his clunker was about to get piled into. I tried not to be panicky. Sometimes the adrenalin-chatter would scare them off. Cooper seemed to always know when I had guests. Occasionally, I would play it cool, forgo the crash gear, and invite my company for a leisurely drive. This was risky, though, for if Cooper came upon me, the two of us would fall into deathly maneuvers, to his advantage, for I couldn't cream him while carrying guests. I often accused him of scouting, which he denied.

During the last several months of it I was dating a woman who could put up with air-raid procedures. Cally accepted those occasions, I suppose, much the same as did Cooper's wife, Latty—as a disrupting nuisance. What Cooper and I actually got from the jousting matches, beyond adrenalin thrill, was hard to see. At odd moments I would find myself smiling over the thought of crunching Cooper's old beater.

Latty would sometimes try to seduce Coop after one of my calls, so that the old Plymouth would perish, empty-seated, out in the yard, ending the stupid game. He once discovered that the distributor cap was missing and disconnected the telephone until it was found. (Several days later it was "mysteriously" returned.) To be fair, I had, on occasion, sent him and his wife and kid packing into the old car, driving as fast as they could out of the neighborhood on their way to some cross-town engagement. I heard about these things after the fact. All Cooper said during the call was "I'm sorry, you must have the wrong number."

What began idly—when we each were certain that our clunkers were in their last hours anyway—grew into something more. Our old cars kept running, staying alive month after month, beyond one year. I was seriously involved, but Cooper, he showed a kind of zeal, what I imagine followed from a married man plotting doom for a young, single fellow. To both of us it was a test of persistence, an honorable challenge of fortitude, and a duel to junker death.

Earlier that final week I had returned from Cally's in a dark mood, put on the crash suit, and called in a bogey. "Would you like some sour cream on that mashed potato, sir?"

"I think you've got the wrong number, buddy."

It was almost midnight, and I was wound tight. Cally was talking about that time when you either make some kind of commitment or go your separate ways. I felt as if I'd been chased with rope. I would have liked very much to broadside Cooper coming out of his cul-de-sac, or better, catch him stalled in the grass beside his driveway. I could see myself jumping the curb two lawns back, getting up enough speed across the grass to knock the Plymouth over and roll her a couple of times down the little slope.

Beyond Nineteenth Street I slowed, as any pair of approaching headlights could be his. I quickly scanned each car as it passed, expecting to see that familiar, rumpled frame.

Due mainly to bad timing and shyness around other traffic, we had done little more than bust out our own headlights a number of times and bang up each other's trunks. I had caught Cooper a couple of times on the back side panel, pinching off the rear of his Plymouth into jagged metal tips. He had closed my passenger door for good, once broadsiding and spinning me into a ditch. After that one we got out, grinning like idiots, to survey the damage. We shook hands and drove home, happy in the way that madmen can get.

Now, as I turned into Cooper's street, I spotted him, beneath the hood, fiddling about the engine in agitation. When he noticed my headlights he froze, staring like a deer caught by a jacklight.

I idled a moment, gauging a path across the driveways and letting his fear sink in.

Suddenly I realized that this would be the end. If I plowed over the old Plymouth right here, I would be putting the lid on this part of my life, this duel with a friend and family man.

Slowly I backed out of the street, so that Cooper wouldn't see the car in profile and know that it was me.

Thursday night Cally was over and after about an hour of hard discourse, we were ready to pitch everything into the pot. The phone rang, and I should have left it ringing, but I picked it up.

"Hello?"

"The check's in the mail, old boy."

"You bum."

Cally knew the routine well and simply watched as I scuttled about, gathering up the crash suit. I had the boots, gloves, and jumpsuit on when she finally spoke, making it clear that if I walked out the door, that would be that.

I opened the door about six inches. For some time I had morbidly considered how Cooper would finish the Rambler if he caught her parked on the street. I didn't think he would strike head on but drive forward in the opposing lane, at the last instant swerving into its front side quarter, bashing the hub over into the engine and raking up the fender. At least that's how I would have done it.

"I'm going," I said. "I have to." I tried to explain what it was like nursing a first car through the years, caring for it, keeping it going, and I made the unfortunate comparison to first love.

I closed the door very gently.

A minute or two later, I could hear the guttural cough of Cooper's Valiant, the whine as it gathered speed and then sooner than I was prepared for, BANG! Various metal devices could be heard clinking on the pavement. The quiet was interrupted by Cooper hollering "Whoo-hoo!" a couple of times, and then it was quiet again.

I had broken a sweat, bundled in the insane, padded suit.

"I suppose I'm through with this crazy thing," I said at last, and began to peel off my protection.

# Hardy's Blind Rattler

EVAN MOORE

He was sitting on a five-gallon lard can smoothing pie dough into a Dutch oven when I first saw him. Six-foot-four and skinny as a stretched worm. Crouched crablike before a giant wood stove in a cow camp, all arms and legs protruding from a white apron, topped by a worn-out baseball cap that had once been red.

Shedrick Hardy III didn't look like a king that day, but more like the camp cook for the 6666 Ranch near Guthrie. A fire glowed at his feet, and the blackened, cast-iron wood stove sat behind him. Dozens of pots and skillets of the same hue hung from a wooden rack, and a small boy of eight or ten was busily scrubbing one in a tin tub. A chuck wagon that could easily have been a hundred years old was parked by the stove, and the mules that had pulled it there were standing in a pen, downwind from the camp.

Just beyond the mules in a huge corral were about a hundred bawling, muling, steer calves. All cut and branded and voicing pain and indignity to their mothers, who waited impatiently outside the fence. It was a late fall roundup in 1959 on the Sixes. A dozen cowboys had been working this pasture for three days, and Hardy was the cook.

He looked up from the pie dough, and his eyes shone in a face of carved mahogany. Then, he started to rise. He did it with grandeur, slowly, from the knees and waist in the manner of a man comfortable with great power. When he'd reached his height, he folded his arms, and I could see the gauzelike webbing of the worn shirt on his elbows. He was dusted with flour. His jeans were faded and frayed. The baseball cap sat back on his head like some mechanic's rag, and a callused big toe showed through a crack in his right boot.

He was magnificent.

"Will you gentlemen be havin' lunch?" he asked.

I wasn't a gentleman. I was barely twelve and wouldn't have deserved the title if I were older, but I realized this man would call me one nonetheless. We were three quail hunters there by invitation of the ranch owner. We'd planned on sardines and crackers, but we'd seen the camp and the wood smoke, and something in the massive oven smelled inviting, so we agreed. He grinned then and announced both lunch and himself.

"I got fried steak, beans, potatoes, and peach pie," he said. "I'm Hardy."

It was then that I saw Hardy was a potentate, albeit one with a small empire. He was a black man in a white man's world, somehow self-educated to the one job that would afford him a unique dignity. Within the circle of the cook's wagon, no one outranked him. There were a dozen cowboys and a few of those who doubled as horse wranglers, two swampers, and a few assorted laborers in the camp, but there was only one cook.

We squatted on the ground in Hardy's kingdom and feasted. Huge slabs of fried steak sat by a pot of beans, laden with onions and green peppers. The peach pie, a kind of cobbler with a thick, brown crust, swam under a pool of butter in a Dutch oven. There were biscuits: sourdough, two inches thick and four inches square, browned top and bottom with a golden glow in the center, so laden with butter it ran in a golden stream if you squeezed one.

We ate and Hardy talked. He'd cooked on all the big ranches in the northwest but he'd been on the Sixes more than thirty years, and his wife, Katy Bell, was the cook at the headquarters house. Hardy stayed with the chuck wagon when it was out. That was partially because he could cook for large numbers of men and partially because he liked the job and the authority it carried. It was also because he could not abandon a container of whiskey until it was empty—a tendency more easily controlled away from town.

"But I'm stayin' sober now. Yes, sir," he said. "I ain't had a drink in two weeks. Been out with this wagon a week or more.

"This morning a man come drivin' up, got out of his truck, and walked up to the wagon. I gave him a cup of coffee, and he pulled out a bottle and asked did I want some, and I told him, 'No, thank you.' It wasn't easy, but I said it.

"Well, he sat down and poured some in his coffee and set the bottle by his boot. I looked over a couple of times, and I'd see that bottle and it was the biggest bottle I'd ever seen. It stood up all the way to the top of his boot. I kept lookin' back at it every now and then, and it kept lookin' too big. He asked me again did I want some, and I told him 'no' and, when I looked over again, it was even bigger than I'd thought. It was all the way up to his knee.

"Well, that fella finally got up to leave and he asked me once more and I still said 'no.' I was feelin' pretty good about then, but I watched that man leave, and that bottle had growed so big he had to carry it out over his shoulder."

The sky had darkened, and a light rain started to fall. Hardy stood and yelled "rag house!" and, as we left, he was standing imperiously by his stove as a group of cowboys hustled to raise a tent over the wagon.

I saw Hardy off and on again over the next few years, and he became embedded in my mind with all my other impressions of big ranches and open, lonely country. I heard tales from the cowboys about the time he rode one of the mules bareback ten miles on a moonless night in a clandestine jaunt to see Katy Bell and retrieve a bottle of whiskey. His marital strife was legend. Hardy would drink and Katy Bell would get angry. Hardy would drink more in defiance, and she would get angrier until one of their bouts ended with her chasing him around the headquarters' kitchen with a butcher knife. She'd finally thrown that knife, and there was a hole where it had lodged in the wall.

But all agreed there was no better cook than Hardy. He was illiterate and carried his recipes in his memory. He measured by pounds and ounces, rather than cups and teaspoons, but his biscuits won sourdough competitions and men spoke of his peach pies with reverence. He was good with mules and always trained his own, and he could repair machinery.

In fact, the ranch might have been his home for life if it hadn't been for the blind rattlesnake.

Fifteen years after I'd first seen him sitting on the lard can, I was driving from Fort Worth to Santa Fe, New Mexico, when I made the capricious decision to stop and find Hardy. I soon learned that Katy Bell was dead, and Hardy was no longer on the ranch but had moved to the outskirts of Paducah, about forty miles to the north.

There, after a few inquiries, I was guided to a leaning weathered shack. The dirt yard had the distinct smell of poverty, of mildew, stale urine, and rotting wood. Whiskey bottles were strewn under the porch, and I could see a lone figure seated on a bed in the dim light inside.

It was the familiar form, thin and lean, but something was different. There was no right hand this time, only a metal hook that extended from the wrist.

"Hardy?" I said. "You remember me?"

He did, or at least was too polite to admit he didn't, and we sat on a log in the front yard.

"The hand?" he said. "Aw, I was doin' a little extra work up at the cotton gin about two years ago, and it got hung up in the gears of the thing. It was just me and the boss man, and we couldn't get it out. I knowed it was ruined, so I'd best tear it off before I bled to death. Boss man just passed out trying, so I done it myself. Then I passed out, too.

"They fixed me with this hook. It'll pick things up. Got this strap here goes around your back and you can hunch your shoulder and make it open and close, but I can't do nothin' with it that way.

"Only thing I can see it's really good for is, when you're shootin' craps. You know, you got the dice in one hand, you're fixin' to make a pass and you look down, and there's another hand reachin' for your money. Well, you can whomp that other hand with it.

"But, no I didn't lose my cook job over the hand. No. I lost that before. It was over my snake.

"You see, I was livin' behind the big house and I came out one mornin' early, and there was a big rattlesnake just outside my door at the bottom of the steps. All rared back with his teeth pointin' at me. Well, I just reached inside the screen door real slow where I had a kettle of water boilin' on the stove and I got it and I throwed that water square at that snake. Got him all over the head and he writhed around, but it didn't kill him.

"It made him blind. Couldn't see nothin'. I don't know why I didn't just kill him then, but I didn't. I just reached down and caught him behind the head and took him inside and put him in a garbage can. Later on I made that snake a cage and I kept him up in the house with me. He was still blind as could be, but he was gentled. I'd catch some mice and feed him one every now and then, and he was just like a pet. Never would try to bite me.

"See, that snake kind of reminded me of me. Didn't nobody

want him and he didn't quite belong anywhere. He was crippled and ugly and old, but he could still rare back and chomp at you if he wanted to. He just didn't want to no more. He wouldn't hurt nobody.

"But the boss lady at the ranch, she didn't like it. She said if I was to keep somethin' like that, she didn't want me or that snake around there. And, if I was gonna keep that snake, I'd best pick up and go.

"So, here I am. I kept the snake for a while, but he finally died."

I left Hardy on that log with a pint and my good wishes, but not before he let me take his picture. He put his hat on for that, a new one. Then he stood, slowly, and, for a moment, he was majestic again.

Still, driving out of Paducah, the snake story bothered me. It sounded too strange. I kept wondering if there had been too many bottles, too much loneliness, and, maybe, a little senility; if those had combined to plant the snake in his imagination where it had grown to a reality. For whatever reason I'd taken the time to find Hardy, I wanted to be sure of what I'd found.

I turned the car and drove toward the Sixes. There, I turned in at the headquarters and drove to the back door, where I found the foreman's wife. She was a pleasant woman and remembered me after a few minutes, so I asked, feeling a little strange.

"Ma'am? I was just curious. Whatever happened to Hardy?"

"Well, he's crazy," she said. "I just couldn't keep the man around here. He's lost a hand, but that wouldn't be a problem. He could still work. Hardy worked awfully well, too, when he wasn't drinking. But he wouldn't do what I told him. He was living in one of the bunkhouses, and I told him, 'If you're going to stay around this ranch, there are some things you simply can't do.'

"Well, you won't believe it, but he insisted on keeping a blind rattlesnake."

# On Being Mistaken for a Tree

JIM LANGDON

It was a small thing, a gentle tugging at the sleeve – not something to be bothered with right away.

A chill wind out of the north beat across the Bolivar Flats, hammering the breakers into corrugated ripples along the shore. The sky was empty, except for two thin wisps of vapor trail beneath a faint thumbnail moon, still visible in the early morning light.

My arms grew weary as I panned with my binoculars the huge concentration of shorebirds beyond the tide line. Great rafts of white pelicans cluttered the horizon, the tankers on Galveston Bay floating above them like a watery mirage. A flush of pink at the vision's edge – roseate spoonbills, reflecting the dawn. And the legions of sandpipers, plovers, willets, dowitchers, and ruddy turnstones, while above, the confetti-like swirls of gulls and terns, playthings of the April wind.

The enormity of the scene was overwhelming – trying to sort the snowy plovers from the piping variety, the long-billed from the short-billed dowitchers, and the westerns from the God-knows-how-many-other-kinds of sandpipers that ran the beach. I lowered the glasses in frustration and once again felt the light brush against my sleeve.

This time I caught a flash of color, a fluff of sunburst yellow and bold black. At first I thought it must be a butterfly, perhaps a tiger swallowtail. But then the tiny bird dropped to the sand at my feet, exhausted. I knelt down for a closer look, remembering the brightly colored illustrations in the field guides. Dime-sized brilliant yellow face surrounded by the black executioner's hood – no question, it was a male hooded warbler, and he had just journeyed non-stop across the vast Gulf of Mexico.

On the last leg of his flight, he had bucked merciless headwinds and his body still heaved though his eyes were already closed. When at last he made landfall, I was the first thing he saw. How conspicuous I must have been, sticking up from this flat, beige surface in my spring green nylon windbreaker and my camouflage green gimme cap. Clearly, the little fellow must have mistaken me for a tree!

I shivered as the sense of pride and elation took hold.

For this is what drives a person to a lonely plot of sand on a chilly morning in early April to walk the beach alone. It is more than the wonder of the myriad variety of birds, more than the lure of solitude, seductive though each may be.

It is a longing, a yearning for something that is missing, something that has been lost. And more, a drive toward the unexpected yet hoped-for encounter.

But encounter with what?

With some trace of our origins, perhaps, some tangible reminder of our history, our roots in the natural world – a return to a sensibility hopelessly lost in the workaday world of automobiles and freeways and offices and computers and television screens and newspaper headlines.

Such encounters are rare, but when they occur, they are indelibly stamped in the consciousness, where they remain forever, reminders of another reality concurrent with our own.

Once, beside an illuminated cove on the Kona coast of the Big Island of Hawaii, I crouched beneath the tropical stars on rough lava rock that cut my feet and watched as two huge manta rays circled within arm's reach, straining the crystalline water for plankton and other microscopic morsels.

I could have reached out and touched their wingtips had I wished, but instead I rushed to the house for face mask and snorkel. They were still circling the cove when I returned, but when I tried to enter the water, I found I could not.

It was not so much a matter of fear – after all, these creatures meant me no harm, though their size alone was intimidating.

Rather, it was a sense of awe – that, and a profound respect for the bond I felt had been established between me and these great animals. I was honored to bear witness to their graceful, if curious, ballet, but as badly as I wanted to enter the water with them, I knew that to do so would be a violation of that bond.

Suddenly I felt very old and alone, watching in silence as the great fish glided round and round like the wheels of time.

Years later, in the jungles of Guatemala, standing atop an ancient Mayan ruin overgrown with vegetation, I once again was jolted into that other time zone, this time by an unexpected chorus of roars from a band of howler monkeys in the canopy below.

To the uninitiated ear, it sounded like the voice of the jaguar, and for an instant I knew the terror and loneliness of what it is to be human, naked in the pitiless gaze of the natural world.

In the dripping jungle heat, my blood ran cold, and I felt the icy blast from the mouth of a cave a million years in the past.

In that inexplicable, terrifying moment, I felt like the last man on earth. Or perhaps the first.

But here, on the Bolivar Flats, I was the last "tree" on earth, at least as far as the sleeping aviator at my feet was concerned.

And so it was, on this stark, alluvial plain, that I began to think of my life as a tree. First my toes became roots, probing deep into the sand and black gumbo mud. Then my arms became branches, and my beard turned to moss, and all the while the warbler slept, secure in the shadow of my hoary trunk.

And the earth turned, and the seasons came and went—sun, moon, stars, rain—and the bond between us was welded fast.

I stood this way for eons, though in reality it could not have been more than twenty minutes. Slowly, reluctantly, I returned to the world in which I lived, a world in which a lone man stood on the sand, staring down at a sleeping bird.

Now there was the roar of a diesel from the highway, and farther down the beach, the first pickup truck, still a good way off but heading in this direction. What to do?

I worried about the bird's vulnerability, so bright and so small in the middle of this wide, open expanse. Maybe he would be sufficiently exhausted to let me carry him, at least as far as the tall grass which might afford him some protection.

But even as I entertained this thought I knew it could not be. To touch him would be to break the mystical bond between us.

Still, I had to try. I could think of nothing else to do. I stooped down beside him. He was breathing more normally now, but his eyes were still closed. Slowly I reached out my hand to pick him up.

There was an explosion of sunlight, and before a finger had touched a feather, he was gone, flitting unevenly and low over the sand, fluttering like a stone skipped across the water, until he landed on a narrow isthmus between two tidal pools.

He looked like a wildflower, solitary and out of place, surrounded by a large flock of laughing gulls with a few royal terns mixed in.

I wished him the best and turned and headed for my car, resisting the urge to look back to see if he was still there, or if the gulls had moved in for closer inspection. I didn't want to know about it if they had.

That day, I drove on down Texas 87 through Crystal Beach and Gilchrist and on to High Island, where I got in some fine spring migration birding.

But I return to the Flats from time to time and will continue to do so as the seasons call.

For I am one with the earth, and one with that particular plot of sand.

My roots run deep.

# Alone with a Lion

### MARIA MOSS

I saw a lion once, on a winter day in the high Big Bend desert just above the Mexican border. Perhaps by now he's fallen to a rancher's bullet or to hunger, and his bones have bleached and disappeared into the ancient alluvium pulled down from Colorado by the Rio Grande. I like to think he's out there, padding silently through some rock-strewn wash or panting in the darkness of his lair—a muscular strip of perfect carnivorous evolution.

That he and I came upon each other that day, in the cold blue cloudless light, was at once miraculous and terrifying. Though I still go looking for wild things, I see them differently now, and I don't as often go alone.

Adult lions (also known as cougars, panthers, pumas, catamounts, and, to most American naturalists, simply lions) are roughly the size of a human being; the males average just under 140 pounds. They are highly secretive, territorial predators—mysterious, almost mythical creatures whose existence in present-day America seems unthinkable and wonderful. Each lion requires twenty to thirty-five square miles of land on which to hunt. They travel their terrain in solitude, except when raising cubs and during two-week periods every two to three years when pairs socialize and mate. They are specialized killing organisms, like desert sharks, honed by the millennia to fit as smoothly alongside the rest of the wildlife population as a blade against a whetstone.

I thought of all I'd read about lions as I strode off into the desert that day, but what turned over again and again in my mind was a typed memo I'd seen posted at the trail head. "Danger," it read. "Young lion in the area." The establishment of personal territory is a stressful time in a lion's life, following, as it usually does, the mother's rejection of her nearly grown offspring. Young lions are unpredictable and sometimes dangerous.

The apprehension I felt poised on the brink of titillation, inextricably entwined, as it was, with desire. I knew, as an enraptured adolescent knows when she walks past the house of the boy who fascinates her, that I wanted the lion to find me, as passionately as I feared it would. I thought of an elegant roll of muscle under golden fur. I thought of the crunch of bone, the snapping and tearing of ligament and tissue. I thought of turning back.

I had hiked half the day in the brilliant winter air, breathing and thinking and listening to something and then to nothing at all. The Chihuahuan Desert is clean and efficient, like a coral reef, or a Japanese garden. I could walk among the dagger-plants, the yucca and lichugilla, and the tiny, perfect cacti without disturbing them, over the flat white rocks with barely a rattle. Ten miles away, a dark smear of bluffs on the horizon marked the Rio Grande. Beyond it, the silvery peaks of the Sierra del Carmen rose out of Mexico, impenetrable, vast, and unspeakably wild.

For a quarter-hour or more, I'd heard the softest tapping of stones, now in the rim-rock above me, now in a stand of yucca off to one side and then the other. I would stop, and there it would be—some tiny movement in the corner of my vision, and the sense of something holding its breath.

When I came to the road that split the desert for a narrow strip, the lion left its low cover and walked languidly into the open. It stopped and turned to face me, fifty yards away. I froze, and the delicious cramp of pleasure and fear that accompanies the rapid descent of an airplane shot through my chest and hands.

I've seen more photographs of lions than I can remember, but still I was unprepared for this one's beauty. He was the color of sand, thin and tall as a wolf. The familiar square face and smooth curve of muscle along his shoulders seemed almost reptilian. He switched his tail from side to side, watching me with a kind of single-minded, contemplative interest. I felt small as a rabbit.

He moved closer to me, relaxed and fearless, the loose weight of his body swinging slightly as he took a few steps and then stopped again. There was no sound at all, and the silence was disorienting. I don't know how long we stood there together. I remember thinking of all the things I'd been told to do in a lion encounter—

breathe deeply, swell the body, look as large as possible, and back away slowly – but I simply stood, mesmerized and, now, very much afraid.

I fingered the leather strap of my walking stick. Should I brandish it? I had intruded on him with my foolish solitary advance into his territory, like some suicidal, three-legged doe. What had I expected? That because he was beautiful, and I am enchanted by any feline creature, we would somehow be friends? I had never in my life seen anything so absolutely alien, so feral beyond any sense I could have imagined. In those moments, the vast gulf between what wild is and what we imagine it to be was clear. The lion finally looked away, and with the same graceful detachment with which he'd appeared, walked off into the cacti.

I waited a long time before turning back to the trail head.

# The Woman Who Dated Lawrence Welk

THOM MARSHALL

When I first heard about the town, it seemed like a good idea. College graduation, the end-of-summer version, was looming, and I had no idea what I would do with my shiny new B.A. The future had sneaked up on me.

The parents whose educations and careers had been hit by the Double-D whammy of the '30s—Depression and Dust Bowl—had taught us that college degrees, in whatever subjects, would be our keys to success. Earn them, they preached, and the world would beat paths to our portals. So I had concentrated on obtaining a degree, believing that wealth, success, and security—a rewarding career—would seek me out. However, with only a couple of weeks to go to baccalaureate, I had not been sought.

Then I heard that the school superintendent in a remote little West Texas town was having a difficult time filling all his faculty positions. Back in '67, when the state base pay was $4,700 a year and there was a teacher shortage, almost any college graduate could fall back on a teaching job, if he had to.

So here, recruiting on campus, was a superintendent who was desperate because school was going to start in a couple of weeks and he still was short one teacher for speech and English. And here was I, desperate because I had nowhere to go with my English major and speech minor. A perfect match: the town he offered, which I'd never before visited and of which I'd never even heard, seemed better than nowhere. And the superintendent apparently thought that I, with grades that barely justified a degree, would be better than no teacher at all.

*The WPA Guide to Texas,* a fat book of 718 pages published in 1940, spends few words on the "one-story town. . . . Oil and cattle are the leading interests. . . . The country is rough, with but

127

little vegetation other than those drab, colorless, stunted growths which exist in this arid, alkaline country."

Time had not done for the place what it does for prized grape juices and strong cheeses. When I drove my battered Comet into town and cruised about for a quick once-over, I saw no improvements upon that 1940 description. Streets were empty. Air conditioners in windows hummed. Everybody was staying home, keeping cool, watching TV. Welcome to our town, buddy. Never had loneliness cut that deep. The end of the next nine months seemed as distant as the sun setting in that strange and empty horizon. If I'd been a coyote, I'd have howled.

Next evening there was a welcoming dinner for new teachers at the high school. The other two were a Spanish teacher and a typing teacher. There were many couples among the veterans on the staff. The home-economics teacher's husband was the football coach. The math teacher's wife taught science. It was a sensible arrangement, certainly better than facing life in the town alone.

The dinner featured a goat barbecued by the shop teacher in a smoker he'd fashioned from an old water heater. The meat was provided by the maintenance man at the school, who also was mayor of the town and had been for many years. He said he had goats on a piece of land a few miles away. The shop teacher said his-honor-the-maintenance-man hunted and shot his goats as though they were wild deer. The principal said I should get my hair cut.

"We don't let our students wear their hair that long," he said.

I went to school Monday with whitewalls, a little boy's haircut, so short it wouldn't stay down right. I was twenty-three, but with that haircut looked younger than some of the students. I was nervous when the first bell sounded, but stood at the blackboard and talked about what we would do, what we would study, what we would learn. And as I talked I began to relax. They seemed to be listening. They seemed receptive. A hand went up. I had inspired some student to a question; my opening monologue had planted a seed that already was growing; I was going to be a great teacher.

She was lovely, that student. Pretty smile and twinkling eyes that studied my reaction as she said, "What's your name?"

"El Estupido." I had forgotten to introduce myself. Blushing, I turned to face the blackboard, and when I started to write my name the chalk squeaked. They laughed. I was no teacher; I was faking it.

As often as I could afford the gas, I got out of town. When my hair grew back enough, I fled to my old college campus and a post–football-game fraternity party. I laughed a lot, said I was doing great, said I loved the place, said I loved the job, wondered if they believed it.

Most weekends I couldn't afford to leave and was stuck in town without much to do. Single women my age were gone; when they left home for college, they stayed away for good. There were a couple of seniors in my speech class that I could have enjoyed knowing better–they were, after all, just a few years younger than I–but dating them was against the rules. The principal and the superintendent and the school board and the PTA and the rest of the town wouldn't have liked it, and they all would have known about it by noon the following day. It was difficult to keep secrets there.

One night I caught a trio of eighth graders checking my garbage for beer cans. I ran them off before they finished counting. But all of those empties were not mine. The superintendent also enjoyed a few beers now and then. The school board was full of tee-totalers, so he couldn't very well be seen in either of the town's roadhouses. Neither could he safely pop tops at home because he had school-age kids who had their friends over, and that gang of eighth graders probably checked his garbage, too.

So he'd drop by my place in the evening, get a beer out of the refrigerator, complain if it was Budweiser instead of Schlitz, pitch some money into the beer kitty, and then we'd talk about politics or the latest jolt of news. There was quite a lot to discuss as 1967 became 1968. Visiting the trouble spots of the nation and world in conversation made it easier to tolerate being stuck in a town where nothing much ever happened.

Running out of beer meant driving nineteen miles to the slightly larger neighboring town where I could dash in and buy a case without being recognized. I drove over there for my haircuts, too, after that first one.

Nine months. Time crawls when you're miserable. Oh, I got to know some good people and occasionally feasted on more barbecued goat. But I longed for the end of school when I could point the Comet's tailpipe at Main Street and watch the town shrink to nothing in the rear-view mirror. I didn't belong any more than Lawrence Welk had.

That was a story that haunted me the whole time I was there.

At the end of that welcome-new-teachers dinner, one of the veterans took me on a tour of the town's highlights. I remember three. Two were large, empty buildings that had been hotels when, like much of the rest of West Texas, the town was bustling with oil exploration activity.

The third had been an exclusive club, a fun way to spend that oil boom money. All that remained was a hole in the ground – the former swimming pool. Wind-blown weeds and trash filled it, and the surfaces were cracked and crumbled. It really had been something, my guide said. It had live music. As a matter of fact, Lawrence Welk's band played there for a long time, no kidding. And Lawrence Welk actually dated a local girl. The guide told me who it was. Everyone in town knew her story.

I never met the woman. I didn't want to. She may have become the town's celebrity because of that brief, long-ago romance, but it had come to nothing. He moved on without her. The town frightened me. Dreams could die there. Hopes and ambitions could wither up and get blown into a crumbling old swimming pool.

By sunset on the last day of school I was two hundred miles away from the job, the town, the hole in the ground, and the woman who dated Lawrence Welk.

# Dixon and the Snowbird

KATHY PIERCE

On my fifth day of being a Texan I walked into Dixon's office in search of a job. He thought I was shivering because I had been out in the cold January wind. Actually, I was trembling because I hadn't been on an interview in years. I had been at home raising two children, but finally decided it was time to return to the work force.

Dixon wasn't a particularly handsome man, but he had a beautiful, contagious smile. And his magnetic personality enabled me to relax instantly.

The job he described sounded ideal. Best of all, his office was one mile away from my apartment in Spring Branch. I knew I could make more money working downtown, but I had seen the Katy Freeway during rush hour.

Dixon admitted I was qualified, but he was still skeptical about hiring me. Reaching for a cigarette, he explained, "Snowbirds – or Northerners – flock down here every winter looking for jobs and warm weather. In the summer, when they discover they didn't make their first million, and when their hands sizzle on the steering wheel, they go back home. I don't want to be looking for your replacement next July."

I am not an aggressive person, but I realized if I didn't sell myself I could kiss that job goodbye. Shyly I began, "Sir, my husband was a pastor who left the ministry last fall. We were convinced we could start a new life in Houston, so we sold our house in Louisville and loaded everything we owned into a U-Haul." I swallowed hard and promised, "This snowbird isn't going to fly away."

Dixon hired me with the stipulation I wouldn't call him "sir" again.

A week later, my husband dropped by my place of business

131

and spoke briefly with my new boss. When he left, Dixon called me into his office. He blew a smoke ring into the air and said, "Your husband has the makings of a great salesman, and I have the perfect place in mind for him. This company rarely hires individuals without experience, but," he said with a sly grin, "I have connections."

He made a few phone calls and scheduled an appointment for the manager of a Fortune 500 company and my husband to meet the next day. Stunned, I asked, "Why are you doing this?"

He replied philosophically, "We aren't on this earth too long. The way I see it, we should try our best to help each other out. Someone may burn you along the way, but it's no big deal." He looked at some pictures of his two daughters on his bookshelf and smiled proudly. "My girls and their mother, my ex-wife, think I'm a pushover, but if I can't help someone, I'm not happy."

If I had second thoughts about relocating to Houston, they vanished at that point. And when that prestigious firm hired my husband at an unbelievable salary I began to wonder if there was anything Dixon couldn't do.

It didn't take me long to learn that Dixon was a creature of habit. Each Monday morning he walked into the office slowly, rubbing his forehead. He removed a bottle of scotch from his desk drawer and handed it to me. "Hide this for me," he'd say. "And if I ask for it, don't give it to me." On Friday afternoons I noticed he had found the bottle and returned it to his drawer.

For some reason, Dixon assumed the role of my protector. He thought of me solely as a small-town girl who shouldn't be exposed to "life in the fast lane." If he accidentally cursed in my presence, he apologized immediately. I might have understood his behavior had he been an older man, but he was only forty-one.

Dixon had a bountiful supply of quotes, one of which was, "Nothing stays the same forever." He wasn't kidding. The oil business bottomed out, and as a result, our corporation went bankrupt. Our company may have fizzled, but not our friendship. It grew more precious to me with each passing year, especially when my marriage crumbled. I'm sure there were nights Dixon dreaded picking up his telephone because he knew I'd be on the other end of the line, but he never made me feel like a pest. Instead, he listened patiently, then assured me I'd survive.

"When I met you six years ago," he reminisced, "You were a quiet little girl who was afraid to go downtown. Now you're independent and feisty—sometimes downright bitchy."

"Stuff it!"

"See what I mean? Kathy, you don't need a husband to make you happy. Happiness comes from within. Haven't I taught you anything?"

Dixon spent so much time focusing on other people's problems that it was easy to forget he had any of his own. Amy, an unemployed college student, had been living with him for four years. He paid all the bills, including her tuition. Shortly before she graduated, Dixon discovered she was having an affair with his best friend. The next thing I knew he moved to Dallas. He claimed business was better there, but I knew he moved to get away from those who had betrayed him.

Jeff and Amy had barely exchanged vows when Jeff died. Instantly, the grieving widow turned to Dixon for comfort—and got it! I was furious with him. "After what that snake did to you?"

Dixon said simply, "Her heart was breaking. What kind of a friend would I be if I turned away in that condition? Besides, if the situation were reversed, she would have let me cry on her shoulder."

"No, she wouldn't, and you know it."

Dixon wouldn't argue with me. If he ever said one cruel word about Amy or Jeff, or anyone else for that matter, I never heard it. Dixon's emptiness was soon filled in a bittersweet way; his ex-wife died, and his daughters moved in with him. He loved playing full-time father and gave up drinking overnight.

Not long after that, he and his girls met me and my kids at AstroWorld. I spent the whole day talking about the incredible new man in my life. For the first time in our friendship, Dixon didn't share my joy. Friends had hinted that he was in love with me, but I laughed at them. I reminded them that he had never done anything to substantiate their rumors.

After that weekend, however, I knew my friends were right. Dixon's phone calls gradually ended, and when I called him, I detected sorrow in his voice. I felt so uncomfortable talking to him that I decided it would be best not to call him again until those awkward feelings went away.

They're gone now—but so is Dixon; cancer recently claimed

his life. It's too late to thank him for believing there's good in everyone, and for giving people hundreds of second chances. It's too late to tell him how lucky I was to have him call me his friend. And it's too late to tell him that in my own way, I loved him, too.

# This Is Not My Beautiful House

MARION WINIK

As I informed the Bureau of the Census earlier this year, I am currently living my middle-income thirty-two-year-old Caucasian life in a house of six rooms in Austin, with one Caucasian husband and one Caucasian son and no unrelated persons who don't normally live here but don't have anyplace else to live either. Is this me? I thought as I filled in the last machine-readable block. A grown-up? A nuclear mom? A Donna Reed for the nineties?

I'll tell you, I didn't start out with this in mind. A born iconoclast, an aspiring artiste, a feminist vegetarian prodigal daughter, from early youth I considered myself destined to lead a startling life far outside the bounds of convention. I would be famous, dangerous, brilliant, and relentlessly cool: a sort of cross between Emma Goldman, Jack Kerouac, and Georgia O'Keeffe. Home ownership, marriage, and gainful employment did not figure into my plans, except as symbols of the wimpy conformism I vowed to avoid. So what happened? Where did this station wagon come from? When did Emma O'Kerouac take up residence at the middle of the American road?

Escorted by The Ghost of Census Past, let us revisit the year 1980. Having graduated from college two years earlier—where I studied Hinduism, Marxism, and poetry to prepare me for what I supposed was my future—I drifted south to Austin. There I got a job teaching creative writing to juvenile delinquents, a position for which I was qualified by virtue of being hardly more than a creative delinquent myself. I lived in a house with the same number of rooms as my current home, but with half the rent and three times the number of inhabitants. Unrelated by blood or marriage, we were entwined instead by coincidence and convenience, by illicit love and left-wing politics, by the overarching need to agree on a single grocery list. I was twentysomething and suffering from delusions of grandeur, having just had my first book of poetry published in an edition of one thousand by a small press in New Braunfels. Convinced that fame and fortune awaited me, I packed up and moved to New York City.

Alas, I not only did not achieve instant celebrity, but could not even find a place to live. At first, I stayed in the heroin-district apartment of a family friend, a Buddhist on retreat with his llama. Later I moved in with a cordial but neurotic woman ten years older than me who charged me half the rent for the opportunity to put a bed in her walk-in closet. At last I found my own place, three tiny rooms up five flights in a commercial neighborhood, where an industrial exhaust fan blew dirty steam through the open windows. I lived there with my best friend, my sister, and my sister's boyfriend. We all hated each other.

But the housing situation was not my worst problem. Even more frustrating was the fact that the city of my birth was a veritable Marion Winik factory, a city overrun by Marion Winiks, all wearing the same cute outfits, writing the same short stories, taking the same trains to the same parties to talk about the same movies with the same people. Living in Texas, I had benefited from a certain émigré mystique; I so rarely met someone "just like me" that I was able to sustain an illusion of uniqueness. In New York, it was another story. All this competition, this constant affront to my cherished individuality, made me feel exceedingly lethargic. I decided to ruin my life by becoming a drug addict.

But midway through my brilliant demise, I was rescued by Destiny, which crammed me into a blue Peugeot full of Manhattanites heading down to Mardi Gras in New Orleans. There I fell madly in love with a sexually ambiguous ice-skating bartender. Though I was not really his type, he couldn't resist my air of passionate excess: "She carries a whole carton of cigarettes in her purse," he bragged to his friends. Enraptured, I sat at his bar every night till he got off at 3:00 A.M., when we'd dance and drink and do drugs in the men's room and walk the smelly, oyster-juice streets until dawn.

My carnival beau had a wonderful apartment in the French Quarter, a second-floor studio with an iron-railed balcony and red brick walls. The kitchen window opened above the courtyard of a guest house for gay men, and bits of gossip and details of meals at Gallatoire's and Arnaud's drifted in all day long. How could I resist? Within a week after returning home, I broke the news to my roommates, quit my job, and made arrangements to finish my master's degree by mail. I knew the relationship was a little iffy, but I had to get out of New York somehow.

The first few months were rocky, complicated by his ex-lovers and my neuroses, but neither of us was ready to give up. Instead, we decided to bid the French Quarter adieu. We would cement our coupledom by starting a new life in a new town, by tossing every last bean into the cooking pot. Soon we were dragging a U-Haul filled with our mutual possessions back to Austin, where low rents and ephemeral job offers beckoned.

We leased an un–air-conditioned house on the Avenue of Confederate Heroes, where airplanes cruised over almost close enough to touch. But what was wrong with this place ran deeper than jet engines, deeper than nautically patterned wallpaper and peeling linoleum. It was sheer exhaustion: the weariness of a rent house that has been filled and emptied too many times, that sprawls on its corner with a beaten look, skirts hitched high, slouch-framed door wide open.

At first, I thought the house was fine. I was right back there in the sweaty kitchen cooking lentil soup on the crooked stove. But gradually, the funkiness of the place came to seem overwhelming, not inspiring. As my zest for anti-materialism began to fade, I lost interest in making do with less. I wanted new things, clean things, things that worked when you turned them on, things with five-year warranties on parts and labor. I wanted central air and heat. What you want, said the real estate agent, is a condominium!

It wasn't painless, leaving post-adolescent bohemia behind, becoming a typical DINC (Double Income, No Children), acquiring the trendy condo that would complete the picture. But suddenly the promise of gracious living—the luminous planes of unspoiled Formica—seemed to outweigh the once-dreaded bourgeois connotations. (My boyfriend, he of the fabulous French Quarter, had no such radical pretensions to wrestle with. Ready for gracious living from the word go, he was delighted that I had finally come around.)

It's OK, I thought. I'm buying a house, not selling my soul.

It's not as if I've started wearing high heels and voting Republican. It's not as if I owned a microwave oven, for God's sake. I may have relaxed my standards, but I haven't lost them altogether.

I looked at one place after another, but most of them had a certain generic, hotel-room feeling that failed to win my heart. Finally the wily real estate agent took me to the construction site of a condominium that had not yet been built. As he suspected, this place had none of the flaws of those which already existed. I could tell from the tiny floor plan with its clever symbols, it was just perfect. The neighborhood was perfect. Even the trees that had to be cut down to make way for the complex were perfect. But what's this here? I asked, pointing to an unfamiliar symbol in the rectangle marked "kitchen." A built-in microwave, the agent told me confidently. Oh well, I rationalized, I'll never use it.

Reversing the pattern followed by previous generations, home ownership led us somehow to marriage. I had always assumed I wouldn't marry. It was just too predictable, too passé. Though I did feel attracted to motherhood, I hoped to pull it off without accumulating a husband in the process. As it turned out, I accepted my first proposal. It came one night while we were lying on the bed after a gin game with my newlywed sister and brother-in-law, holding hands and watching a silent television. Do you think we should get married, too? asked my partner at cards. Yes, I said slowly, I do.

I had finally figured it out—the way my life felt from the inside was more important than how it looked from without. And how I felt was neither predictable nor passé. And so I entered the state of holy matrimony—in ivory lace, no less, champagne in one hand, cigarette in the other. This is the happiest day of my life, I announced to my uncle behind the video camera. I was trying to sound facetious, but my starry eyes gave me away.

A couple of years passed. I quit smoking, had a baby, and the trendy condo was transformed as well. My sunny study became a nursery, the elegant guest bath Diaper Central, our plush silver wall-to-wall carpet a grizzled mat. The flight of steps leading to our front door gradually assumed the aspect of Sisyphus' mountain; a medium-size toddler played the role of the rock. The last straw came one day as I was pushing him to the store for some juice. He jumped out of the stroller and bolted into someone else's backyard. A little slide, a toy car, and a plastic rake—he thought he was in Disney World. Finally I had to drag him away. The owner drove up as we were leaving. I'm sorry, I told her, he doesn't have a yard of his own.

I had the marriage, I had the kid, we had just bought the station wagon, now all I needed was the two-car garage to park it in. To be honest, by this time I didn't give a damn how conventional my dream house might be, I just wanted a place where we could spread out and be a family. Unfortunately, I'd bought my condo right before the biggest real estate crash in Texas history. My only escape route was to rent it out, and lease a house for whatever I could get.

As the first months of the nineties unfurled, my little clan and I moved to a spacious abode with a big kitchen (no microwave!) and a verdant expanse of fenced yard, which we immediately equipped with a plastic rake and a fleet of small engineless vehicles. The rental fee has only three digits, and compared with a thirty-year adjustable-rate mortgage as inescapable as a pact with the devil, the twelve-month lease seems benign. And the fact that I don't own my own home—while depressing to my friends who are in the same boat—is somehow heartening to me. Being part of the first generation of Americans whose standard of living is lower than their parents' pleases my latent anti-capitalist sensibilities.

So that's how it happened. And I'm not the only one it's happened to, either. Most of the people we barbecue with and watch videos with and borrow baby clothes from are erstwhile rebels and renegades, each of whom has a *Big Chill* story like mine. But does it mean we don't care about art or politics or God or what is cool and what is not? Hell, no. It just means we fell in love, and got too old to stay up all night, and moved on, with a little more baggage, to the next hotel.

# A Date with the Last Houston Princess

BOB LEE

As I was nervously dressing to get ready to pick her up, all sorts of thoughts came to me. Remember to open the door for her, walk in front once at the restaurant, don't talk with food in my mouth, and for Mother's sake, place my napkin on my lap. And this time, tip the waiters fairly.

My date was Constance Houston, a friend I've known since I was a teenager. She was my teacher at Phyllis Wheatley High School in the city's old Fifth Ward. She and I were going to have lunch to celebrate her birthday. She was born August 7, 1899. Yes, she was about to turn ninety years old. And, I must admit, it was not just any girl in the classroom I had secretly loved at Wheatley High. It was my Miss Houston.

I arrived at her stately, elegant home built at the turn of the century, amazed—as always—by its grace and beauty. When her father moved here and purchased this house from German builders in 1913, the land around it was prairie. Miss Houston told me that when she first came to the Fifth Ward, there were fields and pastures with cows and horses grazing. I found it hard to imagine a time when the Fifth Ward was not a slum. She told me that most blacks lived near Buffalo Bayou. They farmed the rich soil thrown up from the flooding of the bayou, and this community was called the Bottom.

Her father, Mr. Houston, was a successful blacksmith, and her mother was a teacher. She was born in Huntsville, but her dad moved them to Houston all in one day, she said, when whites lynched a black boy. But soon after that, a black man was lynched in Houston, too. There was no place to run, she said. Lynching and beating went on everywhere.

I walked up the stairs to the long Victorian gallery. I rang the

ancient doorbell promptly at the time I said I'd be there, 11:30 A.M.
My date came to the door, assisted by her walking cane. She looked
like spring, dressed in a beautiful green print dress. She had these
lovely low heels on her little feet, she wore fine jewelry, her hair
shone with health, and she had that warm, welcoming smile that
I am sure hundreds of children looked at and said, "This is the
right place to be. She cares." This is the smile I watched in high
school.

Miss Constance Houston, you see, was my home economics
teacher. I was an athlete, part-time student, and full-time street
professional. I had discovered that the home economics classes had
99 percent girls, and they prepared cakes, cookies, and exotic meals.
I enrolled.

My teammates and friends from the street fraternity thought
I had lost my manhood. I became their joke. But home economics
was the only class I would not cut. I was never late, and I didn't
mind wearing the aprons. I learned to bake my cake and eat it,
too. For one full hour I was surrounded by the prettiest brown
darlings of the Fifth Ward, and I am still a good cook today. It
wasn't long before some of my fellow athletes noticed the advan-
tages of taking home economics. Darrow Dotson, track star at
Wheatley High and later at Southern University in Baton Rouge,
enrolled in the other home ec class. Still others followed our lead.

For Miss Constance Houston, I had made reservations at one
of Houston's finest restaurants, Phillis' Place. While on our way
to the restaurant, I stopped to pick up tickets to a Wheatley re-
union at Bernadette's Scientific Barbershop where generations of
Wheatleyites get their hair trimmed. This was a Friday, and the
shop was wall-to-wall males. I announced with glee, "Fellas, guess
who I am having lunch with today?" They peeked out the window
and in unison—sounding like the Mormon Tabernacle Choir—said
"Miss Houston." They all went outside to greet her as if she were
Lena Horne or the Princess of Houston.

Once we got to the restaurant, we were led to a table overlooking the garden. I was nervous. What would we talk about, I wondered? But being the teacher she is, she took command and opened
up over our meal.

She told me that her grandfather was friend and personal ser-
vant to Gen. Sam Houston in Huntsville, and that General Houston advised him to take his name, for things would surely be eas-

ier for him. She went on to say her grandfather had later founded the Sam Houston Vocational High School for Negroes, in Huntsville. She stated her parents were determined that she and her sister (another Houston princess) would get college educations, and they did. Miss Houston, I believe, has more degrees than a thermometer.

She told me that at the turn of the century, there was only one school for blacks in Houston. It was called the Colored High School and that she was probably the only surviving founder of what is now Jack Yates High School and Booker T. Washington High. And she helped to build the foundation of what is now Texas Southern University.

She gazed out the window, eyes fixed on a beautiful flower, then looked at me with her ancient eyes and said, "I worked at one school when I was a young lady, and there were forty-two teachers. I've outlived them all." She looked away and said, "I cannot believe they are all dead." She told me that the Fourth Ward was the dominant black community built around the Antioch Baptist Church founded by the educator and minister Rev. Jack Yates.

She went on to say that the Fifth Ward at the turn of the century was populated by white, Chinese, Italian, and Irish communities, and that they were the only black family in that circle. I thought to myself, "Integration back then? No way."

She told me with a laugh how she would walk into the whites' restaurants where blacks were not allowed. Even then she dressed like a princess. Her skin was so light, she looked white. She talked about the horse and carriage she owned and would drive to school. On muddy days she would ride by saddle. And with sadness she would talk about her husband Mr. Thompson, who recently died. They were married in 1923 and were together for more than sixty years.

Our waiter came out with the surprise dessert. I had gone by the restaurant the day before to set the stage. The smile on Miss Houston's face never left. It's a smile that lets you know you have a rightful place in her world. But like all good dates, time flies and we soon returned to her home.

As we walked through the old wrought iron gate, I asked if I could help her. She said, "I don't need help. I try to do all I can for myself, and if I need help, I'll ask you, son."

We stood outside under the big Texas sky to chat. I remembered how she had told me this stately house had served as a hotel for some of the most prominent blacks in America who were not allowed in Houston hotels during the time of segregation. Miss Houston hosted people such as Ethel Waters, actress and singer; labor leader A. Philip Randolph, my personal hero; and various members of the Duke Ellington and Count Basie bands. They were brought to town by white demand but could not stay in white hotels.

Miss Houston was pointing out the beautiful plants and flowers in her tropical garden when I spied this huge iron ball. "What is that, Miss Houston?" I asked.

"Oh, that's a cannon ball used in the Civil War. My father, being a blacksmith, appreciated good iron," she said. I walked her to the door and waited until she was inside. I took her little hand and kissed it, like the English gents do, and said "Happy Birthday, Miss Houston." And with that angelic smile she gave me a motherly kiss and said, "I will never forget this day, my boy."

As I walked back to my car I thought to myself, this was a once-in-a-lifetime date. Miss Houston has outlived her sister, scores of friends, neighbors, and even her students. She was born before the turn of this century, and I've known her since I was fifteen years old. Man, I'll never forget the day I actually had lunch with the last Houston princess.

# Ambrose, Mother, and Magic

EVAN MOORE

Jay Gorney died the other day and reminded me of Ambrose and the magic.

I never met Jay Gorney, never even saw him. The little news item about his death said he'd lived most of his ninety-three years in Hollywood and New York City, and I haven't spent much time in either place. But the story said he wrote the music to "Brother Can You Spare a Dime?" and I immediately thought of a lilting, bluesy tune and a strange little man in a weathered old house with "Mother" in Mineral Wells.

Gorney wrote his Depression-era classic in 1932 for a Broadway revue titled *Americana,* and its notes carried across the country. He wrote a number of others too, mostly for musicals, the lavish, gilt-edged kind that took American minds off the ugly reality of a dead economy. Shirley Temple, James Dunn, and a lot of others danced their way through those pictures and created a gossamer, ephemeral relief.

All of which reminded me of Ambrose, who, as far as I know, never made it to Hollywood or New York City, either.

I don't know that he ever left Mineral Wells, and I don't think he wanted to. It was his home, a place of past glories. The old Baker hotel, once a resort retreat with hot, sulfurous baths for Fort Worth's wealthy, loomed closed and vacant on Main Street then. Fort Wolters, the town's Army post, had just been deactivated and it sprawled, empty, just north of the city limits.

The beer joints were on the east end, and I met Ambrose in one of those in 1978. It was a place with a big, roaring evaporative cooler and holes in the screens that let flies in. I was with a singer who called herself "Rattlesnake Annie" and her husband, and we'd gone there to meet Julia.

144

The reasons for meeting Julia have grown hazy with time, but it had something to do with her claim that she was the sixth wife and widow of a dissipated millionaire and that she was one of the first people in Texas to have been given electric shock treatment. She lived in a trailer house behind the bar and kept a pile of fur coats (gifts from the millionaire) in a freezer on the back porch.

On this particular afternoon Julia was holding court at a back table. She was a woman of indeterminate age, somewhere between sixty and ninety. She was wearing red hair that wasn't hers, dark glasses, a lot of jewelry that was either very expensive or very phony and an expression that seemed to oscillate between regal and haggard.

And she was almost wearing the little man on her right. He was soft and shapeless and very white with only a wisp of graying hair that began at his ears and thinned out toward the back of his head. His thin arms protruded from a white, short-sleeved shirt and ended in long, delicate fingers. The fingers danced silently among themselves while his feet shuffled under the table in expensive Italian shoes.

And he had pale blue eyes that never left Julia.

"Hello," she said. "This is Ambrose."

But Ambrose didn't know I was there. As Julia and I talked about the sins of her ex-husband and the therapeutic effects of being wrapped in a wet sheet and hooked to an electric wire, his blue eyes never strayed from her face. They stayed on her lips as she told me fantastic tales of romance ruined by drunkenness and cruelty, and they trailed her as she finally left the table and returned to her trailer.

"You must believe her," he said, with a small smile in my direction. "Even if it's not true. If it's not . . . 'your' reality. You must believe her. It's what makes her wonderful, you see. What makes her unique.

"It's her magic."

"And you must meet Mother," he added, and I realized his hands had stopped moving. "I'd like for you to come to the house and I'll introduce you."

We left the bar and followed Ambrose along the town's hilly streets to what had once been a majestic old house. It sat on a corner, towering inside a fortress of huge oaks in a yard devoid of grass. Gray and old. The paint long since had succumbed to sun and wind.

"You won't meet Mother," Annie told me. "Nobody ever does.

"We think he just wants company. He's brought us over to meet her before, but she never came downstairs and we're not even sure she was up there.

"He's a strange one. He's been mooning over Julia for years, and he's never asked her for a date. Just sits there and watches her no matter what she says. But he's kind of interesting and he plays a mean piano."

Ambrose was beckoning then from the back of the house. We

entered through a butler's pantry, passed through a little kitchen, a dining room with some dark, heavy furniture lining the walls and into a vast living room. The floors rang with the hollow sound of old pier-and-beam houses and there was a scent of age and disuse.

But I couldn't really see. Every shade, blind, and curtain was drawn as though, like its owner, the house retreated from the sun. I could make out the outlines of chairs and a sofa and a huge piano in a corner, but I couldn't determine the mosaic of the old carpet. Ambrose made no move for a light switch, and I made my way to what looked like an overstuffed chair and stayed by it.

"Have a drink," he said, and handed me a water glass full of bourbon with two ice cubes. "I'll go check on Mother."

He returned in a few moments with a crestfallen look and reported that Mother wasn't feeling well.

"She has her good days and her bad ones," he said. "She really should get downstairs more . . . but I can't influence her."

"Would you like some music?" he asked, and sat at the piano. The long white fingers were moving again, gliding over the keys without touching them until they settled on a G-chord.

And he played "Brother Can You Spare a Dime?" He only sang the first bar, maybe less, but the piano was enough. W. C. Handy and Scott Joplin and a hundred other musicians came rolling out of the percussion box. Ambrose's fingers were flawless, and I drank the whiskey and listened and thought about my grandmother seated at another piano, playing the same tunes twenty years before.

He played several more. There were "Harvest Moon" and "Paper Moon" and a medley I didn't know, but Jay Gorney kept applauding through all of them. And Ambrose seemed to pick up other instruments. A banjo from somewhere, a trumpet that faded in. Then drums and cymbals and woodwinds and strings. And a Busby Berkeley chorus line and Shirley Temple and Bojangles and James Cagney danced their way out of the piano and circled the pale man in the dim room.

And as my eyes dilated I could tell that Ambrose was crying. Almost unnoticeably. No sobs. Just two slow streams of tears moving down into the creases of a big, wide smile.

We drank some more of Ambrose's whiskey sometime after that and I don't remember how long he played, but I know it was dusk when he finally stopped. The light was so weak I could barely see the piano and Ambrose had become a ghostly blur behind it.

"You'll have to see the patio now," he said with the first hint of excitement I'd heard in his voice. "It's the only other property we have left. We used to own a lot of property around town, but Mother sold everything else.

"But I just couldn't bear to let her sell the patio."

We piled in my car and drove about a mile to what appeared to be the highest hill in Mineral Wells. On top of it was just what Ambrose had promised, a patio. No house, no utilities. Just a large, level area of about a half-acre, covered with reddish tiles. There were a few trees, surrounded by little, round, brick curbs, two concrete benches, and a brick wall at the south end, overlooking the town.

Below the patio, stretching out like a Chinese fan, was Mineral Wells. It was twilight, still early enough for small-town people to be awake, and the lights of the houses twinkled through the tree-tops in varying sparks of white and yellow with a few reds and blues mixed in.

And immediately below the patio wall, at the curb of the street below, was a brand new incandescent street light. Its colorless light spread upward, cutting through the glimmer of the city and al-most illuminating the tiles.

"Oh, damn," said Ambrose. "Damn. They've put that thing in and they've ruined it. I'd hoped they wouldn't. For years I've come up here and looked out over the lights of this town. It was Xanadu. It was the Ice Castle. It was something beautiful and they've come along and put this damn street light in and they've ruined it.

"They don't understand.

"You don't disturb the magic."

We took Ambrose home after that. He was quiet on the way, inconsolable. Annie tried to say a few things about how great the view from the patio was despite the street light, but it didn't mat-ter. He wasn't responding.

By the time we got to his house, he'd regained a little spirit and he thanked us for spending the afternoon with him. He didn't offer us any more whiskey and he didn't invite us back inside, however. He just said goodbye at the car and shuffled around to the back door.

We waited a few minutes to be sure he'd gotten inside, then drove away, leaving him in his worn mausoleum with Mother and the piano.

When I looked back as we left, the house was completely dark.

# Dialogue with a River Rat

RICHARD STEWART

Coot Swilley was spitting mad.

He sat there in a tattered old folding chair at a table in front of the little house he had built on his island in the middle of an East Texas river and spat out a stream of verbal venom.

It wasn't just a bad day for Coot—more like a bad life, with the whole world as the target of his enmity. Unfortunately, I was an emissary of that world.

He was using language more filthy than any I'd ever heard a sober man use. It was notable not for its inventiveness, but because of Coot's ability to use The Forbidden Word in every conceivable context—and a few that weren't so conceivable.

"No, sir," he sneered, "I don't want to talk to no reporters about no story. I stay out here on my island and I don't bother no person on earth, and all I ask is that nobody bothers me."

This is not exactly how he put it. A reader interested in complete authenticity should mentally insert some form of The Forbidden Word in about every third word of anything Coot said.

Coot Swilley isn't his real name, either. Sometimes writers change the names of their subjects to protect the innocent from trouble or embarrassment. This time the name was changed so Coot wouldn't be tempted to come to town and shoot the writer.

He was a small man with a big reputation. All up and down the river folks had been telling me that Coot was the last of the old-time river rats, a man who lived life on his own terms. Some considered him a harmless old character. Others hinted darkly of people disappearing when they dared enter his territory, or of bodies washing up far downstream.

He seemed harmless enough. While he didn't offer me any of

the coffee he was drinking, he didn't object to me sitting down for a spell. As he talked, he smoked Pall Malls and pointed a gnarled finger at me or in other directions for emphasis. His wrinkled, seventy-four-year-old face showed a wide range of expression, especially anger.

He seemed to be cleaner than I imagined a near-hermit to be. The insulated undershirt that showed through the open collar of his plaid flannel shirt looked only a little yellowed. A stained red cap from a hunting club covered his head. White, close-cropped hair peeked from under the cap.

He was clean-shaven, and the only scent I could detect was from a smoldering log a few feet away or one of the hounds that came by to sniff at me every now and then.

Coot expanded his list of people he didn't want to see show up at his island. He included almost every kind of lawman, conservationists, do-gooders of every sort, and a goodly number of his eleven children and numerous grandchildren, nephews, and more distant relatives.

"I don't care if anybody ever comes out here," he said. "I welcome my friends, and they know who they are. My enemies know who they are, too, and they better stay the hell away from here, because I'll shoot them as quick as look at them."

I noticed a rifle leaning against a tree. It did not look as if it were there just for decoration.

He grinned when he saw me looking at the rifle. "I've nothing against you," he said. "I heard you was looking for me, and I got your phone number. If I'd a-wanted to talk to you I would have called you. I could have saved you a trip way up here."

As Coot talked on, it seemed as if a blue haze of profanity surrounded him. He was kind of like a lawn-mower engine with bad piston rings, making lots of noise and blue smoke.

The blue verbal haze seemed totally out of place with the physical beauty of his island. It was early fall, with just a hint of coolness in the air. The blue sky above the towering pines was punctuated by a few fluffy clouds.

The chocolate-colored river flowed behind Coot, far below the bluff where he built his house. Sandbars on the river shone in the sunlight like snow.

"I had thirteen children," he went on. "Eleven of them lived to adulthood, and I don't have nothing to do with most of them. Most of them are useless to me."

Off to one side were three silent characters dressed in camouflage hunting gear and those gray welding caps that make the wearer's head look pointed. They laughed among themselves as Coot described how useless he considered most of his relatives.

"Of course, I do get along with some of them, like my son, here," Coot said, pointing a thumb at the oldest of the trio. "That's my grandson there with him and one of his friends.

"I know you been talking to my sons about me." The camouflage trio started laughing even harder. "Them that would tell you anything about me are totally useless."

I was fairly sure that I had talked to the camouflage son on the telephone about Coot. It's hard to keep all of Coot's relatives separate since there are a great many of them, and they all seem to share one of about a half-dozen different first names.

I had been hunting for Coot for a long time. It was impossible to telephone him, since his island had no connection, other than boats, with the outside world. I had called several relatives, asking them to pass messages asking him to call me.

Once, a guy who claimed to be some kind of distant relative even took me in a borrowed boat to Coot's island. Even though several local folks said they thought he was on the island, Coot had, on a whim, decided to go to town that day. My guide had warned me that it was best for me to stay in the boat and not go up on the island without express permission from Coot.

"I even know you came out here once," he said. "I don't know who the SOB is who took you out here, but if I'd a been here I would have shot the low-life."

I took a polite tack. Being outnumbered and unarmed, it seemed like the wise thing to do. After all, Coot hadn't actually threatened to shoot me. Not yet, anyhow.

"Gee, Mr. Swilley, I certainly didn't mean to upset you. It's just that out here you are living a life that many people just dream about," I said.

It seemed to placate him a little.

"You have escaped from all the pressures of everyday life. Out here you don't have to put up with crummy bosses or traffic jams or ringing telephones or any of those other things that drive people crazy in modern life today," I said. "A lot of our readers would like to know how you do it."

"I just do it," he said. "I don't need much, and I don't like people messing with me."

"How do you live out here?" I asked.

"Oh, I garden a little. If I need some fish, I just fish a little. There's the chickens."

Several rangy brown chickens clucked around the bare dirt yard.

"Of course, all this corn I left out here isn't for the chickens. Most of it is here for my deer," he said.

"Deer? You've got pet deer? How many?"

"I used to have sixteen head, but some no good, son of a. . . ." His voice trailed off into a mumble of curses. ". . . Shot and killed some of them. How can anybody kill a deer that's got a red collar and a bell around his neck? Worthless, no good. . . ." More cursing.

"I don't wish any harm to any man," he said with a grin, "as long as he don't mess with me." His grin turned into a snarl. "Of course, if God gave me the power to throw a switch and wipe every living thing off the face of the Earth, I'd do it. That's probably why God will never give me the power to throw that switch."

I wasn't sure, but it looked as if the blue haze had formed a dark cloud over Coot's head.

"What do you do for money?" I asked. "I mean, you have to get gas for your boat motor and shells for your guns."

"I get a little draw from the government," he said. "From when I was in the Army and got all shot up."

He later explained: "They were fightin' when I was born (World War I), and I got in on it the next time they was fightin'. I sure as hell did."

The mention of war sent him off into another blue-haze rage, this time against the way the United States treats veterans. "I don't like to talk about it, because most of my buddies are still over there. Sometimes I wonder if it wouldn't a-been better for me if I'd a-been left over there too," he said, settling down in a blue funk.

I decided to change the subject and asked him if he would mind showing me around the place.

He was obviously proud of his island, which he explained was on the tax rolls of neither of the counties on each side of the river. "This here is part of the river. God put it here," he said. He explained that it was impossible for him or anybody else to get a legal title to it, but that it was his because he had established a camp on it long ago and had lived there full-time for several years.

"This here's my kitchen," he said, opening the door to a dirt-floored building the size of a two-car garage. It had a frame and a roof, but the walls were made out of black plastic. A single propane lantern provided dim illumination.

The camouflage boys were inside the kitchen by then, sitting on one of two wooden picnic tables in the middle of the big room. They were eating what looked like some sort of white and yellow glob. From its smell, it seemed likely one of Coot's chickens had ended up in the pot.

"I've got a propane ice box and a propane stove and a wood stove," he said with pride. "And I got all the cabinets I need."

Next door, in a bright red building a little bigger than a two-car garage, were the rest of his living quarters. It had a real plywood floor and windows all around that flooded the interior with sunlight. An old sofa and some chairs were clustered around a portable radio and a small, battery-powered television set.

"I hear you liked to listen to Hank Williams," I said, motioning toward the radio. "But I thought you hated television."

"I keep that devil's box there for my children when they come around," he said. He added that he considers television, long hair, and higher education the most destructive influences in today's society. "I never saw more than the fourth grade myself," he said.

The rear of the big room was crammed with about seven beds of all sizes and descriptions. At the head of a small bed in one corner was a hand-lettered sign:

"This here is Coot Swilley's bed. I am an old man, so please let me alone and let me sleep in peace."

"I put that up there because sometimes I have drunks who come out here and I let them sleep here, and I don't want them to get in my bed," he said.

Outside he showed me an old wringer washing machine he runs with a gasoline engine. He also started up another small engine that powers his water pump. A thick stream of water shot into the air.

By then he was acting so friendly that only about one Forbidden Word per sentence crept into his language. I decided it was safe to ask if I could take a picture of him and his fine water pump.

That reminded him that he doesn't like reporters, and in an instant he had escorted me down to his boat landing and shown me the way to get back into the main river channel without running aground. As I eased my boat out into the stream, I looked around at what was a beautiful, blue-eyed Texas day, free of the hassles of the twentieth century.

Old Coot had come out here to escape those evils, I thought, but perhaps he had brought some far worse with him.

I noticed a blue haze spreading over the water. It wasn't from the boat engine.

The boat motor masked Coot's words, but I had a pretty good idea of what he was saying.

# View from the Third Ward

CHARLES CLAWSON

One evening last fall, my small yellow convertible crammed with everything I owned, I drove into a neighborhood I would later learn is called the Third Ward, near the University of Houston. I hadn't yet learned how this city numbers its ghettos. Located there was the weekly apartment I had called about. It was roughly my last chance to sleep in a bed that night. The sun was almost down.

I followed the street sign into a rutted back road where Hispanic children were playing football in the street, shouting and laughing. They parted for my small Fiat slowly, as if they didn't think it could do them much harm anyway. I stopped in front of the old building, which had divots knocked out of the bricks and a metal stairway that was leaning at a precarious angle. A boy holding the football was near enough to read the expression on my face. *"Ayuda! Ayuda!"* he called in a falsetto, and the other children laughed. I knew that *ayuda* means help.

My landlord was John Wayne living his other life, the one where he didn't get a break but hung on as a broken-down slumlord, propped by drinks. His tongue habitually fiddled with a gap in his side teeth as he was sorting keys, and he had a lot of keys. In this life the swagger had become the walk of a man with one lead foot, and he was slow in everything, without much of a chance in the face of Indians.

The Duke showed me to the neighbors, so that my presence wouldn't startle them. He said that otherwise they would think a young white guy with a car worked for the city. He warned me about Lester, downstairs, saying that if Lester cornered you he'd talk a hole through the lining of your stomach.

Lester shuffled to his door, an old Art Carney, almost transparent, holding onto this life by his nightshirt, it seemed, and he said not one word.

As The Duke led me upstairs to my room he said, "Well, you're lucky."

The door had a padlock outside, two locks on the inside. He said, "We don't get many robberies," and I thought, "My God, who would be desperate enough to rob a place like this?"

I stepped into the dim room and looked at the taped-up couch, the thin paneling that leaned away from the wall. Even in that stale air, I could smell the grease on the walls, and I could make out hair and small insects laminated to the kitchen table.

"It's not a luxury hotel," said The Duke.

I stood there one step in for a long time, my eyes getting accustomed to the dark, feeling vaguely that some sort of inertia had nailed me there, until I realized that my shoes were stuck to the linoleum.

I could hear a mother and daughter arguing out on the landing. They didn't seem to care if I overheard.

"You been next door?"

"Who? With that white man?"

"What you been up to?"

"I don't even know him. He just moved there."

They walked down the landing then, and I thought the girl said she wanted to get married.

"WITH THAT WHITE MAN?"

The world was foreign, and I didn't know what was possible.

I lived in those rooms for four months, becoming so accustomed to the neighborhood that occasionally I wouldn't recognize it. The boy who had held the football in the street asked me one day if I owned the apartment building. One night a stranger helped me push my car back to the apartment and then sprinted out of there.

I met most of the people in the neighborhood because my car kept breaking down. I became friends with the girl next door and found it pretty interesting to eavesdrop as boys tried to wheedle their way into her whims. Once I unplugged the refrigerator to hear better.

"There. You got your hug. Now go on."

"Just another minute."

"No, there! I saw you."

"You're not going to leave me like this. Are you?"

"Yes I will. Believe me."

"Aw, I can see why you be cold to anyone else. But I can't see why you be cold to me."

"Goodbye, Nick."

"Aw."

"I SAW YOU."

After Nick left, I plugged in the refrigerator and went back to sorting beans, wondering why anyone would choose to live in the suburbs.

Early on, Lester would wave, moving his lips as if to speak, and I would pause, but he wouldn't say anything. We became pretty huge friends, although for the sake of my own work production, I generally avoided him. He liked to talk about his hernia, to explain in graphic detail how his guts were down where his testicles should be.

Lester and I hung out in his place, where the walls were papered with National Geographic maps, and he showed me his stack of Reader's Digests and the few naked-lady magazines he recommended halfheartedly. He had boxes and boxes of canned food, an insane amount, which he added to each day because, it seemed, he had nothing else to do. Out of doors he used a shopping cart as a walker, so a bag of groceries may have been camouflage for a strict athletic routine. Once, though, he shook his head at the craziness of hoarding so much food, as if it were the actions of someone else, and he said that when he was young there wasn't enough to go around. Later, as we became better friends, he showed me his closet, the gift shirts and shoes, still in their boxes, that he would never wear.

According to Lester—and I believed him—he was a wealthy man, owning several hundred thousand dollars in property. When I asked him why he lived here, he said that he had signed the first week's lease while he was drunk and couldn't tell what a rat hole the place was. He said that ten years later his eyes gave out from cataracts, so he just stayed here. That sounded about right, too.

I finally moved out because the darkness and shabbiness of the rooms were depressing me. What I had visited was my other life, the one enacted in broken rooms about three light years from the disinfected apartments of southwest Houston. I won't forget making eye contact with The Duke—the surprise of blue specks still in his eyes, the jawline not completely staggered by alcoholic slumber—and understanding then that my own shadow life, if it should return, would revolve around such fallen heroes as these.

# We All Walk on Bones

NAOMI SHIHAB NYE

Recently an artist friend who has lived a long time in Galveston told me how hard it is, especially during hurricane season each year, to bear the echoes.

"We walk on bones," she said. "Do you realize that? The wind is filled with cries."

I was fascinated by this because I, too, have felt haunted by places such as Galveston, where vast numbers of people perished tragically in the past. You feel that catch in the throat that says, "something unfinished here, still lingering." If you tilt your head just a little bit to one side, you can hear it, like the hush of a broom sweeping across the streets. I've felt it in Guatemala and Mexico City after earthquakes, and in Bangladesh, where whole villages are swept out to sea by annual tidal monsoons, disasters becoming almost punctual in that poor land. The air grows so meshed with the presence of the dead it feels like a heavy tapestry strung between sky and Earth.

We all walk on bones. In San Antonio, my family lives downtown across from a park that covers one of the original *acequias,* stone irrigation ditches that channeled water from the San Antonio River hundreds of years ago. Indians camped by it, early Texas settlers watered their horses, washed their clothes in it.

We know that the intricate walls of the *acequia* still tunnel under the park's mowed green expanses because an archaeological team from the University of Texas arrived a few years ago and dug it up. They studied it and decided little children might topple in if they left it open, so closed it over again. People who had lived on this street for fifty years said, "I had no idea."

It's impossible to walk in my neighborhood without being asked directions to the Alamo. Inside its thick walls the echoes are so loud you can almost interpret them. Bones of the Alamo defenders are buried at San Fernando Cathedral a few blocks down. Bones of a lunatic neighbor are said to be buried under a concrete slab just over our fence, but I try not to think about it.

Once a workman burrowing under our house emerged with a tiny white teacup, unchipped, the china so old it seemed to have turned to stone. He set the cup on the table tenderly, this huge fellow smeared with dirt, as if he heard what it said: "Another world, gone. And you are all so full of yourselves."

What happens to contemporary people not only full of ourselves but also full of more slices-of-world-news than we know what to do with? Daily we gulp headlines, glimpse flashes of staggering episodes, turn the page. We can't stay long anywhere because there's too much of it. China, the Middle East, Armenia, our hearts are tugged twenty directions, stretched. You could almost feel homesick for those days when our ancestors knew what was happening at their own farm, and maybe the next farm down the road.

In a poem called "Evening News," William Stafford speaks of watching "the whole world alive in glass," and turning away from the television toward his own backyard. He beseeches birds, wind, "unscheduled grass," to "please help to make everything go deep again."

But it might be too much if everything went deep. We feel for the people we know, and we feel a little more for the places we have been, but we also develop by necessity, a remarkable capacity to hear and think without feeling too much.

Occasionally we embrace a particular cause and follow it closely. A friend of mine, who happens to have AIDS, also has Central American bumper-stickers shouting off every fender and slope of his ancient Ford. A group of local women friends has recently decided to convince everyone they know in Texas to recycle trash. "If the state doesn't make us, we'll make ourselves!" They print up sheaves of pamphlets and reports, distributing them across the town. They can't heal the injuries of far-off oil spills, but by golly, they can do something about the mayonnaise jars on the next block.

Or are we prey to other echoes by way of heritage – in a sense, doomed by our own blood to care. I follow news of the uprising on the West Bank with keener interest than anything else in the paper, clipping horrific stories: "Ibtisam Bozieh woke from a nap and peered through the green shutter when the Jewish settlers began shooting—the shy thirteen-year-old had wanted to be a doctor, but she became a martyr, instead." I write endless numbers of letters to congressmen and editors. Why? Because my grandmother still lives high in the hills of her small Palestinian village, because my cousin's husband was recently rounded up in a large group arrested "without charges" by Israeli soldiers, and because I know what the stones there smell like: a rich, dusky soup of smoke, and sun, and thyme. Those people can never be headlines to me, nor to anyone who has visited them, sat with them, broken huge flat wheels of bread with them.

I know how my grandmother's throaty giggle dances off the walls of her cool, high-ceiling, centuries-old rooms. She can't tell us how old she is because she comes from a time when people didn't bother with such things. She wears long, lushly embroidered dresses and a billowing white headdress. Sometimes, when she's upset about something, she sleeps sitting up in bed. She says it's in case she dies from her anger and the angels whisk her off during the night. She doesn't want to have to talk to the angels lying down.

My grandmother moved with her family to these rooms after being displaced by Israelis from her Jerusalem home in 1948. I know what she says about politics: "Bad politics means you have bad dreams."

Then she goes on talking about the softness of a sweater, or the lemon tree in the courtyards, or the people who go away, far, far away, and never come back. Sometimes in the night I feel the far-flung ripples of our dreams intersecting high above the earth and I wake with her laughter in my ears.

Once I asked the oldest man in her village what he thought about politics and he said, "Boring, boring. I just want to know that my fig tree will still be my fig tree when I get up in the morning. That's what politics means to me." And he offered a bowl of ripe figs and plums from his garden, sweeter and more sensible than any rhetoric.

I felt I had to do something with his love of growing things, with my grandmother's clear-eyed simplicity, or my silence would betray them. So now I speak to Zionists if invited. I carry poems by both Arab and Jewish women to read to a women's group at a local synagogue. The audience's arms are folded when I begin and all the hands are open in their laps when I end. I hold up the shared images of the writers: arid land peppered with stones, deep wells, the olive trees unfurling their roots. I plot with Jewish friends toward more readings, collections of work, ways to heal.

Somehow just listening seems to link me to other people and traditions; we've all suffered, paid homage, held hope. It's hard to feel alone if you listen closely enough. The people I understand least are those who embrace only their own issues, closing in, narrowing their ears.

When our son was born, we gave him a Native American middle name, Cloud Feather. We have no ethnic tie with Native Americans other than the ground we stand on. When people ask us why, we say it's the least we can do.

# A Place to Call Home

MARTHA A. HOWARD

I can't remember where I put the list of social service agencies. It contains the phone numbers of every Skid Row mission and soup kitchen in a two-mile radius of downtown. I usually start at the top and just say, "When Mark Bonner shows up, have him call his sister. It's important. Thanks. No, no number. He knows it." One or two days later, Mark gets back to me.

This time it is a family death that makes the connection necessary. I had just seen Mark at Christmas, when he spent the holiday with me and my family and our sister and hers. We did quite well. He refers to us as his "Junior League" sisters, and he is our "Skid Row" brother. He doesn't drink or shoot up; he just can't hold a job. Doctors have termed it a social problem. He can't get along with anyone, and since he generally stays mildly depressed and has at times been suicidal, I'd say his problem isn't other people – he just doesn't like himself.

I usually try not to involve him in anything remotely uncomfortable, but lately I've changed my philosophy. Who am I to make his decisions? Am I protecting him or making things easier on myself? If he wants to go, I'll take him with me.

Here it is. How did it get there? Oh well, at least I don't have to call Social Services to get these numbers. A lot of them aren't even listed in the phone book. And the hassle isn't worth the information you receive half the time. And that is only when you can get through to them.

"Agape (center)."

"Yes. If Mark Bonner comes by, leave a message for him to call his sister."

"Sure, lady. What's the number?"

"He knows it. Thanks."

163

"Sure, yeah."

"Catholic Charities Soup Kitchen, Don here."

"Hi, Don. Is Father Freeman in?"

"Nope, just me. Can I help you?"

"Sure. This is Martha Howard. Tell Mark Bonner to call me if he comes in. This is his sister. It's important."

"No problem. I'll leave the message on the board."

"Thanks."

My son asked, " Mom, what's wrong? Why do you need to talk to Uncle Mark?"

"My dad's brother died this morning, honey, and I need to let him know. The services aren't until Friday, so I have a couple of days to find him."

"I think Erin is putting bubble bath in the toilet."

"Brian, go stop her!"

"She told me I'm next."

"What? To die?"

"No. To go into the toilet, Mom."

"Brian, I think that at eleven you are perfectly capable of stopping Erin from sudsing the sewers of Houston. Give me a break, will you?"

"Sure, Mom. Sure."

"Christian Community Center."

And so it goes. I finally get to the "Ms" and decide to take a break. It will be cold tonight. Supposed to get into the mid-twenties, so I know he'll want to get in off the street. Get in somewhere warm. I hope he'll stay at a place in the first half of the alphabet. I can't face any more calls tonight. Seventeen so far. I'll do the other ten or so tomorrow morning after I get the kids off to school.

What I despise are the news commentaries concerning the welfare of the street people whenever the temperature drops like this. Usually I see Mark's face. One time it was just the back of his head but I recognized him because of the faded Mr. Shine Car Wash T-shirt he wore. I went into the bathroom and threw up.

Mark finally gets back to me the next evening. I explain my plans for attending the funeral. He seems appreciative that I'm including him. Fleetingly, I consider offering to buy him a new suit of clothes but quickly dismiss that idea, realizing I'll need to fund lunch and will probably need to leave several dollars with him when I drop him off after the service.

I psyche myself up for the service so I won't become emotional. I haven't seen a lot of the people present in years, and as a favor to me, I'd asked my husband to please put in an appearance so his absence wouldn't be noticed. We are in the process of a divorce, and I do not want to deal with that drama on this particular day.

I pick Mark up at the McDonald's across from the bus station. He is outside drinking a cup of coffee. He looks clean and warm (our sister's husband, John, had given him a heavy coat at Christmas) but he is terribly ragged. I try to focus on clean and warm. I am a study in gray. Gray leather pumps, matching leather handbag and gray wool shirtwaist. With my black trench coat I look every bit the Junior Leaguer. There is such disparity between us.

We drive into the parking lot of the church at the same time my soon-to-be ex-husband, Ray, does. We exchange greetings, he and Mark speak, and the three of us walk in together.

We spot our sister, and before we know it we are being reintroduced to people we haven't seen since childhood.

It is obvious Mark doesn't exactly fit in. Our cousin Allen walks over and asks him where he is working. Mark answers, "here and there." I am relieved that he doesn't mention that he does odd jobs for the various missions. Maybe I should start thinking of him as a missionary. I had never considered that before . . .

Sitting between Mark and Ray, I attempt not to think of the reality of the moment: my father's last brother dead, the fact that my husband is sitting next to me and we look so perfect (only last week I'd filed an injunction against him for financial records, so we could move on with the divorce he wants); listening to my sister making inane conversation about how wonderful it is to be a teacher and to be able to take personal leave days—as she and her husband are both doing today.

The service is brief, the strains of "In the Garden" haunting, the weather biting. As we leave the church, I brush Ray's face with my lips, thank him for coming and get in line for the trip to the cemetery.

This is a Masonic service and one foreign to my Catholic upbringing. The men in their aprons and hats are peculiar. Mark and

I had exchanged a few sacrilegious comments regarding this as we had driven the twenty-odd miles outside of town to the cemetery.

I am about to freeze. Mark says that it isn't bad, that he had slept in a box the week before and his eyebrows were frozen when he woke up. He tells me that once when it was raining hard, an icicle grew off his left ear. At times like these I have to realize that Mark is choosing a life-style.

Across the highway from the cemetery is a great home-style restaurant, and I invite my sister and her husband to join us. We used to go there on Sunday afternoons after mass as kids. The interstate was being built, and we'd go play on the hills of the overpasses. It was great fun. Our parents would be inside with the wife of the uncle we had just buried, having a final few cups of coffee; their son was with the rest of us kids.

But they decline the invitation; so does Mark. He says that what he'd really like is just a hamburger and a cup of good coffee. We stop at a drive-through franchise and eat as we drive back into the city.

"Sis, what are you planning to do with your old Pinto?"

"I don't think I can get a lot for it. I'll keep it in the driveway awhile longer. Maybe early in the spring Ray can get it running. Why?"

"Just wondered. I lived in an old Chevy for about six weeks once."

I think of establishing a sort of "apartment community" for the homeless. Gather about eight to ten old cars, place them on a downtown lot and provide shelter to at least that many street people. (Later, when I mention this to my counselor, he considers commitment—mine.) Plant some zinnias in the bumpers, put numbers on the fenders. It sure as hell would beat a box.

Mark directs me to the mission. It's going to be cold again tonight, and he wants to get in early to get a bed. I drop him off and again my breath is taken away by the desolateness of this area of downtown. He warns me to lock my car doors. I hand him some one dollar bills, half of which he hands back, and we tell each other "bye."

Tears stream down my face as I drive through town. It's getting late. I pass InterFirst Plaza. So sleek, polished, almost a city within a city. Attempting to avoid the seedier areas of the city, I drive down Main and through the park. I wonder as I drive whether my tears would turn into icicles hanging off my eyelashes if I were walking. I pass the museum area and drive through the Medical Center. Miracles are performed there daily. I wonder what is happening in those buildings. Surely one building would have enough rooms to house our homeless. Wouldn't that be a small miracle? I think of all the hours over the past year and a half that I've spent in one of those rooms in one of those buildings, in counseling, attempting to come to terms with a divorce and a homeless brother.

I turn right on Sunset and drive past Rice University into the Village. This is familiar and safe. No cars that could be slept in. No boxes that could provide shelter. No doorways to call home.

I turn into my driveway. I see lights on. I park the car and walk up the back walk. I hear the television and the children. Our baby sitter, Mrs. Adamson, is reading a story to Erin. It smells as if a casserole is in the oven. How nice. How safe. I'm home.

# Walter and the Sharks

PETE BARTHELME

I got my first red reel by lying, publicly.

In my long-gone youth, the Swedish-built red Ambassadeur fishing reels were a badge of the expert, a much-desired symbol of commitment to the sport. They were more precisely made, worked better than other reels, and showed the influence of clever and practical design. They also cost two or three times their competition.

I remember going on a fishing trip to Port O'Connor the year after Hurricane Carla in the company of some grizzled experts who barely tolerated a smooth-faced youth. They all carried custom popping rods and red Ambassadeur reels; I had a clumsy Penn reel and was shamed.

I caught less fish too, although one can't imagine the fish really care what sort of reel one uses. Or do they?

I wanted a red reel badly.

My chance came when I was asked to "star" in a TV commercial. The producer was looking for "real people." Being reasonably real and willing to work cheap, I was selected, and a talent fee was proffered. This was well before the time of FTC interference and truth-in-advertising and consumer morality and such. I wandered into the barn of a TV studio wearing a white shirt, which would never do, and I stepped on the seamless background paper with shoes, which was worse. These wrongs righted, I stood before one of the bulky cameras of the day and said earnestly, "I had my car painted at Name Withheld Auto Bake and it looks fine!"

The fact that my aging car was in its original rust, and I had never even seen the painting establishment in question seemed not relevant.

It was wrong and I wouldn't do it again, but the reel sure did

cast well. I managed to deal with guilt and took the grocery money to buy an equally handsome rod.

It was obvious that conventional morality and sense of proper behavior were easily cast aside when it came to fish. I would not flinch at the word "obsession." With me, it began in college when I established an unlimited world record in cutting Chemistry 103 because the University of Houston was on the Gulf Freeway, and the Gulf Freeway led to Galveston, saltwater, and fish.

I learned a bit as I went along, and I read, and I studied and caught an occasional fish. I came into the possession of an aluminum car-top boat, twelve feet of passport to all sorts of adventures, only one or two of which threatened to drown me. The small boat led to a larger boat and a larger one yet, and I was forced to learn a bit about navigation, a touch about radios, a smidgen about the weather and boat handling and knots and brass fittings versus aluminum and what to do when the bilge fills up with escaping gasoline twelve miles offshore. It was a heck of a lot more fun than Chemistry 103.

I discovered an essential truth or two, a very real appreciation of the wind and the waves and the almost staggering indifference both have toward the life and safety of a small human speck out playing among them.

This fixation has continued for the past two decades and more with no letup in sight. As a bonus, my fishing career has exposed me to a variety of wonderful people. Like the Walterses at Olivia, a little-known hamlet about 120 miles southwest of here, between Palacios and Port Lavaca. They were old and tough, she more than he. He was stringy and slow and didn't say much but would wrinkle up his eyes in polite amazement as I explained some fish theory or other. Then he would reach down in the bottom of their old boat and pull up a stringer to boggle the mind.

Even the game wardens were scared of Mrs. Walters' tongue, and the bait camp operators treated them as equals. Stories about the couple reached their peak when Mr. Walters misjudged the turn coming into the boat slips and ran abruptly aground. The impact threw Mrs. Walters—talking a blue streak, it is reported, headfirst into the mud on the bank. "And he just smiled," is the universal punch line.

Another notable was John Townsend, unofficial king of Olivia for years. John was a gruff and forthright individual, with plenty of bark on his burly frame. He did not mince words. When I was sneaking around the tiny village with a new wife, not quite sure of the reactions of my friends there, John stuck his head out of his house trailer and roared at me, "Well, bring her in. She's too damn big to hide!"

John was also the person who, when caught by the local warden out on the bay at night with something illegal in the way of nets or gigs or something, had the perfect Middle Coast answer to the peace office's reprimand when the warden said reproachfully, "John, you know better."

John replied, "I know better, but I didn't do better. Take me in."

The Walterses and John Townsend were strange, Middle Coast beings whom I eyed with a peculiar combination of fear and respect and affection. Equally strange, somewhat smaller beings, were my own children, none of whom are currently in jail. Nor do they have any serious habits or afflictions frowned upon by society.

I think fishing may have had something to do with that. All three kids rode in Emma, the pickup from hell, down to Olivia on a weekly weekend basis, braving rain and cold and gale-force winds, sharing my enthusiasm for the chase. In some secret place in my heart, I know it wasn't my superb parenting as much as live shrimp under a popping cork that made the kids skirt a large majority of the illegal and immoral temptations that abound today.

Fishing keeps your head straight.

Even after all these years, I do not consider myself a finished fisherperson. Not compared to some. Like Walter.

I have no idea of Walter's occupation, religion, political leanings. I do not know if he was nice to his kids, polite to his wife, paid his taxes, or had a pet. I know this. Walter was a fisherman. I encountered him in the Freeport surf, Bryan Beach, one summer day when the wind had died and the water was flat and green to the beach. It was the kind of day when a surf fisherman's heart leaps because the normally brownish water is clear and beautiful and holds nearly infinite fishy promise.

I stopped my faithful Volkswagen next to another observer in a pickup to watch Walter fishing waist deep in the surf and was puzzled to see him flail the water with his rod. It seemed a rough way to treat equipment but he would cast and catch something, string it, and then beat the bejabbers out of the water. I readied my equipment to wade out with him.

Ready to go, I walked over to the pickup and asked, "Why is he beatin' up on the water?"

I quote the answer verbatim: "Oh, that's just Ol' Walter. He's catching those little trout out there and the damn sharks are eating them off his stringer and he's trying to run them off."

That was Walter. A fisherman.

On a modest scale, I have attempted to emulate Walter all my adult life.

# Deja Vu and Old Deceits

BILLY PORTERFIELD

I came in from the day's rounds exhausted, aware of a twitch in
my left eye. Everything I touched, I fumbled. Slammed the car
door on my coattail. Dropped the letter I'd dug from the mailbox.
Couldn't get the door key in the hole. Tripped over a throw rug.
One of those days.

I was famished. At least I had had the foresight that morning
to defrost a Cornish game hen. I laid her on a grill in the oven,
set the temperature to cook her to a golden brown in an hour,
placed a bottle of Chablis in the freezer for a quick chill, and sprang
for the bathroom, where, in a steamy foam of suds and bath oil,
I intended to relax until the bird was done.

I awoke three hours later with a sore throat, lying in cold water,
smelling something burning in the kitchen. I dumped the cindered
bird in the trash. At least the wine had not frozen. But now it
was not what I wanted. I needed stiff shots of sour mash to warm
my throat and knock me out for the night. But what I wanted
I didn't have. A weekend party had wiped out my liquor cabinet.

Grumbling, I jumped into jeans and walked to the nearest bar.
Fall was in the air. There was a snap to things, and I was sorry my
throat ached because I was ready for sweaters and Sundays in the
grandstand. This year, I wouldn't just sit home and watch the Cowboys on TV. I would get out to Texas Stadium for a few of the
home games. Deja vu hit me. I had experienced this before, somewhere, and it wasn't the usual excitement of a new season. It was
something specific, and, curiously, it came back to me.

It must have been the fall of 1960. I was in Houston, walking
with a great tide of people toward Jeppesen Stadium, trying to forget the fever in my throat so that I could enjoy what lay in store
for us. By some miracle, Lamar Hunt and Bud Adams had man-

aged to bring professional football to Texas, and Bud's team, the gushing new Houston Oilers, were about to open the season that very night. There was excitement in the air, anticipation. Bud and his coach, Lou Rymkus, had gotten Heisman Trophy winner Billy Cannon, the LSU bullet, to run with the Oilers behind that old Chicago bear, George Blanda.

Our hopes had not been in vain. I yelled myself hoarse from September through January, for the Oilers went on to a great season, winning the first American Football League Championship in a stunning game against the Los Angeles Chargers. The winning touchdown was an eighty-eight-yard pass and run from Blanda to Cannon. Ah, sweet football falls in the heartland of America. Even with sore throats they were wonderful.

The lights along Greenville burned away my reverie. I could have gone to a bar where I was sure to run into friends, but I didn't want that. I found a quiet place where no one knew me, settled into a dark corner over my bourbon. I sipped it without ice, letting the gentle fire numb my throat.

I was having my second whiskey, pleased I had not eaten, and just about ready for the walk home and bed, when I saw this fellow bearing down on me. My first thought was annoyance. I did not want company. My second thought was as discomforting. He looked familiar, but I couldn't place him.

"William," he said lightly. "Long time no see. May I join you?"

"Pull up a chair," I said, dismayed.

He was a nice enough looking man, rather tall and slight, youngish middle-age.

"I've been keeping up with you," he said, "but I bet you've wondered about me."

"That," I said with irony, "is true. I was asking myself that very thing when I saw you coming."

"Well," he said, "the wife and I split some years ago. My girls are grown and on their own. I'm still hacking. Getting by, waiting for the big break. I moved to Dallas about a year ago. It's funny we would meet here tonight. I've been nursing a beer and waiting to go home and open the mail. Expecting something important."

"What's that?"

"You remember that short story collection I was working on in Houston? Well, I think, at long last, that I've sold it to a publisher. I'm supposed to have a letter from my agent when I get home. I'm a little nervous about it, frankly. That's why I'm putting it off. It's been a long time, as you know."

Houston? Now that was a coincidence, considering my reverie of the moment before. But this guy? His short stories? I hadn't an idea what he was talking about. "How long has it been?" I ventured.

"Oh, it was '64, at least, sometime before you left Houston for Detroit. I remember we had a goodbye beer at the Navigation Bar." The Navigation! I remembered that place, remembered hanging out there, but this man? I knew him well enough to have said farewell? I went on making small talk while trying to track him in my memory. It was no use. I grew bored with it, with his cloying intimacy. I was afraid he was going to buy me a drink and keep me there, but he didn't.

Oh, he kept me there, but not with whiskey.

"I'd buy you a round," he said, "but I'm a little short tonight. That's why I've nursed this beer."

"Don't worry about it," I said. "I'm running late as it is, really have to down this and go."

"But not before you've seen this," he said, fishing something out of a worn briefcase. It was a typed manuscript, not new, not clean. It had been passed from hand to hand for years. "Remember?" he said, thrusting it before me.

I looked at it blankly.

"My collection," he went on, "the one you read at the Navigation. I've changed it considerably, rearranged the stories, and rewritten some. But the title piece is the same as it was. It was the one you said was as good a story as you'd ever read."

Curious now, my eyes fell upon the story. I read but a few words before I recognized it and remembered, with a flash, this pushy fellow out of the past who sat before me.

My mind went back years. Age fell away from our faces. He had approached me in the Navigation with his manuscript, perhaps this very copy, and had insisted I read the closing story, the one I now gazed upon. It was called "The Night Visitor," and it was a story about a white man, a recluse living among Indians in the jungles of Mexico. He violates a burial ground and has to face the wrath of a ghost, a medicine man of the dead tribe. It was a spooky tale, beautifully written.

The only problem was that it had been written by someone

else, a once-famous but now obscure and mysterious German who went by the pen name of B. Traven. The story had not been in circulation for years, and the imposter felt safe showing it about in bars as evidence of his genius. I had seen that his deceit was harmless, at least to others, that it never would sober up and face the light of day, that he never would dare to try to publish his theft. And so I had gone along with it, saying quite truthfully that it was one of the best stories I had read.

But what was I to do with it now, eighteen years later? Shove it in his face and call him a liar?

I looked up from the pages and appraised him. He was waiting for a word from me, as if he had ripped the story fresh from his typewriter. My old praise had worn out over time. His heart would break if I would not repeat it and restore him.

"What do you think?" he said. "Does it still hold up? I have always valued your opinion."

I said nothing for a long moment. At the very least, I had to see him squirm a little. And he did.

"It is as gorgeous as ever," I finally said. "Reads as fresh and new as Genesis."

"Thank you," he said. "Thank you."

# The Ghost That Lives Within

EVAN MOORE

The ghost was sitting in a doorway of the long-closed Rice Hotel the last time I saw him, looking out through the pale blue eyes of an old man.

It was midafternoon and the old man was hunched casually in one of the bum's cradles that line that slowly decaying edifice, smoking a cigarette. He wasn't obviously drunk, but he seemed oblivious to the filth around him and was carrying on an animated argument with himself. He looked just this side of disheveled, but clean, with a brown suit coat, a pair of gray trousers, a white shirt and a dark-colored vest that didn't quite match any other part of the outfit. Somehow, he'd had the flair to add a loosely knotted red tie and a dark brown, felt hat with a red feather.

The old man glanced up at me and spoke to himself. I could tell he didn't really see me, but the ghost did and there was instant recognition. I'd seen him before.

And I was momentarily twenty-one again on a sidewalk in down-town Fort Worth.

I think I knew him before then, though not as well. When I was a small child, he was the one who set loose the thing that lived in the dark in my closet, or under my bed – the thing that immediately disappeared when the light was turned on or anyone else came into the room, but always slid back with a low, mean giggle when it was dark and I was alone. Later, he was the one who stood in the misty background of my first real failure, shaking with mocking laughter. It was his voice that whispered to me at my first introduction to death that death is irrevocable and the living are the ones most truly alone.

But I wouldn't have recognized the ghost then, not at the age of five, or ten, or fifteen. In fact, I might never have known him by sight if it hadn't been for J. C.

J. C. was my first hero. Not the overwhelming, larger-than-life type who lived in the pages of comics, or one of the celebrities, or athletes, or even an infamous bad guy. He was just a tall, laconic dentist from east Tennessee with sparkling brown eyes and his own sense of what made the world turn. He was a friend of my father and he taught me, among other things, to gig frogs.

That was in 1957 when I was ten. Dwight Eisenhower was beginning a second term as president. Chevrolet was selling a classic. And J. C. was teaching me the romance of stumbling around a stock tank in the dark in a pair of rubber boots with a flashlight and a spear. He taught me to listen for the low, resonant bellow of a big bullfrog, just how close and at what angle to hold the light so the beam would mesmerize one, just where to aim so the gig would grab. He taught me how to clean one of the squirming things without losing it, how to grip the slippery skin, how to look within the folds of ivory muscle to find and extract the sciatic nerve so the legs wouldn't be tough.

He kept me out all night and he looked the other way when I stole a drink from his bottle.

He was one of the men who taught me the rules and unspoken etiquette of a quail hunt: where to stand on a covey rise, when to shoot at another man's bird, and when not to. When I made a decent shot, I'd look over through the smell of shotgun smoke in the cold air toward him—tall, skinny, standing by in his worn khakis wearing a grin like a sullied Jimmy Stewart.

He also taught me his own brand of irreverence. Once, at the repeated requests of my father, who had to be out of town, he took my mother to a formal dance. First, he arrived cold sober in a tuxedo, allaying the two biggest fears she'd been suffering. Once there, he conducted himself as a perfect gentleman and offended no one, calming her into further complacency. Finally, he impressed her with the way in which he swept her around the entire dance floor in long, graceful steps to one song after another, gliding from corner to corner, barely brushing by the potted ferns. That was until she realized he was dancing from one plant to another, unloading a mouthful of tobacco juice in each.

There was the time he brought a party of drunken hunters to

his house, sat them in the living room with a fresh bottle, then prepared a meat loaf made from dog food that they raved about for hours; the time he made his "special beans" on a camping trip and they exploded; the time he saved two hundred square feet of our yard by impersonating a lawyer . . .

But that requires explanation. Each year, for decades, my father, J. C., and a few others had gone fishing in a somewhat remote part of Oklahoma called Three Rivers. These were not overnight, civilized jaunts, but two-week, rustic affairs. To eat, they had to cook. To have clean clothes, they had to wash.

And on one particular trip, J. C. decided not to wash. He didn't wash his clothes, change his clothes, or shave. My father wasn't sure he took off his hat. In fact, by the time they were ready for the return trip, J. C.'s appearance had taken on a shocking aspect. Red, Oklahoma clay stained his khakis. Fish scales clung to his shirt. He'd grown a ratty, two-week beard and his hair hung in uncombed strands from beneath his drooping old hat. He was frightening enough that, as my father was passing two middle-aged women in another car on the return trip, J. C. turned and leered and the women ran off the road.

When they finally arrived back in Fort Worth, they were greeted with the sight of a man carefully hammering stakes along a two-foot-wide strip of our yard.

"Just what do you think you're doing?" my father asked.

"Well, I'm the architect for this project," the man replied, cheerfully gesturing toward a church addition next door. "This yard is actually two feet into the church property. We'll be building a wall along here. . . . Uh, who are you?"

"Well, I'm Dr. Moore and this is my yard."

"Who is that?"

J. C. loomed above the squatting architect, a tower of filth. His muddy boots blended upward into the soiled fabric of his ragged pants, leading up to his magnificently stained shirt. Above that was the grizzled, sun-burned, unwashed, unshaven face wearing a deranged grin.

"I am his 'lawyer'," said J. C. "And you are going to get the hell off this property."

As the architect bowed to discretion, stammered something unintelligible, and left, J. C. grew a little larger in my fifteen-year-old eyes. I marveled at a giant who could dismiss an authority figure with only dirt and audacity. I was enough of an adult to appreciate the humor of the situation and enough of a child to revel in the thought of him pulling it off. Being with a grown-up who would do something that brazen filled me with a strange feeling of pride and appreciation that I later recognized as awe.

Awe is difficult to diminish. When it's instilled in youth, it sometimes never dies. As I grew older, so did J. C., but he never seemed to shrink like other men. When he argued with a garage owner over a car warranty, wound up hitting the man over the head with a shotgun barrel, and was subsequently sued for ruining his hat, he was a warrior. When he gave up dentistry in favor of gin rummy, he was a romantic. When he physically heaved a card player out of an exclusive men's club for cheating, he became a defender of all that was moral.

And when he dropped out of sight, he was mysterious. My father told me he was finally "on the bottle." His wife, the only woman he'd ever seemed to change around, was long dead. His children were grown and gone and, somewhere along the way, J. C. had given up his interest in life. He didn't hunt, he didn't fish, and the camping trips were a thing of the past. When his friends called him he was half-drunk and only half-interested. He didn't call them and, eventually, they forgot him.

I suppose I did too. As it became more likely that I wouldn't see him, it became less likely that I'd remember him when I didn't. Little by little, he was relegated to the part of my memory reserved for the things that never change.

Then, I was twenty-one, walking down the sidewalk on Henderson Street in the late afternoon when I saw the familiar figure approaching. The gait was different, it had changed from a loose, freewheeling stride to a slow drag. And the head wasn't held the same way. And the shoulders didn't seem as straight. . . . But it was him. He shuffled toward me in a rumpled suit, an open shirt, and a pair of house shoes. He wasn't obviously drunk, but he looked at me and spoke to himself.

And something that wasn't J. C. looked out through an old man's eyes and all the things I'd ever been truly afraid of poured in on me in one cold moment. I watched him walk slowly past and I didn't speak. He opened the door to his old car and got in and drove away and I didn't call out or follow. Some sense told me he wouldn't want me to, or, maybe, that neither of us wanted me to. I just walked on to my car and got in and sat there for a while.

I thought I was afraid of the ghost, then I thought it was J. C. Finally, I realized it wasn't either one. What I was afraid of was inside me, fear of myself, fear of failure or, more likely, fear that I'd never be in awe of anything again.

It's a fear that lives in mirrors. And it looks back in the reflection of my own eyes.

# Good Ol' Tolie

## H. R. BRATTON

Ol' Tolie had only one eye, no teeth, and he limped.

He had lost his eye in a knife fight over a girl when he was nine-teen. The girl went ahead and married the boy who had knifed him, which she was going to do anyhow, so Tolie lost his eye for nothing. He lost his teeth, because he stopped brushing them when he got too old to mind his ma. He got his limp from an accident in the logging woods.

A lawyer from the county seat had come to see him in the hospital. And while he was looking down at Tolie and seeing how bad he was hurting, he said, "Tolie, I think you ought to sue. I'll bet we could get judgment against them for at least ten thousand dollars."

"Go ahead," Tolie said. "I sure could use it."

The lawyer handed Tolie a piece of paper to sign, then he smiled and left. Tolie got all excited and started thinking about a new car. A sporty red one. The lawyer settled with the big logging company out of court. He got eight thousand dollars. The hospital got fifteen hundred dollars. Tolie got five hundred dollars. It was the lawyer who got the sporty red car.

Tolie put his five hundred dollars down on a used truck and started hauling logs. One day, when he was going back to the woods for another load, he saw a girl walking down the road. Bettijean said, yes, she'd like a ride as far as the store. She had seen Tolie driving back and forth, and had timed her trip to the store just right.

A month later Tolie and Bettijean were married. Three months after that, Tolie's truck was repossessed.

Bettijean suggested that they go to Houston and look for work. They did, and they both got jobs at a big hospital: Tolie as a maintenance man; she as a maid. Four years later, when they had two kids to look out for, the workers at the hospital voted to strike.

They wanted to go on working and tried to cross the picket line. But they were beaten up and chased away. Out of money and behind in their rent, they had to go home to Bettijean's mother.

It was slack time in the woods, and nobody wanted to hire a man with a bad leg for logging work, anyway. That was when Tolie applied for a job as janitor at the school in the county seat. The school hired him, and they moved into a little shack out on the seamier side of town.

The next five years or so were the happiest years of Tolie's life – home every night with Bettijean, playing ball and going fishing with Tommy and Davey, their two boys. But then one day in the fall of the year the boys were in the second and third grades, Bettijean went to work at the cafe out on the highway. She said she wanted to make some money to buy some things for the house.

She usually came home at ten or eleven, and Tolie always waited up for her. But one night she didn't come home at all. The folks at the cafe told Tolie that she had left in a big truck with an over-the-road trucker.

The boys cried. Tolie tried not to, but he finally broke down and cried along with them. He learned to cook a little better, how to wash clothes, make up beds, and get the boys off to school. Two years later, when the boys had stopped asking every night when their mother was coming home, she walked in the door just as they were sitting down to supper.

The boys both tried to hug and kiss her at the same time, while Tolie stood by his chair and waited. Finally Bettijean looked up at Tolie and said, "Do you think you might have enough beans in the pot for me?"

"Yeah," Tolie said. "I always cook enough to have some left over." He looked away when he realized he had been about to say, "So you can have some if you was to come back."

After supper, when they had more or less closed the gap in their lives with a few minutes of talk, they all went to bed as if Bettijean had never been away.

When she saw the anxious looks on the boys' faces the next afternoon as they walked into the house, she started meeting them at school and walking home with them. On days when she couldn't, she made sure they got a note telling them not to worry; she would get home as soon as she could.

One evening she went with Tolie and the boys to a PTA function and was treated like some trashy interloper—and Tolie wasn't treated much better. Pretty soon Bettijean said, "I'm not feelin' well. I'm goin' home." Tolie said, "Go ahead. I'll find the boys, and we'll be comin' along right behind you."

When Tolie and the boys got home, Bettijean wasn't there. Tolie called the cafe out on the highway and the owner, Charlie Lawson, said, "Yes, I saw her get in a truck headed west just a few minutes ago."

It didn't hurt quite as much this time. The boys were older, and for Tolie, it wasn't totally unexpected. He had seen the wanderlust that came to Bettijean's eyes when she heard a big truck out on the interstate. He was just glad for the few days she had stayed with them.

She was back to see the boys graduate from junior high school. (Tommy had dropped back a year so he could help Davey with his studies.) She stayed nearly a year, and was loved every day as much as any mother could be loved, before she went away again. But this time, for some reason, she didn't come back to see the boys graduate from high school. Tolie didn't say anything to the boys, but he figured, after not hearing anything from her mother, that Bettijean was dead.

The boys went off to Houston to find jobs, and ol' Tolie was left alone in the little shack he wisely had bought before property in every little town in East Texas had quadrupled. It was about this time that my wife and I moved into a house just down the road from him.

Our early evening walk took us by his little house (ol' Tolie had improved it until it couldn't be called a shack anymore), and since he was nearly always sitting out on his front porch, ready to talk when we'd come by, we soon got to know him.

He loved it when we bragged on his house. He came down from the porch to take us around to show us the improvements he had made. Especially the new lean-to bathroom he had added. When we came back around to the front, ol' Tolie stopped and said, "I have been thinkin' about puttin' up a white picket fence here in front. Bettijean was always talkin' about one." We assumed that Bettijean was dead, just as his words and demeanor implied.

Ol' Tolie sat on his porch every evening and listened for big trucks out on the highway. If he heard one stop at the cafe, he'd get excited and start straining his eyes to see if he might see Bettijean walking up the road toward him. He'd sit and listen until the cafe closed up, and he knew no more trucks would be stopping, before he'd finally go into the lonely house and go to bed.

But one night, after he had gone to sleep, a truck stopped out on the highway. And a few minutes later, Bettijean was tapping on his door.

The next evening, they were sitting together on ol' Tolie's porch as we came walking by. He stopped us, and, with a big, toothless smile, introduced us to the wife he had thought he would never see again. Bettijean smiled and was pleasant, but whatever good looks she might have had once, were now all gone. With the competition out there in the truck stops along the way, she might have trouble finding another trucker willing to take her along. But from the way ol' Tolie was looking at her, it was obvious he thought she was still as lovely as ever.

The boys came to see her, and she was still with Tolie when we moved away a few weeks later. It has been nearly a year, and we don't know if Bettijean is still with Tolie. We hope she is. But if she isn't, we are sure that ol' Tolie goes out on his little porch every evening to sit and listen.

# Stopping by a Town in Texas

BEN EZZELL

He was an old friend, a black man now dead, named L. A. Mc-
Iver, who lived in Oklahoma City. Over a period of perhaps twenty-
five years, he visited Canadian, Texas, a couple of times a year to
gather funds for the support of a children's home in which he was
interested – spending his own vacation time (and his own money)
to carry on his mission.

In the early 1950s, Mr. McIver stopped overnight in our home,
having arrived here behind schedule in the late evening, and I came
face to face with what it meant to be a black and a traveler through
southern America. Although I had been born in Texas and spent
most of my life in the state, I hadn't fully realized what problems
my black friends faced simply traveling from town to town.

Mac's custom, I learned, was to time his trips through the Panhandle so he could reach Pampa by night, because Pampa had a
community of blacks and he could find lodging there. He could
not check into a hotel or motel room in Canadian or eat a meal
in a restaurant here or even, I was shamed to learn, make use of
a public restroom (although the Santa Fe Railway Station did, at
one time, have a restroom marked "Colored"). It wasn't that Canadian was specially unwelcoming to blacks, not any more than any
other small town in the region, but there were no blacks living
in the community; it was a question that just didn't come up, not
if you were white.

In some areas of Texas, Mexican people were treated almost as
badly, but Canadian had a resident Mexican population, thanks
largely to the Santa Fe Railroad, which maintained a division point
here. The local people of Mexican descent were, for the most part,
longtime residents who had become socially accepted, at least on
the day-to-day levels of social contact. Their children attended the

public schools, became cheerleaders and football and basketball players, occasionally dated Anglo boys and girls, and grew up with them on friendly terms.

Not so the blacks. With the exception of a legendary cowboy from the early days here, there weren't any.

So it was that Mr. McIver, finding the editor working late at the office, dropped in for a visit and asked if I thought it would be "all right" if he parked his car in the alley and slept there.

I assured him that it would be all right, and nobody would object (but wasn't at all sure that this was so) and also told him that it would be unnecessary because he would be welcome to spend the night at our home.

We were friends, but he was hesitant at first because he thought our neighbors wouldn't like it and might make trouble for my family. That hadn't occurred to me (because I wasn't black and a stranger), and it came as a shock to realize that my friend, Mr. McIver, was more concerned about the safety of my family than with his own safety. I assured him that my neighbors wouldn't mind (and didn't tell him that it would matter mighty little if they did), and he accepted my invitation, spent a pleasant evening in our home with Nan and the children and breakfasted with us before he traveled on. The roof didn't fall in and no crosses were burned on the lawn, although in some towns in the South, this could have happened in the 1950s in free America.

In the 1960s, shortly after the Civil Rights Act had passed Congress, opening public dining places and motels and hotels to black people as well as whites, Mac arrived in Canadian one day in midafternoon. Neither he nor this editor had taken time for lunch. I invited him to join me for lunch at a downtown restaurant and again, he was hesitant, not sure that the restaurant would like my bringing him in as my guest. He was not concerned about himself (he was used to that sort of treatment), but about his host.

To relieve his mind, I called the restaurant, knowing that the law of the land now required all races be served. But the law was new, and custom was old, and the restaurant owners were nervous. They proposed that I bring my guest to the kitchen door, and I proposed that I might bring him by way of the courthouse door and, to avoid a scene, we compromised—much to the relief of both Mac and the restaurant owner—and two hot dinners were delivered to the newspaper offices, where we lunched in friendly quiet.

A few years later, in the early 1970s, Mac called me at my home one evening to invite me to meet him and visit in his room at a Canadian motel, where he was a registered guest. I started to suggest that he come to my home instead, in the interest of comfort, and stopped quickly because I realized how important it was for him to be able to extend the invitation to me.

The reason for his visit to Canadian was one of the most humbling experiences of my life. When I went to his motel, he explained the mission that had led him to make the two-hundred-mile drive from Oklahoma City. In addition to his longtime volunteer work for the children's home, this gentle man was also a lay leader in his church, and the church had a problem with the bureaucracy.

He explained that the church served a congregation of people in the inner-city area, and that it had been built and maintained with loving care. It was a neat brick building (he showed me pictures) which was, unfortunately, located in the path of that sometimes monster known as "urban renewal." The bureaucrats wanted to buy the church property so they could tear it down. McIver and his fellow church members wanted to keep their church in their neighborhood and were not interested in selling.

His problem: he was scheduled to meet with a city board to plead the case for the congregation, and he had made the long drive to see me because, as he explained gravely, "You know how to use words."

He wanted me to write a speech for him to explain why his people wanted to keep their church where it was.

I promised to have it for him next morning, and I came soberly to my office and sat down to write, and I guess God was with both of us because I did, and Mac was pleased and called me a few days later to tell me that it had worked, and the church would be left alone. I suspected that the words were far less effective than that tall, aging, gentle man who delivered them—probably his last mission on the Earth for his church and his people. Mac died not long after that.

# Prying into the Secrets of a Dead House

BOBBYE S. WICKE

They say it's haunted. It creaks and flaps and sighs enough to send
me back outside to see if someone drove up or the wind picked
up. No. Old houses are like that. This one could be crying out
in pain, wounded by the mindless smashing of vandals. Bone-tired
from standing up to that old hag, Mother Nature, all alone.

The tin front-porch roof has fallen square and flush onto the
porch, and the shed roof has almost, unevenly, reached the ground.
The roofs are rusted, but intact; the exposed wood has dried out
gray and hard as stone, but straight and undecayed.

Everything else is chaos. Someone broke the windows and ripped
out the frames, chopped up stair steps, pulled the exterior siding
off, smashed bottles, and strewed everywhere the shabby clothes
left by the last residents. There is a difference between nature's in-
sidious destruction and that wrought by man. Nature kills with
dignity.

I have long been an aficionado of old houses, pulling off the
road in the middle of long trips and short errands to investigate
quaint roof lines, obsolete architectural styles that served – and still
serve – practical purposes, and barns meant to serve generations.
I like porches buffering against the elements, letting the homeowner
set a spell at once sheltered and part of the neighborhood. I like
central hallways that provide privacy as well as communication between sleeping and working and sitting rooms, windows meant
to admit light, kitchens meant for gathering family and friends.
It seems appropriate to me to raise houses on piers, leaving space
for ventilation and sleeping dogs and less attractive happenings that
awaken the homeowner in the middle of the night; it seems right
to "go up" into one's home. I wonder who came up with the no-

tion of plunking houses on slabs on warm, wet unstable ground,
like slabs in graveyards.

Abandoned houses have mysterious ambiences apart from architecture. They can be hostile, kind, cold, neutral. I have walked
away backward, literally, from some, unable to explain my revul-
sion, but sure that few people could feel at home there. I have
bought and loved a few friendly, hoary homes and invested so much
sweat equity in them that they should have become mansions. Remembering, I wonder if I left an ambience there. I still see past
the destruction and decay in old houses, seeing what could be restored, and how, and what it should cost, but I avoid those houses
now. As a realtor, I find few buyers receptive to fixing or painting,
let alone refurbishing or restoring. As an aficionado, I realize that
the status of old houses has changed ominously.

I should have resisted this old wreck barely glimpsed through
the trees, should not have come here, looking over my shoulder,
to pry into the secrets of a dead house. Outside, I tread lightly,
watching for signs of old wells, crumbling cisterns, or collapsing
septic tanks, lest I become the newest resident ghost.

This was never a fancy house. Its modest history is revealed where
vandals have peeled away its layers. Around the middle of the century, the plain, wood-plank exterior fell victim to an asbestos siding salesman, but you can see that the owners had kept the wood
painted. Instead of deadbolts and burglar bars, the front door has
an old-fashioned keyhole that any key from a bin at the general
store might have fitted, and it once had nine glass panes where
a visitor could tap on the glass and peep in to see who's home.

On my right, two large rooms open off the center hall. In the
second room, there's a stained and chipped kitchen sink with porcelain drainboards like wings. On my left, three smaller rooms
boasting fireplaces of native stone might be dining room, parlor,
and spare bedroom; other rooms have tin-lined chimney flues for
wood-burning stoves. The ceilings and walls are rough wood planks
with wallpaper pasted right on the wood. The interior doors were
homemade of random-width boards fastened together with three
crosspieces and too-long nails bent over on the other side. A tiny
bathroom at the end of the hall looks like a converted closet; its
footed bathtub is filled with broken toilets and sinks.

Upstairs, two small bedrooms, no bath. Large, faded blue cabbage roses still bloom bravely on one wall of the cozy bedroom with the fireplace. Shreds of a more subdued pink rose-patterned wallpaper cling to the walls of the other bedroom. "Look here," the roses call. "See how pretty we were, imagine what we have seen!"

Windows are everywhere, reaching from the floor almost to the ceiling in the downstairs rooms; the builder of this house did not want to shut the world out. Even in its mutilation, this old house has the ambience of a kind house once filled with sunshine and happy spirits.

Haunted? Not by its past. Its evil spirits are modern, acquired when it lingered past the stage where a new life was practical. Not like a bare-bones-plain old farmhouse I owned for a decade. Our old farmhouse was infested with equal invisible energy by powder post beetles and a mischievous spirit. At night I thought I could hear the beetles boring through the eight-inch, rough-cut beams in the basement. Our ghost—we came to think of him as one of us—was neither a day nor a night person. At any hour that suited his whimsy, he might set odd objects like a jar of pennies or a bell pepper on the stairs, or stomp about a vacant room or materialize as an invisible ice-cold patch one could walk through. He might lock all the outside house doors while we were outside working. We had no keys, for no one locked doors then. He might play wheezy hymns on a ghostly pump organ at midnight, or stand in the moonlight beside the old outhouse (patiently awaiting his turn?). We grew accustomed to this random nonsense, quit trying to find logical explanations, and never, never mentioned him to house guests—unless they mentioned him first. The powder post beetles were exorcised by the next owners of our old farmhouse. Our sociable ghost left a year before that, for reasons I may never understand.

Despite the jaunty angle of the Queen Anne roof line and the blooming flowers planted by caring hands, this is a sad house: no history or architecture worth saving, hardly enough brick and stone and good wood to salvage. Standing a stone's throw from an elementary school in a rural refuge for commuters who reap the good salaries of the petrochemical center and leave its troubles behind at five o'clock, it suddenly seems a dangerous house. It may be too visible to attract criminals, with light streaming through its windows and its lopsided one-hinged front door; it may survive until a curious child is injured here, or a trusting one is raped; then the bulldozers will come to obliterate its shame.

The old house creaks and sighs again, more loudly than before, sending a chill down my back. The blue cabbage roses become gaudy and sinister; are those bones in the ashes of the tiny fireplace? I tiptoe to the windows to peer into the lengthening shadows in the yard before I move stealthily to the top of the stairs to listen . . . for what? I have been frightened by my own thoughts. A last look from the safety of my locked car. With its windows and lopsided front door blackened by the last shadows of the day, the old house has turned forbidding, even angry and reproachful. What nonsense; it's only a soulless jumble of wood and tin and faded roses. Only an abandoned house, awaiting its turn on the evening news.

# Feelings of Guilt over Aunt Lucile

IRL MOWERY

The dainty little shopping bag full of letters silently reproaches me. It has perched in my bookcase for over three years, ever since my Aunt Lucile's funeral. I have put off going through them because the cousin who found them in my aunt's house told me they were my letters, saved for who knows how many years. Once I have put them in chronological order (which my aunt is unlikely to have done), I won't be able to resist reading them; the longer I delay, the more I dread that experience.

I think about my Aunt Lucile at least once a month – with conflicting emotions of gratitude and guilt – when I deposit the check from the trust officer who invested what I inherited from her. I postpone thinking about my relationship with Lucile, though, because I suspect that most of the letters in that decorative shopping bag were written to thank her for the birthday checks she used to send me.

I was her only nephew. By calling her Lucile, without the customary "Aunt," I set a precedent in my mother's family. Being the first grandchild, thus having no peers, I imitated the elders I heard using first names; they, in the free and easy twenties, never corrected me. When my uncle's four daughters came along, they imitated me. We five cousins, destined to become Lucile's surrogate children, thought of her not as an authority figure but a playmate.

Professionally, Lucile was a schoolteacher; temperamentally, she was a flapper, the main attraction of the summers when my mother and I would flee sweltering Houston for the airy sleeping porches of Granmaw's hilltop house near Dallas. I would loiter in the upstairs hall, knowing that whenever I heard giggling on the other side of Lucile's bedroom door, something fun was about to happen—like my mother bobbing her sister's hair with the kitchen scissors. Self-liberated from a Bible-thumping background, Lucile taught my mother to dance, even to play cards—but not on Sundays, of course.

When Lucile married a Houston swain who had shuttled countless miles over gravel roads in an open racer to court her, she became part of my everyday life in the flat country, but without losing a shred of allure. She spent a wicked amount of time in the roadster her husband gave her, killing the time formerly spent in the classroom; I was her gleeful accomplice, crouching in the rumble seat as she sped aimlessly around the coastal plain. In Houston, a city of lawn-bordered bungalows, Lucile chose to live glamorously, in a two-story apartment house! Among my most exotic memories are the nights I was allowed to spend at Lucile's, sleeping on her Murphy bed, breakfasting on her drop-leaf table, watching her icebox being replenished through a special iceman's door in the hall.

When Lucile went back to Dallas to reclaim her teaching job, the words "divorce" and "grass-widow" entered my young vocabulary. After that, I only got to see her summers and Christmases at Granmaw's house, where she lived until she remarried. Although a color print of her retirement photo sits on my desk, I still visualize Lucile as she was between her first two husbands. In a period that coincided with the Great Depression, it was her innate restlessness which kept the family from sinking into lethargy and despair.

While factory workers and bookkeepers were being laid off in droves, postmen and teachers were exempt from joblessness, so Lucile always had money. One scorching August she impulsively bought a new Chevrolet, into which she piled me and her four nieces (all of us too young to drive) and took off for Carlsbad Caverns. We slept in tourist cabins and thrived on bologna sandwiches and Orange Crush. The abandon with which she bought that car (schoolteacher's special—no down payment until October) typified her casual attitude toward money. When the five of us gathered as her heirs for the reading of Lucile's will, we were astounded by the assets she had accumulated, without apparently trying.

Lucile never seemed to think about money but she always had more than enough. As our lawyer plodded through the inventory of Lucile's estate, which included numerous small rent-houses, he explained that they had been deeded to her by grateful people who couldn't repay the money she had lent them. We inheritors toured the rent-houses, sized up the tenants, and decided to get out of the real estate business lest we be dubbed slumlords. When our agent sold the tacky little houses on the fringes of downtown Dallas for the value of the land on which they stood, I finally understood the meaning of casting bread upon the water.

As I sort these thank-you letters, thinking about gratitude, I puzzle over the pang of guilt I feel every time I receive the monthly check from my trust. Do I suffer because I'm unable to thank my aunt for the inheritance that established that income? Not really. I have to confess that, during the preacher's eulogy at Lucile's funeral, I was feeling not grief, but release from having to write and tell her what I had bought with her birthday money.

Without reading these letters spread over my desk, I clearly remember how I used some of Lucile's early checks. They began to arrive after the death of my mother (at whose bedside Lucile kept vigil with me) had left me an adult "orphan." The first check, a complete surprise, replaced the wobbly card-table in our East Side cold-water flat with an unfinished dining table, which my wife lovingly stained and waxed. The second check replaced my ancient Underwood upright with the reconditioned portable typewriter that went with me when I directed plays in summer stock. When my wife's running part in a soap opera enabled us to move to an elevator building on the West Side, Lucile's birthday check (which we had begun to anticipate by then) bought chairs for our scrap of terrace.

In later years, after I had traded the uncertainty of show business for the steady income of what I laughingly called "real business," thanking Lucile gradually became a burden. The amount of the check steadily increased, and when we bought things for ourselves during the year, my wife and I began to say to one another, "This will be Lucile's next present."

I began to feel terribly dishonest when I wrote the annual letter, trying to remember which of the many things we had intermittently splurged on had theoretically been paid for by Lucile's birthday check. After the death of her third, and final husband, I finally admitted to Lucile that her money had bought our dinner in a three-star restaurant on the tour of Provence, which we had already taken. My belated attack of candor seemed to relieve her as much as it did me; she responded with a postcard from Nairobi, telling about the rhino she had photographed on an elegant safari with a white hunter.

As I check the sequence of postmarks on my letters to her, I feel a bit shabby about not having saved Lucile's letters to me. I don't know why I should; I have never saved anybody's letters. Besides, the checks were not accompanied by letters; they were enclosed in birthday cards embellished with birds and flowers. Opposite the rhymed sentiments, Lucile would write her own message, to her "only son," in her rounded teacher's hand. Why had those cards made me feel uncomfortable? I was her only son, albeit an involuntary substitute for the stillborn infant sired by her first husband.

Why should I feel guilty, as her only son, to inherit my share of Lucile's estate? Could it be that, despite years of therapy, I am subliminally swayed by Granmaw's preaching "by the sweat of thy brow shalt thou earn thy daily bread," or words to that effect? Why should I feel undeserving of my inheritance from Lucile? By simply being myself, the only male in my generation of her family, I seem to have qualified as her surrogate son and heir. True, I never gave her anything, as did the debtors who repaid her with bits of real estate, but I never asked her for anything, either. Or did I?

The diamond! I forgot the diamond. Early in World War II, yearning to formalize the engagement to my fiancee but unable to afford a ring on a cadet's pay, I asked Lucile to sell me the diamond from her old engagement ring. By then she was happily remarried and, knowing how much she had hated her first husband, I thought she would probably give me the stone. She did the next best thing by letting me have it for half its real value, on the installment plan; I sent her ten dollars a month while training for the overseas duty that would separate me from my war bride.

The collection of my letters doesn't go back quite that far, mercifully, and now that they are neatly stacked, I may as well tackle them. The one on top, to my surprise, is dated in October instead of August, right after my birthday. It concerns a check that I have sent to Lucile, instead of the other way 'round. I had completely forgotten borrowing two hundred to pay a psychiatrist. She must have been anxious about my resorting to psychotherapy, because my letter takes pains to explain how much I have benefited from the ten sessions paid for by the money she lent me. As I read this letter, I hear rain stripping brilliant foliage from the big maple beside a house in Vermont, to which I had withdrawn, isolating my unsuccessful self from my soap-actress wife, seeking out a country psychiatrist to referee my battle against the inevitable abandonment of my own theatrical aspirations.

The next letter dates from February of the following year. I have found a steady job, we now live in a genteel apartment on the West Side, and I am repaying the money she lent for moving expenses. How could I have forgotten this period of adjustment, when my Aunt Lucile came to my rescue, underwriting my struggle to realign my life with reality? By turning to her for help, I had done something for her that no other kinsman was in a position to do; I had silently declared her to be my "other mother," thus earning the title "only son."

The next letter, written in August of the same year, thanks Lucile for the terrace furniture. I have to remove my reading glasses and dry them. I now recall that I, who had moved in a dry-eyed trance through the deaths of my father and my mother, began to weep at my Aunt Lucile's funeral when the preacher interrupted his eulogy—to praise the Lord for the air conditioning she had given the little country church in memory of Granmaw.

# Taking Care of Birdie

MARTHA BOETHEL

We're sitting on the porch at the nursing home—me perched at attention in a white wrought-iron rocker, Birdie strapped into her wheelchair so she can't slide out. I'm facing a busy Dallas street, a line of decaying condos on the other side. They were big sellers in the seventies, each with a different brick facade. Now they're empty, pasted with official notices and surrounded by a chain-link fence. Birdie's facing me. She's rolling back and forth in her wheelchair, threatening my feet at one end of the roll and a line of shrubbery at the other. I reach out to set the brake.

"Bird, you're about to roll off the porch," I tell her.

"At least then I'd be somewhere else," she replies.

She's trying to persuade me to take her home with me. We've had this conversation many times, several within the past half-hour. I counter with practical observations about money and nurses and my own aging parents. None of it matters. She wants out—and who can blame her?

Friends sometimes ask me how I came to have charge of a ninety-year-old woman not my mother. I tell them the stork dropped her on me—and from quite a ways up. Actually, that's not far from the truth. My folks called me one evening last June, each parent in his or her bedroom shouting at a speakerphone from his or her recliner. Along with their hellos I could hear J. R. screaming at Bobby about mineral rights and Harry Caray giving the closing stats on the Cubs' latest loss.

"You remember your cousin Bird," my mother shouted over the competition.

"Mom, you ask me that every time you mention her."

"Don't get huffy. I don't mention her that often. Anyway, she's dying."

197

Birdie is my mother's cousin – mine, too, of course, but "cousin" implies contemporaries, and Birdie's age more than doubles mine. I remembered her mostly from childhood holidays. She and her suave stockbroker husband would breeze in from Dallas on Christmas Day, sip some eggnog, dispense magnificent gifts, and breeze out again, mysteriously free of the baggage of complaints and whiny children and camera equipment dragged in by the other relatives.

Bird gave me books: *Rabbit Hill* and *Misty of Chincoteague*. She brought me a carved wooden box from Malaysia, a soapstone Fu dog from Hong Kong. She was smart, independent; she traveled. I wanted to be exactly like her. But her husband died, and she stopped coming to see us.

Now she was dying, and someone from the family needed to wish her goodbye. My mother made her usual excuses.

"You know I can't go–I just had my other knee replaced."

"Mom, that was four months ago."

"Well, I'm still a cripple–I barely make it to bingo and back."

So I went–doing the family duty as I always do. I found Birdie unconscious, sharing a room with a diabetic who had just had her foot amputated. I sat with Birdie while her neighbor moaned and howled. Birdie looked ancient, diminished, as fragile as the bone-china milkmaid she'd sent me from London. After a time I bent over to kiss her forehead, tell her goodbye. She opened her eyes, "Get me out of this hellhole," she whispered.

Turns out that Birdie, who never had children, long ago alienated every relative on the planet, living or dead–except for my family, whom she hadn't seen since the sixties. Her brother and sister were long dead–one drowned while fishing, the other choked to death on a bite of flank steak–though it wouldn't have mattered if they were alive, since she'd excommunicated them both in a fight over the location of their mother's grave. Half a dozen nieces and nephews–all blacklisted for reasons unknown. And her friends were as geriatric as she was. One of them took me to lunch in the hospital cafeteria, announcing, over her plate of chicken a la king, "Look, I'm the youngest of the bunch, and I've got two plastic hips and a pacemaker. We can't look after Birdie. It's you or some greedy stranger."

So now I visit her in the fancy nursing home my mother and I picked out, and we argue about her alternatives in life. She can't tell me what county she lives in, can't even call up my mother's name. But she knows what she knows: "This place is pure hell."

And, of course, it's true: This nursing home has lovely French provincial furniture, good food in the dining room, bingo three times a week. But Birdie's half blind; she can't swallow even a sip of water (don't ask–it's all done with tubes); and bingo's for idiots anyway. She's had three roommates in the past seven months. The latest is comatose, but as Birdie points out, at least she's quiet. Birdie rolls around the corridors in her wheelchair. I figure she makes at least thirty laps a day, and then she's ready to go back to bed. No wonder she begs me to bring her a gun. I might actually do it if I didn't think she'd take a couple of nurses with her.

So we sit on the porch. She rolls back and forth. I lean forward, ready to grab the wheelchair before she goes sailing into the pyracantha.

"I found a photograph of you the other day," I tell her.

"So?" she says suspiciously. She's caught on to the tricks I use to distract her. "It was a picture of you on an elephant."

The photo had been tucked into a folder filled with speeches she'd made as state president of the Catholic Daughters of America. I read the speeches. They were full not of the mystery and spirit I'd imagined, but of the Old Testament and obedience, the daily, muddy road to grace. But the photograph, that was the Birdie I'd known, perched on an elephant, wearing jodhpurs, a scarf streaming from her neck like Isadora Duncan, waving fiercely at the camera.

"I remember that elephant," she tells me, rolling to a stop half an inch from my toe. "We were in Delhi. Wendell paid a dollar so I could ride."

"How was it?" I ask her.

"A hell of a lot better than this," she answers, rolling on.

# Secrets of an Unquiet House

TEE LURRY

Mr. Smith, the realtor, said, "The house has been vacant for years. I have newer houses you might be interested in seeing. . . ."

"We really want to see this one," I insisted for both my husband, Tom, and me.

Mr. Smith searched the rubble of keys in his desk drawer and finally found a single key. We parked in the driveway and followed the stepping-stones through the tall, thick grass and weeds.

An old bougainvillea vine spread a curtain of purple bloom across the small front porch. Tom pulled the vines aside and we ducked under to reach the front door.

The key fit into the lock but failed to turn. Mr. Smith said, "Key doesn't fit. Sorry." He didn't sound sorry at all. I took the key from his hand and worked it back and forth in the lock. The lock turned. The door opened quietly, no squeaks, no drags, no sound except that of our footsteps against the tile that floored the entry.

Inside, the light was gloomy. The brightness of early July sunshine was dimmed by dirty windowpanes. There was no electricity. Mr. Smith pulled a small flashlight from his pocket and waved a slender streak of light across the room.

Spiders had long since staked territorial claims to corners and over chandeliers. The windows lifted with ease, as though rain and cold and heat had not swelled their wooden frames. Old hardwood floors resounded sharply from our heels.

Tom said, "Needs carpets." I knew he hated bare floors.

"We can get carpets," I said willingly but believing I could argue later for cleaning and refurbishing the beautiful old hardwood floors. Already, I was planning, and I had not even seen the rest of the house.

Rear windows offered a view of uncut grass and weeds spreading to reach a raised bricked flower bed built along the high stone wall circling the backyard. A gardener's dream. Tom, not a gardener, said "That yard's a mess." I thought it a wonderful challenge. Imagine, a raised flower bed! What a back saver!

I followed Tom, as he examined the kitchen cabinets closely. "Good oak. And that wall paneling looks like old curly pine, the kind we used to use. Did you see this big pantry? There's room enough for that round table you like so well. We could breakfast in the kitchen."

I let him discover the good things. I could already feel the warmth and smell fresh bread and hear pleasant laughter in that kitchen.

Mr. Smith stood by idly, letting us make our own discoveries. I thought I saw a twinkle in his eye.

Tom opened the window above the sink. The view was free of tree branches that hung outside and the long shadows of the afternoon. "Is that direction east?"

Mr. Smith agreed it was. Then I knew—standing there early mornings looking out, I could watch the sun rise while making coffee for the two of us. I had wished for an east window many times, having to face a neighbor's brick wall while living in our town house.

Secretly, I was ready to buy. But I followed Mr. Smith as he walked ahead, apologizing for the cobwebs and dirty windows. "This house has been managed by an attorney who handles the estate for the heirs. He took it off the market several years ago." An uneasiness hit me. "Maybe it's not for sale?"

"I'll check it out," he assured me. "I believe it could be sold to the right party."

An odd statement. What kind of a party? A buyer would have to qualify financially, I knew. What, other than that?

Tom interrupted my thoughts, pulling down the attic ladder to climb up and walk around, then come down again. "That attic is completely floored, and the roof is planked underside all the way. All the pipes and ducts are wrapped for protection. The air conditioner and heater will have to be checked out. I think I've found the plans to the house."

He unrolled a yellowed tube of blueprints, held them spread out. I left the two men inspecting the faded sheets and talking.

I trailed through the bedrooms and baths dreamily placing furniture, adding curtains. The closets were large, the windows were the dormer type and a window seat in the master bedroom looked out over the garden. Both baths had sliding glass doors, each etched with a pattern of cranes, standing amid cattails. I smiled, remembering the same crane pattern from my grandmother's bath. The walls were tiled up to the ceiling and across the floor with old-fashioned large tile, well-caulked. The porcelain faucets had a pattern of painted flowers.

Tom came behind me. "The plans show the house is built on a solid four-foot foundation. Unbelievable in this day and time! The contractor was named Weimer, and the house was built in 1944 for Adolph Hermann. That was forty-six years ago. You wouldn't expect a house that old to be in such good shape."

I defended, "It's a wonderful house."

Tom talked on, "They insulated the outside walls. That's why it's so quiet and we can't hear the traffic outside."

None of this influenced me, but I nodded. I stood in the hall and looked about. The house already possessed me.

The men walked ahead, outside. It seemed strange that their voices should seemingly come not from the front porch where they stood but from above my head, muffled in tone, indistinguishable. I imagined I heard a woman laugh.

It took two months for Mr. Smith to reach the heirs and for the paperwork to be finished. At the closing, the attorney for the estate was old and palsied. He asked me twice if I really liked the house. "I love it," I said, curious why he should inquire. Why else would we buy it?

Before moving, Tom insisted upon a new steel garage door with an opener. The inside of the house was painted, the paneling cleaned and waxed. The windows sparkled when they were cleaned. I lost my argument about carpets and agreed to new ones, wall to wall. Small concession, I thought. Tom insisted the wooden cornices and top siding be covered with aluminum siding.

The expense had been much more than we had anticipated, so I asked, "Why don't we wait until next summer?"

"No. Now. If anything happens I want the house secured for you to live here the rest of your life."

We both smiled. It was an old game between us. We joked a

lot about such matters, each of us remembering our previous spouses had died suddenly, and those experiences had left us cautious about losing each other.

Now I reassured Tom. "Nothing's going to happen to you. I want us to live in this house for a long time, enjoying it together." I put my arms around him for a hug. "Let's hope so," he said.

It was September before we settled in. The sun came up with bright rosy colors that first morning I stood at my east window making coffee. I planted fall bulbs and mulched the flower gardens for spring planting. Tom got acquainted with a new fishing buddy next door. We found a church nearby.

We learned our way around the neighborhood. At night, after we were in bed, we spoke together sometimes about how quiet the house was in spite of being on the corner, with traffic outside.

Tom slept soundly. But I heard. The voices usually began after midnight, awakening me. Muffled sounds, with indistinguishable words, pleasant happy sounds, voices always speaking together, sometimes soft with laughter. About four o'clock they would cease. It was not a regular nightly pattern but a frequent one. Sometimes I would rise and go out into the hall, but no one was there. Sometimes being awakened annoyed me, and I would call out, "Stop! Let me sleep!" and they would stop. Strangely, they did not frighten me. They only caused me to wonder. I knew the voices were only for me, since Tom had not mentioned hearing them.

A happy year passed. Then Tom died. Suddenly. Not in the house but in the hospital emergency room, where 911 had taken him after my call. A stroke, the doctor said. My children came and took me home and I sat, trying to accept what had happened. My daughters stayed for a while. They folded Tom's clothing into boxes and called Goodwill. They repainted our bedroom, put up bright new curtains, changed the furniture, made a new room out of the old, made it my bedroom—no longer Tom's and mine. I was grateful to them. I slept, intermittently, with pills.

My daughter said, "This is the quietest house! No sound at all at night."

I had heard the voices and wondered if she had. They moaned and cried, no longer happy. I did not mention them to my daughter. After she left I took the pills regularly so I would not have to listen to their sorrow. Mine was enough.

I was alone again. I deliberately replanted the flower garden, planted roses, Tom's favorite, well knowing they would die with the coming winter's freeze. I hosed down the dusty new siding, remembering what Tom had said when he had it put there. Mornings, when the sun came up in all its glory through my east window, I made coffee—for one. I set the timing of my days by trivial duties. The house seemed to always need me. And somehow Tom's presence was always there.

I welcomed the voices when they returned. One night I thought I heard Tom calling me. Imagination, I told myself, but I listened each night hoping to hear his voice again.

I consoled myself that death was natural, a blessed passage ordained for us all. Now Tom was at peace. I said all these things over and over. I thought about telling my daughters about the voices but dreaded their thinking me senile. Actually, I had reached the point of believing this myself.

I was suddenly awakened from a deep sleep one morning just before dawn. The house was quiet. I turned in my bed and opened my eyes and there was Tom's face, suspended in air about two feet from me. Tom's face, with its familiar contours, his deep brown eyes, the sparse hair and the familiar cowlick. The face was tanned darker than I remembered, and I saw dirt on his forehead, his chin and down his cheeks, and my first thought was "He has come back from the grave!" I stared into his eyes and he stared back.

Then without warning or sound he disappeared.

I sat up, turned on the light, well knowing he was not there. I had the strangest feeling of calm, of wonder. I told myself it could not be true. Still, the happening was very real to me, and I could not deny it.

The next day I talked to my minister. He was a tolerant, kind young man who reassured me. He quoted scriptures. He said, "Grief affects people in different ways." He asked kindly, "Why don't you go see your physician?" He said a prayer for me.

I went to see my doctor, an old friend. He asked what kind of sleeping pills I was taking. I confessed to buying them over the counter. "Stop them," he said. "You are depressed." He wrote a note on his Rx pad. "This is the name of a psychiatrist I want you to see. This particular one, none other. Tell him I sent you. Don't worry. You are of sound mind."

His last remark was cheering. But a psychiatrist? Sane-minded people didn't need a psychiatrist. I determined to learn the history of the house first, to try to reasonably understand the voices, the face, and what was happening to me.

I called Mr. Smith. "All I know about the man who built the house is hearsay," he said. "It was rumored that his wife was a very strange lady, who spent most of her time at home, not very sociable. I do know Jean Baker, some distant kin of the family. If anyone knows the history of that house, she does. I believe she is listed as Josephine Baker in Garden Oaks."

I found her number. She was friendly and listened patiently. "Yes, Adolph Hermann and my father were distant cousins. I remember when the house was being built. Adolph owned a brick and cement yard and he told my father the house was a wedding gift to his new bride. His first wife had died and he had no children. I don't think she had any children either, although she had been married previously. They were in their sixties when they married. I was a teenager then and really wasn't too interested, but I heard my mother talking about how, after Adolph's death, the woman had made her will stating the house could not be sold to anyone unless they promised to care for it and to love it. My mother used to say, 'What would it matter to her? After she died, she wouldn't know anything about it.' Adolph died suddenly at work. Sometime after that she was killed in an automobile accident. I do remember that."

"Did you know the second family to live in the house?"

"The attorney leased it to a friend of ours, but they moved out of the place after two months. Why, I don't know."

I knew why. Voices. I said, "We bought it from the Porters. Did you know them?"

"No. My mother kinda kept up with that house because of the will. I don't even know how she found out about the will. Why don't you ask Mr. Talley, the attorney? I think he could tell you about the Porters."

Already, with her information, I could understand several things. But I called the number Mr. Talley had listed on our closing papers. "You sold the property to the Porters?" I asked.

His voice was old and as unsteady as I had remembered it.

"Yes. Like your deal. The house was locked up and someone told them I was handling the estate, so they called. When I showed them the house Mrs. Porter fell in love with it. She and Mr. Porter were middle-aged, and it was their second marriage and I remember he said the house was a wedding present. Nice folks. Then he died of a heart attack sometime later. I don't remember how long. Time slips by me. But I sorta kept up with them because they joined our church."

"Did he die in the house?"

"No. In the hospital. She lived in the house alone for several years, then died in the hospital, too."

"Then no children have ever lived in the house?"

"No. Mrs. Porter had me rewrite her will after he died. She stipulated no one with children could buy the house from her estate. She also put the same clause in the will that whoever bought the house must love it and promise to care for it."

I was beginning to understand. Did the voices belong to the two women who had lived there before me? How coincidental that the house had been owned by persons of middle age in second marriages.

I went to see the psychiatrist, Dr. Jacques Bordelon. He was kind, interested. My one hour's time extended into two hours. Finally, he said, "Your problem is quite simple. Your house is haunted. I was raised in a haunted house in the south of France. Our family lived downstairs, and my grandmother lived upstairs, with the spirits. We never heard the spirits, but she did.

"They were her company, and they left when she died, at ninety years of age. There are many houses, all over the world, where spirits are only present to certain people. My contemporaries think me touched when I tell them this story, but it is true. Who can prove there aren't any spirits among us?"

I was astonished. No wonder my physician had told me to see this man, none other. I needed further assurance, and I asked him about doing tests. "No need," he said. "I can give you a diagnosis: It is called hypnagogic imagery. We call it Doppelganger Disorder, where the brain lies about what comes through the senses."

"But it was so real to me . . . Tom's face. . . ."

"Of course. That doesn't mean you are mentally sick. This is usually brought on by stress such as grief or extreme fatigue or by medications. Your doctor told you to stop taking those sleeping pills, which, I suspect, added to your problem. Outwardly you are calm and give the appearance of self-control. But inwardly you are grieving. You have never let your husband go."

I knew he was right. I had kept Tom beside me ever since he died.

"Accept his death. Just keep the memory of your happiness and let him go now. The face you saw was from your imaginary mind, wanting to see him again. A real vision to you. As to the voices, your house is haunted, simple as that. If you are too disturbed by this phenomenon, then take a long vacation – get away for a while, and if they are there when you return, then sell the house."

I didn't want to take a vacation. I knew I would never sell the house. Leaving, I thanked him. I had to think about all these things, sort out my life. A life without Tom.

I went home and walked around the yard. The bougainvillea was purple again. Periwinkles were a lovely mass of pink and white. And the rose bushes had spectacular buds.

Inside, the house embraced me with warmth and comfort. I was home. I dumped the sleeping pills down the drain.

That night I went to bed early, began a new book. At midnight I put the book aside, turned off the light, and waited. Finally, the voices began. I rose and went into the hall and called aloud, "Go away. Let me alone. I promise you I will care for the house and the flowers. I love this place. It is mine now. You may stay if you want, but if you do stay, then do it quietly and enjoy the house with me. If you are satisfied to believe my promises, then go. But you must leave me alone."

If others had heard me that night, they would have most certainly believed me crazy. I did not care. I went back to bed, calm and ready for a night of peaceful sleep.

The house was Tom's last gift of love to me. I could live with happy spirits, if the voices returned, but somehow I did not believe they would.

# Monty Comes Home

## H. R. BRATTON

One morning last week Gracie Tackett called to tell me that ol'
Monty had just had a stroke. I got to the hospital just in time to
see them loading him back in the ambulance to take him to the
VA hospital in Houston. Our local hospital wouldn't take him because somebody had told them he didn't have any money, and not
a nickel's worth of insurance. I went inside to ask the doctor about
Monty. He shrugged and said Monty might last two, maybe three
days, but no longer.

I drove on over to where Monty lived to see if everything had
been turned off and locked up. He lived on the far side of town
in a little rundown shack on a dirt road that ran along the railroad
tracks. He had told me where he had hidden an emergency key
that I could use.

I got the key, unlocked the door, and went in. Everything was
off, and I couldn't see that any of his few belongings were missing:
His little old portable typewriter was still on the box in front of
the cane-bottomed chair where I usually found him sitting and
typing when I came by to visit. Most of the time he'd mumble,
"Come in," and go right on with his two-fingered typing until the
*o* key stuck again. He'd cuss, flick it back in place with his finger,
and finish typing the word he was on before he'd look up to greet
his visitor.

I could never tell, when I found him all hunched over writing
like that, if he was glad I had come or not. But on the days when
I'd find him sitting out on his little front porch, he was always ready
to talk and tell his stories. But even if he was right in the middle
of one, if he heard a train coming, he'd jump to his feet and walk
to the far side of the dirt road, where he'd stand and watch until
the last car had gone by. If it was a freight train, as it usually was,

and he saw some old hobo sitting in an open boxcar door, he'd wave and holler at him as if he were an old friend—and some of them may have been.

When Monty had watched the train out of sight, he'd come back to his chair on the porch and start another story. Almost invariably it would be about the time the railroad bulls had jumped some 'bos he was with in California. But this time the 'bos had been ready for them. And he'd go on to tell in detail how they had beaten "the livin' hell out of the bulls!" I don't guess there had been many really big triumphs in ol' Monty's life for him to crow about.

Sometimes when he had finished his story, he'd gaze way down the tracks and say, "One of these days, when I finish the book I'm workin' on, I'm goin' to hop another freight and do some more travelin' around."

I didn't figure anybody had seen anything they wanted to steal, even if they'd had the chance, but I went on looking around anyway. Besides the battered typewriter, there was an old radio that Monty loved to listen to late at night so he could hoot at "the loonies who called in to say stupid things" on the late-night talk shows. I wondered if Monty might've been a regular caller if he'd had a phone.

On a table in a corner I saw a picture of his son and daughter, when his son was about four and his daughter about five. Monty had married and fathered the two kids as quick as he could to stay out of the World War II draft. But he'd been drafted, anyway, near the end of the war and had served enough non-volunteer time to qualify as a veteran. When they mustered him out, he didn't come straight home. When he finally did come back to town, some five or six years later, he found that Ellie had gotten a divorce and re-married. His kids had forgotten him, or else Ellie had turned them so hard against him they pretended they had.

I had never been in Monty's bedroom before, and I was a little surprised when I saw a picture of our 1938 high school football team hanging on the wall. I was the quarterback, Monty was the center, and one of the cheerleaders kneeling down in front was Gracie Tackett.

Hanging on another wall was the shrunken head Monty had picked up in Borneo on his round-the-world cruise with the well-off widow he had conned into marrying him back in the late fifties. And there was a picture of Monty on a camel in Egypt, a shot of the two lovers at the Taj Mahal, and another one of him and Rosa standing in front of the Eiffel Tower with Monty all decked out in white pants and a designer sport coat. Rosa looked quite fetching in her sporty fashion duds, too. The disillusioned widow had kicked him out a few months after the cruise, when she found out he was having some high times on checks he was signing her name to.

I opened a scrapbook that was lying on his dresser and one of the first things I saw was an old flier that Monty and a female comrade had written during his "commune year" in Oregon.

In a box in a corner were two dusty manuscripts that had been rejected ten or twelve times. One was about a reluctant young soldier who had become a hero in the Korean War. The other was about a young writer in Hollywood whose award-winning script had been stolen by an unscrupulous producer. Monty had thought he would eventually get them published. I thought he would, too. I wondered if I should try to get them into the hands of his son or daughter.

Monty finally had come back to his East Texas hometown to stay about two years back, and he'd been living in the shack by the railroad ever since. He hadn't gone out of his way to re-establish any old friendships, and he hadn't tried to get in touch with his kids or grandkids. I had provided most of the effort that had more or less re-established friendly relations between the two of us. He and Gracie, who had been through three rough marriages and was living alone in another shack up the road when Monty moved into his, had become friends mostly through her efforts, too.

As I relocked the door, I remembered that I hadn't looked in Monty's mailbox. When I opened it, I found a letter with a return address, but the sender hadn't put a name on it. I debated the matter for a moment, then decided that under the circumstances I should go ahead and open it. It was from Rob, Monty's son, and he was coming to see him. He would be there Friday. Friday was the next day. I put the letter in my pocket and went on home, saddened by the thought of Rob being a day too late.

The next afternoon I sat down and tried to think of some old acquaintances of Monty who might be willing to chip in a few dollars to help bury him. I had thought of only two when the phone rang. It was Gracie, but she was carrying on so I couldn't at first make out what she was trying to say. Finally I made out the words: "He's back! Monty is back! He is sittin' right here talkin' to me! But don't come here to see him," she said. "He wants to go on home."

At the VA hospital there had been this young doctor who had, as a last recourse, shot ol' Monty full of a still-experimental drug for the treatment of strokes. It had cleared the last little clot out of his brain, and they'd found him sitting up in bed Friday morning hollering for breakfast. After eating a plateful of ham, eggs, and grits, he had slipped out of the hospital, hitchhiked back to town and had walked into Gracie's shack just a few minutes before she had called.

I got over to Monty's shack as quickly as I could, thinking that I might have been able somehow to soften the shock of Rob coming. Gracie was there with him, and they were celebrating with a bottle of Strawberry Hill.

Monty invited me to sit down and have a sip with them. As I was seating myself at the table, I told him that I'd been worried about him and was glad to see him back.

He smiled and said, "Ah, it wasn't all that bad. They just had to unstick my *o* key!"

I was reaching for the letter in my pocket when a car stopped out front. It was Rob. I wouldn't have time to soften any shock, and I sat a little tense as I waited. I didn't expect either of them to recognize the other, and I was wondering if I should introduce them. But their hearts must've told them, because when they met on the porch they grabbed each other in big bear hugs.

I got up and left quietly by the back door. Gracie followed, and neither father nor son took any notice. Monty wasn't showing any signs of shock, and it was plain to see that after thirty years of searching, he finally had found what he'd been looking for—a son to love and talk to.

# Bury Me in the Country

JENNIFER KING MOODY

Narcissa had been buried in 1920. Seventy years later I watched as her eighty-three-year-old granddaughter held on to a cane and tried to pull the weeds off her grave.

Narcissa had been buried with a cradle, which is a cement oval that people used to put around graves to raise them up. Maybe to protect them from being walked on . . . or it could have been just because they looked nice.

Modern cemetery maintenance doesn't allow for such sentiment. Now they prefer, or even mandate, that the headstone be flat against the ground, making it easier to run lawn mowers right over them. Whatever came up inside the old cradles was simply left to grow unchecked.

Narcissa's granddaughter happened to be a friend of mine, so I thought I should do something to help her. I loaded up my van and drove out to the cemetery one day. I climbed up the man-made hillside, dragging behind me fifty-pound bags of white marble rocks, rolls of landscaping mesh, and sacks of bark nuggets. A cemetery worker drove by and waved hello.

I sat down in the heat with my steak knife and began sawing my way through decades of dandelions. Thorns, stickers, and fire ants put their two bits in, along with an occasional spider.

Two hours later, I was looking at five old cradle graves boasting clean, bare ground. I took a break and tried to remember who my friend said they were. Two were baby cousins, twins I think, born small and weak during the Depression, a time when you needed to be tough. Two of the adults were the grandparents. The third was an uncle who was not really an uncle, but because he had no family of his own, they had let him be buried with theirs. Such were the kindnesses people used to share with one another. He had been a neighbor. We can hardly remember a time of know-ing neighbors so well—or holding them in such high regard.

I filled in low spots with the bark, covered the surface with mesh to stop the weeds from coming back and filled the cradles with new, shiny white marble rocks, so bright they sparkled in the sun. I tucked in red flowers at the headstones.

It looked great. It looked as if they had been buried only yes-terday. It would look pretty for my friend when she came again. There would be no weeds to bend her eighty-three-year-old back for. For a few moments I was truly proud. Then the cemetery guy pulled up in his truck and got out.

"You can't do that!"

I acted like I didn't hear him; that way I could at least hold on to the hope that I had heard him wrong.

"Excuse me, lady, you can't do that."

I resisted the cuss words that first sprang to mind and instead choked out, "I've been doing it all day."

"Well I didn't know what you were doing."

"What did you think I was doing with 250 pounds of rock in the middle of a graveyard—building a pyramid?"

"Well, I didn't know what you were doing until you had it done."

The world flashed before me, a great blank wall of idiocy, and I, the only intelligent living thing in it, stood struck numb and silent, sweat filling my Target-store tennis shoes. Only idiots pay one hundred smackers for sneakers. I bet he was wearing some really expensive ones.

"Those rocks might get thrown by the mowers."

"You don't mow inside these things, anyway. That was the origi-nal problem."

"They might get thrown by the mowers."

Again the flash; the tennis shoes overflowed.

"You should have checked with the office first," were his last words as he drove away.

"Office?"

I had been raised with churchyards and country family plots. It had never crossed my mind to look for an office. Didn't know dead people needed one. Offices probably killed most of them. Wouldn't have gone in it if I'd have seen it. Only office you'll catch me in is a doctor's office, and I've got to be real sick at that. I had an office job once. It lasted about two whole weeks. Been allergic to them ever since.

I got back in my van and drove to the gate. The man in the truck yelled, "You gotta pick those rocks up!"

I yelled back, "You and your office people pick them up if you want them up!"

"Bozo" was tacked onto the end of that sentence, but I didn't say it out loud. Tell me to go to the office. Like I was a little kid in school. That's exactly where everybody sent me when I was a little kid.

I drove home fuming; all that work I had intended to be permanent, some jerk in an office was going to take right back down. The feeling when the guy said, "You can't do that." The pride had flowed out of me like water to the ground. I revved my engine at a few innocent people, shot around a few more and generally, and stupidly, took my anger out on the freeway. God was patient and decided to let me live. After all, I wasn't the only idiot on this planet. The place is covered with them.

Anger gradually subsided to sadness when I started thinking about the country graveyards so familiar and comfortable to me. So easy, no rules to control what you can see or can't.

Seashells brought from hundreds of miles away, lovingly laid by five-year-old hands in a circle around a grandpa. A foil-wrapped coffee can filled with dirt, the bean inside sprouting into a pretty vine for grandma. I saw fifty rocks one time, each painted like an American flag, surrounding the grave of a soldier who died in Vietnam.

I've seen mock orange and morning glory, old roses and trumpet vines speaking eloquently of love with color and fragrance, no matter how long left untended. Cement angels and old wooden crosses on graves where nobody could afford a headstone. I have an uncle lying on a mountainside somewhere under a rock on which someone has scratched just his name, Cecil. I still mean to find him and fix him up a little better. Somebody'll probably try to tell me I can't do it, or they'll have taken his rock away, because of mowers.

I was out in the woods of East Texas once, miles from anywhere. I stumbled across a row of very old graves. There were eight little babies, and at the end the lady who had died trying so hard to fulfill her "duty" as a wife. They had buried her with the ninth.

They were all alone, her husband probably buried elsewhere with a woman who finally did give him children. I found them some pine cones and branches with red berries. For a few moments I reflected on a life lived so long ago and so hard. I thought about my microwave. City cemeteries don't seem to have such stories to tell.

I thought of the time my older sister had rented a room on Galveston Island for me and my friends, a grand finale to a graduation weekend. The other girls partied, walking the streets and beaches from guy to beer and beer to guy. I walked the old cemetery on Broadway. My friends thought I was weird and more than a tad spooky. I thought they were dumb and unbelievably shallow. I didn't understand why they didn't understand how interesting it was. A world of stories and angels and people "lost in the storm"–like me at eighteen.

I have never seen graveyards as dark or scary places. They are to me places of history, of families, and of love. Or at least that's what they used to be. Now they have rules and tiny little squares of land that cost thousands of dollars each. I'm glad most of my family rests more casually.

I'm going to North Carolina to see my own grandfather. I won't take him any fake silk flowers. I've already gathered up most of what I am taking. There's an arrowhead and a buckeye, and a pretty piece of flaky mica. I'll run up some hickory nuts so the squirrels will come see him, and I'll buy some wild birdseed to throw all around. Nobody'll tell me I can't do it.

I'm probably a long way from dying, but when I do, I hope they bury me in the country somewhere. If seventy years later, someone still cares about me, tell them to bring me seashells, pretty rocks, and flowering dogwood branches. I believe I'd like some birdseed myself. Tell them to do just whatever they want, and tell them I would have said, "Thank you for not putting me in a place that had rules."

Narcissa's rocks and red flowers, along with those of her family's, still lie right where I put them months ago. Rules are like witches. If you don't believe in their power, they can't get you.

# Hellfire in a Can of Paint

T. LURRY ROBERTS

At the age of six months, June of 1915, I inherited three uncles, not by wills or court decree, but by family agreement, following my parents' accident. My growing time was divided equally among them, four months of each year in each uncle's home and care.

Until I was seven, no one ever explained that my parents had been killed. Then Uncle Josh spoke truthfully to say my parents were drowned near West Beach in Galveston. Uncle Josh always spoke truthfully, after he quit his job at the lumber yard, when God called him to save souls. I envisioned God's voice booming down from the sky to command him to stop loading boards and start loading souls for Him to bring up.

Of the three, I liked Uncle Josh's home the best, a parsonage next door to the Calvary Baptist Church. My summers were spent there, on Third Street in the Heights, in a shabby little house I did not know was shabby or little because there I knew Aunt Bertha loved me.

Listening to family accountings, I learned Uncle Josh had chosen his wife, Bertha, very carefully after his call to preach. Her volunteer church work and her splendid choir voice helped to decide him. He was forty-two at the time, single, and had not exactly thought about marriage until he needed a wife to help in the matters of the Lord.

Family members discussed Aunt Bertha among themselves in brief sentences: "She's turned out to be a good wife, after all," or "She's set a good example in spite of her beginnings."

When I lived with the other families, I learned that Aunt Bertha had come from a poor family who lived near the railroad yards. She quit school when she was big and strong enough to clean other people's homes. She learned to sew, and this led to the job of doing alterations on men's suits at a clothing store on Congress Avenue. The families said this was held against her because men, not ladies, were tailors in a men's store.

They asked one another, "Didn't men have to pull off their pants for a fitting and stand half dressed for the alternations to be pinned?"

However, word got around that she was very modest and conducted herself like a lady, and that M. Levy, the owner, was pleased with her work and conduct. The families always stressed this compliment but sometimes, forgetting I was listening, they said she had planned that job all along, just to get a husband. Anyhow, she got Uncle Josh.

Aunt Bertha was tall, with long blond hair which she braided and coiled around her head. She had brown eyes with wrinkles spiking out to her temples and deepening when she smiled. She was kind to me, as the other aunts were, but her kindness included hugs and kisses and laughter, and I always believed this was why Uncle Josh married her, even if I never saw hugs and kisses and laughter between them.

When I was a baby, she kept me cushioned in a bureau drawer on the floor beside her own bed. As I outgrew the drawer, she tucked me onto the parlor sofa. The small house had only a bedroom for them and another for Andrew, their son, twelve years older than me. While very young, I learned not to bother Andrew, who only noticed me if I got in his way. Aunt Bertha always regretted having begat only one son for Uncle Josh. I always thought of her as having done her duty and being wise enough to stop begatting.

Among the families, Uncle Josh was called stingy. He often said he had accepted the Lord's call without thought of worldly compensations. Aunt Bertha told me she understood this. She had accepted Uncle Josh in the same way. I never repeated to her what the other families said – that their marriage was a step up from the poverty she had always known and a settling down for him – recalling his sprees during his lumberman's years before God changed his life pattern.

In spite of what they said, I came to understand why she cooked and carefully portioned foods so that each person had only one share, with counted potatoes, measured beans, one piece of corn bread, or one biscuit each. Variations from this menu came only when the church women brought their favorite casseroles or smoked hams or jars of canned vegetables. These were always welcomed, particularly by Uncle Josh. He depended on God's arranging a full pantry, not his gardening efforts or his pocketbook.

Aunt Bertha always visited cordially at family gatherings, but the families seldom came to the little house. If they noticed the shabbiness and lack of repair, they never spoke of it later. But when it was my turn to live there, I saw the sagging front porch, the rotting steps and the scaling paint and the rusted screens on the windows, with holes at the inside latch hooks. When the windows begrudgingly opened for strong arms, I helped stuff paper into the screen holes to keep out the flies.

The outhouse in the backyard was a tribute to Aunt Bertha's effort toward better living. Most outhouses were the same inside, with dirt-dauber cones in corners and the usual bucket of lime to be dippered up and tossed down the hole. Inside this one, the walls were whitewashed and kept brushed to prevent waspy corners. A shoe box was filled with tissue dress patterns cut into squares to use instead of pages from catalogs. Wooden lids covered the seat holes, and sprays of pine branches hung inside the door, their fresh scent clearing the air.

When I told the other aunts about this outhouse grandeur, they said that Aunt Bertha had a few uppity ways for a minister's wife. I did not tell them that the oven in Aunt Bertha's stove had rusted through on the bottom, and Uncle Josh had laid a piece of tin across the hole so the bread would bake. Nor did I tell them the ceilings in some of the rooms were circled with rainwater that had dripped through the leaky roof. When Aunt Bertha talked to Uncle Josh about repairs, he always said he would talk to the church committee, reminding her the rent was free.

That September the committee approved painting the church, never mentioning repairs or painting the house. When I returned the following June, the church job was just being finished. Aunt Bertha explained that the delay was because volunteers did the work.

A perk of the church painting was the surplus can of white paint. Aunt Bertha immediately confiscated the can, carrying it over to the back porch. Uncle Josh objected, saying this was like stealing. It was his duty, he said, to notify the deacons and to let them decide whether to return the unused paint for credit or to agree it could be used to paint the house.

For the first time, I heard Aunt Bertha argue with Uncle Josh. Their dispute continued for days. The can of paint sat on the back stoop, a symbol of disagreement and a beacon of righteousness.

Then one morning after Uncle Josh left to begin his weekly rounds to visit the sick, Aunt Bertha opened the paint can, stirred it vigorously with a stick, and started to work.

She put Andrew to scraping down the scaling old paint before they took turns with the only brush they had. I was set to sweeping up the debris of paint chips and to keep the can of paint stirred.

I supposed if God called it stealing, He would take care of Aunt Bertha's sin later on, in His judgment. I worried a lot about it. I imagined wicked licks of hot flame against Aunt Bertha's legs as she stood on burning coals of hell. I really hated to have this happen to Aunt Bertha. I wished there was a way Uncle Josh could take off the new paint and pour it back into the can for the deacons' decision.

On the following Sunday the bright clean front of the house glared out from the rest of the dingy boards. After church was over, the committee stood around observing and talking. Then without further meetings, they voted for more paint to cover the rest of the house.

Neither Aunt Bertha nor Andrew offered to do the work. Their arms and backs were still sore, and however long volunteers took to finish the job, they would wait.

The following Sunday Uncle Josh preached on forgiveness. I listened as I sat beside Aunt Bertha, and I squeezed her hand. She looked down at me and smiled. I knew then she had won, and I stopped worrying about hellfire.

# About the Authors

Houston novelist Pete Barthelme's latest thriller, awaiting publication, is *Rat-Killin'*. His earlier books are *Push, Meet Shove; Tart, with a Silken Finish;* and *Brainfade*.

Steven Barthelme, formerly of Houston, teaches at the Center for Writers at the Univeristy of Southern Mississippi in Hattiesburg. His short-story book, *And He Tells the Little Horse the Whole Story*, was published by Johns Hopkins University Press in 1987.

Author and essayist Rick Bass lives on a ranch in Montana. His latest book is *Winter: Notes from Montana*, published by Houghton Mifflin Co.

Michael Berryhill, formerly fine arts editor of the *Houston Chronicle*, is executive director of news and publications at Rice University.

Marthat Boethel writes essays, poetry, and fiction. She lives in Austin.

H. R. Bratton is a free-lance writer in Point Blank, Texas.

Teresa Kyle Cage is a free-lance writer in Houston.

Charles Clawson, formerly of Houston, is a free-lance writer in Seattle, where he teaches English at Highline Community College.

William Cobb is a Houston free-lance writer and teacher. His novel, *The Fire Eaters,* is scheduled for publication by W. W. Norton & Co.

The late Ben Ezzell was editor and publisher of the *Canadian Record* in Canadian, Texas.

Adelaide Ferguson is a Houston free-lance writer.

Lionel G. Garcia is a novelist in Seabrook, Texas. His latest books, *Remembrances of Childhood* and *To a Widow with Children,* are scheduled for publication by Arte Publico Press.

Leon Hale is a columnist for the *Houston Chronicle* and author of several books, including *Turn Left at the Second Bridge* (published by Texas A&M University Press).

Gunnar Hansen, formerly of Texas, is a free-lance writer in Northeast Harbor, Maine.

Michael Hargraves is a free-lance writer in Coldspring, Texas.

Martha Anne Howard is a Houston free-lance writer. She is working on a novel about the homeless. Since this article was written, her brother has died.

Barbara Karkabi is a reporter for the *Houston Chronicle*.

Jim Langdon is a copy editor for the *Houston Chronicle*.

Rolf Laub, of Houston, has been drawing the illustrations for State Lines in the *Houston Chronicle*'s *Texas Magazine* almost since the feature began in July, 1989. His style and execution reflect the wide range of mood and tone of the essays.

Bob Lee of Houston, a community organizer and free-lance writer, is a social worker for the Harris County Hospital District.

Tee Lurry is the pen name for a Houston writer.

Thom Marshall is a columnist for the *Houston Chronicle*.

Jennifer King Moody is a free-lance writer in Pasadena, Texas.

Evan Moore is a reporter for the *Houston Chronicle*.

Maria Moss is a former writer and researcher for the Houston bureau of the *New York Times*. She has been managing editor of *Houston Metropolitan* magazine since 1991.

Irl Mowery of Houston is a former actor, Broadway producer, opera company manager, and ballet fundraiser who retired to write fiction, poetry, and plays.

Sunny Nash is a free-lance writer and photographer in Hearne, Texas.

Naomi Shihab Nye of San Antonio is an essayist and poet who has published three collections of poetry: *Yellow Glove*, *Different Ways to Pray*, and *Hugging the Jukebox*. She is editor of *This Same Sky*, a collection of poems from around the world by Macmillan Publishing Co.

Kathy Pierce is a Houston free-lance writer.

Billy Porterfield is a columnist for the *Austin American-Statesman*.

Rachel Herrera Reed is a Houston-area schoolteacher.

Dallas novelist C. C. Risenhoover teaches journalism and communications at Chemeketa Community College in Salem, Oregon. His latest book is *White Heat*, by Baskerville Publishers.

T. Lurry Roberts of Houston is a free-lance writer of poetry and short stories.

Barbara Wilson Shallue, a former chemical plant operator, is a student at San Jacinto College.

Richard Stewart is a Beaumont-based reporter for the *Houston Chronicle*.

Edward Swift is a New York–based novelist who writes about his home region of East Texas. This essay is from a work in progress, *Grandfather's Finger and Other East Texas Memories*.

Margaret Symmank is a playwright and free-lance writer in Santa Fe, Texas.

David Theis is a staff writer for the *Houston Press*.

Bobby S. Wicke is a realtor and free-lance writer in Manvel, Texas.

Allen Wier is director of the creative writing program at the University of Alabama in Tuscaloosa. He is a former NEA Fellow, Guggenheim Fellow, and author of *Departing as Air, Things About to Happen, Blanco,* and *A Place for Outlaws*. His latest book in progress is *A Cloud of Witnesses*.

Essayist Marion Winik of Austin is heard on National Public Radio's *All Things Considered*.

*State Lines* was composed into type on a Compugraphic digital phototypesetter in ten and one half point Galliard with one and one half points of spacing between the lines. Galliard was also selected for display. The book was designed by Jim Billingsley, typeset by Metricomp, Inc., printed offset by Thomson-Shore, Inc., and bound by John H. Dekker & Sons, Inc. The paper on which this book is printed carries acid-free characteristics for an effective life of at least three hundred years.

TEXAS A&M UNIVERSITY PRESS : COLLEGE STATION